Herbert Corey's
GREAT WAR

FROM OUR OWN CORRESPONDENT
John Maxwell Hamilton, Series Editor

Herbert Corey's
GREAT WAR

A Memoir of World War I
by the American Reporter
Who Saw It All

Edited by PETER FINN
and JOHN MAXWELL HAMILTON

LOUISIANA STATE UNIVERSITY PRESS
BATON ROUGE

Published by Louisiana State University Press
lsupress.org

Copyright © 2022 by Peter Finn and John Maxwell Hamilton
Herbert Corey's original, unedited typescript, titled "Perfectly Irresponsible,"
is held at the Library of Congress.

All rights reserved. Except in the case of brief quotations used in articles or reviews,
no part of this publication may be reproduced or transmitted in any format or by
any means without written permission of Louisiana State University Press.

DESIGNER: Michelle A. Neustrom
TYPEFACE: OFL Sorts Mill Goudy

COVER IMAGE: Corey using binoculars to look out from a fortified trench.
Undated. (Library of Congress)

LIBRARY OF CONGRESS CATALOGING-IN-PUBLICATION DATA

Names: Corey, Herbert, 1872–1954. | Finn, Peter, editor. | Hamilton, John Maxwell, editor.
Title: Herbert Corey's Great War : a memoir of World War I, by the American reporter who saw it all / edited by Peter Finn and John Maxwell Hamilton.
Other titles: Perfectly Irresponsible
Description: Baton Rouge : Louisiana State University Press, [2022] | Series: From our own correspondent | Includes bibliographical references and index
Identifiers: LCCN 2021053987 (print) | LCCN 2021053988 (ebook) | ISBN 978-0-8071-7794-5 (cloth) | ISBN 978-0-8071-7795-2 (paperback) | ISBN 978-0-8071-7808-9 (pdf) | ISBN 978-0-8071-7807-2 (epub)
Subjects: LCSH: World War, 1914–1918—Press coverage—United States. | World War, 1914–1918—Journalists—Europe. | World War, 1914–1918—Personal narratives, America. | War correspondents—Europe—History—20th century. | World War, 1914–1918—Censorship—United States. | Journalists—United States—Biography. | Corey, Herbert, 1872–1954. Herbert Corey papers, 1847–1954.
Classification: LCC D631 .C67 2022 (print) | LCC D631 (ebook) | DDC 940.4/24—dc23/eng/20211123
LC record available at https://lccn.loc.gov/2021053987
LC ebook record available at https://lccn.loc.gov/2021053988

Contents

Introduction
vii

Herbert Corey's Great War
1

"Runaway Correspondents":
Editors' Postscript
209

Index
213

Photographs follow page 104.

Introduction

In 1914, Herbert Corey was writing breezy stories in New York for Associated Newspapers. It was a big jump for him. Three years earlier, Corey, thirty-nine and little known, had moved to Manhattan as a correspondent for the *Cincinnati Times-Star*, where he quickly established himself as an amusing, quirky, and sometimes cantankerous observer of New York's foibles in a column titled "New York Day by Day." The newly formed Associated Newspapers, which was trying to establish itself as a national syndicator of columns and comic strips, poached him from the *Times-Star* and gave him a major platform—and $85 a week—for his musings.[1]

Corey had finally reached the main stage of American journalism after a peripatetic existence in the West and Midwest. After working and getting fired from a small newspaper in his native Ohio, he had moved out west as a young man and worked various jobs as a cowboy, sheepherder, stagecoach driver, bartender, and editor of the *Bonanza Rustler* in Wyoming.

Corey returned to his home state in 1900, where he worked for the *Cincinnati Enquirer* and the *Times-Star*. In a story Corey liked to tell, he distinguished himself by contributing to the loss of three handwritten short stories entrusted to him by an inmate at the State Penitentiary in Columbus, the soon-to-be famous writer O. Henry. The circumstances of the loss were of a kind O. Henry would have enjoyed, if it had not been his work that was lost: Corey submitted the stories to the Sunday editor of the *Cincinnati Inquirer*, who misplaced them while he was on one of his periodic alcoholic benders.[2]

Corey became one of the highest paid reporters in Cincinnati, and the *Times-Star*'s choice for New York correspondent—a plum assignment—when the job came open in 1911.

Corey's popularity only grew at the fledgling Associated Newspapers. The service sent him to Britain and France early in 1914 to write entertaining features as well as to cover the heavyweight championship fight between Black boxer Jack Johnson and Frank Moran, an American dentist, in Paris's Vélodrome d'Hiver. Again, he proved adept at mastering an assignment. "My letters," Corey recalled, "had sold very well."[3]

Happy with that success, the Associated Newspapers sent Corey back to Europe after an irredentist Serb nationalist, Gavrilo Princip, assassinated the heir to Austro-Hungarian throne, Archduke Franz Ferdinand. Corey boarded the *Lusitania* in New York harbor on August 6, 1914, the day the British declared war on Germany.

With Corey on the luxury liner were three American journalists whose standing far eclipsed his. Richard Harding Davis was the first journalist-celebrity, much of his fame earned reporting abroad. Picture-book handsome and impeccably dressed, he was the model for the male counterpart to the beautiful "Gibson Girls" drawn by his artist friend Charles Dana Gibson.[4] The second man was Frederick Palmer, who by the time of his retirement some years later was credited with reporting from more battlefields around the globe than any other American correspondent. President Theodore Roosevelt called him "our best war correspondent."[5] Frederick Roy Martin, the third man, did not have the byline recognition of Davis and Palmer, but he was more influential by one significant measure. He was the assistant general manager of the Associated Press, which sent him to reinforce the wire service's bureaus in Europe. His luggage included a leather hatbox containing $20,000 in gold.[6]

"I had broken into the big time," Corey said of his passage to the war in Europe.[7]

As it turned out, Corey saw more of the war than his three famous traveling companions. Davis had his usual spellbinding adventures in Europe. His report of the Germans marching into Brussels was one of the most celebrated pieces of America reporting in the war. The Germans arrested him in Belgium as a supposed British spy, which gave him another famous story. Davis went home in 1916 and died of a heart attack, age fifty-one, that year. When the British agreed to accredit one American reporter to the British army, Secretary of State William Jennings Bryan, who made the selection, named Palmer. After the United States entered the war in 1917, Palmer turned down a stunning $40,000-a-year contract—about the equivalent of $820,000 in 2021 dollars—plus expenses to cover the war for the *New York Herald*. Donning an American army uniform, adorned with the insignia of a

INTRODUCTION   ix

major, he instead headed the press section of the American Expeditionary Force (AEF) on a soldier's salary. Martin did not stay in Europe very long. He returned to his management duties in New York, where at war's end he was elevated to general manager of the AP.

Corey spent considerable time in France and Britain, but he also went to Berlin and visited the German lines on both the Western and Eastern Fronts. He was given enormous latitude by his editors to go where he thought best. He reported from the Netherlands, Italy, Switzerland, Spain, Andorra, Greece, Croatia, Serbia, and elsewhere. In July 1917, he was one of the first reporters accredited to the U.S. fighting forces in Europe, the AEF. By the end of the war, the AEF considered him "the dean of the correspondents with the American Army."[8] When the Armistice was signed in November 1918, he returned to Germany. He was in Paris during some of the peace negotiations the next year.

A handful of correspondents were working in American news bureaus when the war broke. Some, like Paul Scott Mowrer, bureau chief in Paris for the *Chicago Daily News*, and Wythe Williams, who headed bureaus in London and Paris for the *New York Times*, did notably good war reporting in the field. (Later in the war, Williams jumped to *Collier's* and then a British newspaper, Lord Northcliffe's *Daily Mail*). But only a tiny number of correspondents— maybe one or two others—came expressly to cover the war at its inception and stayed past the end. Records for correspondents' tenure in Europe are scattered or nonexistent, but Corey likely was the very first of them to arrive on those shores. And while he came home occasionally and expected anytime to be recalled for good, few if anyone covered the war as long as he did.

Yet Herbert Corey is largely forgotten. His name appears in few histories, and when it does, it is almost without exception in passing and without color. *The Historical Dictionary of War Journalism* carries long entries for Davis and Palmer, as well as Mowrer and Williams. It has none for Corey.[9]

How does one explain his frequent absence from the honor roll of correspondents? He was not an anonymous reporter by any means. On the side, he wrote stories about the war for *National Geographic*, *Harper's Monthly*, and *Everybody's Magazine*. He was the subject of news reports for denouncing British tampering with correspondents' dispatches. His reporting from Germany was controversial at a moment when Allied propaganda dominated Americans' understanding of the war. The American ambassador to Germany, James Gerard, wrote Secretary of State Robert Lansing that Corey's articles from the front were "violently pro-German."[10] They were not, but they did not demonize his subjects. The AEF believed that Corey's "suspected pro-German proclivities . . . prior to the entry of the United States into the war made him persona non grata with the French Government authorities."[11]

But if Corey was courageous and far from anonymous, he was not a correspondent for a major national newspaper, where the greatest national visibility was possible. Nor did the Associated Newspapers, which he represented, have the clout of the big three wire services—the Associated Press, United Press, and the International News Service. The Associated Newspapers is as forgotten as Corey. A shrewd newspaper entrepreneur, Jason Rogers, publisher of the *New York Globe*, started the feature syndicate in 1912 as a cooperative between the *Chicago Daily News*, *Kansas City Star*, *Boston Globe*, and *Philadelphia Bulletin*. In a short time, Rogers acquired nearly thirty other members, and by the time of the war it increased to forty. Rogers's *Globe* was one of the finest newspapers in New York and was known for its features, which he believed were essential to growing readership, as news was common to all papers.

The Associated Newspapers specialized in *Dickey Dippy's Diary* and other comic strips; *Ripley's Believe It or Not!*; Presbyterian minister Dr. Frank Crane's sermons; and columns on home nursing, the outdoors, and bedtime stories. With its emphasis on features, it was somewhat surprising that Associated Newspapers sent Corey to cover the most serious issue of the day, the war. But if his editors could not expect Corey to write lightheartedly about grim wartime conditions and bloody combat, they still wanted the human touch he was so adept at capturing. With few exceptions Corey sent his stories by mail since he normally did not provide the sort of front-page breaking news that deserved the high cost of cable transmission. The AEF files describe him as writing "so-called 'human interest' stuff, rather than actual news."[12]

Another reason for Corey's absence from the lists of war correspondents relates to memoir writing. Every hero needs a Homer, and many of Corey's contemporaries served as their own bards. Some of these journalists had been writing about themselves for years. Richard Harding Davis, author of *Notes of a War Correspondent* and many other books on the wars he covered, was finishing *With the French in France and Salonika* when he died. Frederick Palmer wrote five books during the war and twenty-nine books in all during his career. Even his novels focused on war. The war spawned a slew of new authors. Never before had so many American reporters, many of them marquee names in the biggest newspapers, covered a foreign story of such intense interest to people back home. Publishers clamored for their work. Any visit to Europe, no matter how brief, seemed worthy of a memoir. *Chicago Tribune* sports columnist Ring Lardner wrote *My Four Weeks in France*.

Corey didn't answer the call. In 1919 the trade journal *Editor & Publisher* reported, "Mr. Corey is the most modest of men. He cherishes with a sort of pride his record of never having written a book or delivered a lecture on the war—and he does not propose to mar this record."[13]

Corey did not explain why he shunned memoir writing. Perhaps it was his independence of mind and a reluctance to air his contrarian view of the war and America's allies. It certainly could not have been because he was shy about writing in the first person or that he had an objection to book writing in general. After the war, Corey wrote books on a variety of subjects. His publication list was eclectic: a book about Herbert Hoover, with whom he was friendly, *The Truth about Hoover* (1932); a mystery novel, *Crime at Cobb's House* (1934); *Farewell, Mr. Gangster! America's War on Crime* (1936), written with J. Edgar Hoover; an as-told-to book about a naval architect, *Submarine: The Autobiography of Simon Lake* (1938); and *The Army Means Business* (1942), which deals with World War II.

Corey stayed with the Associated Newspapers through the 1920s, some of the time working abroad, and continued to contribute to such magazines as the *Saturday Evening Post*, *American Mercury*, and *Outlook*. At the end of the decade he moved to Washington, D.C., where he lived in a cozy two-and-a-half story brick and stone home on the slopes of Rock Creek. After leaving Associated Newspapers in 1930, he became a contributing editor for the *Nation's Business*, the magazine of the Washington-based Chamber of Commerce of the United States.

At some point, probably in the 1930s, Corey gave in. Putting aside his aversion to writing memoirs, he worked on two. One covered the war and the other his time as a young man out west and other stories. These personal histories did not get beyond the typewriter stage of production. He was still tinkering with them when he died in 1954 at the age of eighty-two.

Corey's widow gave his papers to the Manuscript Collection of the Library of Congress. The manuscript dealing with the war has an appearance that harkens to journalism's yesteryear. It was produced on cheap paper with a typewriter that cried out for a fresh ribbon. The pages are heavily marked up with his scribbled edits. It was a first draft, with some sections or chapters being repeats of others, and a couple of the last chapters had nothing to do with the war. This would-be book carried the working title "Perfectly Irresponsible," which captures the ironic way Corey thought and wrote about what he saw, but it was hardly suitable for selling books by the yard, as Wythe Williams did with *Dusk of Empire*. The book you are holding in your hands—*Herbert Corey's Great War*—is that book, renamed, edited, and annotated.

War correspondents come in all stripes. Some write perceptively about strategic moves on the battlefield, as Homer Bigart of the *New York Herald-Tribune* did in drawing attention to the failures of military leadership in the Allied landing at Anzio in World War II. At the other end are correspondents sent by their newspapers in search of servicemen whose families are subscribers. "Anybody here from Wisconsin?" the *Milwaukee Journal*'s Robert Doyle would say when he came upon a military unit in the Pacific during World War II.

Corey defies easy comparison. He approximates Ernie Pyle of Scripps Howard in his sympathetic interest in the American foot soldier, but he also told stories about troops on the other side and about noncombatants. A contemporary profile of Corey said he had "a Poesque style."[14] But one might more aptly pick for comparison O. Henry, whose stories he had a hand in losing. Corey, whose passport picture shows a round-faced man wearing a pince-nez and a mildly ironic smile, was brilliant at poignant human yarns, often with a twist. A long, adoring profile in *Pearson's Magazine* in 1915 called him the "premier anecdote man of the United States."[15]

Corey's search for these stories had a lot in common with the best battlefield reporters. He was intrepid. He frequently went where he was not supposed to, the authorities be damned. He did not duck peril and risked his life to get near the fighting. He was in the front trench in October 1917 when the first American soldiers went "over the top." (By an amazing coincidence, the commander of the unit was a high school friend of Corey.)[16] On another occasion a shell fragment hit his helmet.[17] Toward the end of the fighting he was riding two hundred to three hundred kilometers by car in a single day in pursuit of stories.[18]

Corey consistently roughed it to stay near the action. Here is Corey describing his time with Serbs in the winter of 1916–1917. "If it was raining—it usually was raining—it ordinarily fell to my lot to ride on a flat car," he wrote in *National Geographic*. "Sometimes I crouched under a canvassed gun on its way to the front. It was no drier under that gun. It did not even seem drier. But the silent guardsman gave me the place as the place of honor. It was the one courtesy in their power to show."[19]

Corey's offhand, sometimes cranky style in this war memoir was common among feature writers in his time. It is not today. But his vivid reporting is time-honored. Here, in *Harper's Monthly*, he recounts the decimated Serbian army coming down from the Macedonia hills to Monastir Road, the historic highway linking the Adriatic and the Aegean seas that would take them home:

> On the trails thin lines of men move slowly toward the road. As they come nearer it may be seen many are of middle age and some are almost old. Some walk erect under the blue shrapnel helmet furnished to the Serbia army by the French. Others slouch along at precisely the speed of an ox-team. All their lives these Serb peasants have marched by their oxen, goad in hand. Today the pace of the army remains the same. Their faces are deeply lined and covered with many days' growth of gray beard. Once their uniforms were of the horizon blue of the French army. Today they are of a nondescript gray, bleached almost to white in places by a winter's weather. These men are sad and quiet. Bundles hang about them in unmilitary fashion. There are eighteen thousand of them. They are all that are left of the army of four hundred and fifty thousand with which Serbia began the war.[20]

Corey shows us what it felt like on both sides of the lines. His revealing interactions with military and civilian leaders, as well as with fellow reporters, add to our historical understanding. But he is especially illuminating on the impediments that reporters faced in conveying the story of the war to Americans. Corey's frustrations are bold threads running through his memoir.

Censorship was often arbitrary. AEF censors killed stories that reported soldiers' fondness for French wine or implied their sexual fraternization with the locals. The guidelines given to censors called for stopping stories that would "weaken [French] faith in our cooperation."[21] As his colleagues did, Corey decried this attitude as well as the difficulty of getting to the front lines. The British and French especially preferred their own nationals—and then on a limited scale. In Italy, he was "under surveillance all the time," he wrote home, and repeatedly detained when he broke loose in the vain hope of reaching the battle lines.[22]

"Newspaper correspondents do not go to war anymore," Corey wrote in an undated story in his papers. "They are taken to war. Most of their time they spend in sitting about such haunts of luxury as the [Hotel] Adlon at Berlin or the Savoy in London, railing at the folly of the constituting authorities in refusing to take advantage of the opportunity offered them to mold public opinion.... Then one day they get the order" to be escorted to the front.[23]

Corey does not stop with these obvious attempts by the authorities to distort the truth. He dwells repeatedly in his memoir on the efforts of the British to bend American thinking to theirs. This story rarely gets the attention it deserves. In internal memoranda, British officials continually assured each other they were ingénues when it came to propaganda and manipulating the masses; deviousness they told themselves was a German specialty. In fact, the British were far more duplicitous and inventive in courting American opinion leaders, planting stories in the American press, and suppressing news that they did not like.[24]

Equally revealing is Corey's commentary on censorship by American editors. At one point in 1918 he remarked to his mother that he was likely to have trouble because "I am getting away from the vein of soothing syrup which my newspapers have insisted on."[25] They squelched news that did not conform to their patriotic views, or that put them out of step with the government, or that might offend their readers. As Corey shows us, what readers want to believe shapes what they get. He is interesting and balanced on the Committee on Public Information, President Woodrow Wilson's often over-the-top propaganda ministry, but more than once notes how university professors working with the CPI eagerly gave up scholarly detachment to become propagandists.

Corey glibly talks about the war as an adventure. But no reader will put down this book without an acute awareness of his intense disappointment at not being able to fully report on the conflict. In private letters he was harsher. He told his friend Henry Suydam of the *Brooklyn Eagle*, "The fear is growing on me that one of these days I shall go to telling the truth about our gallant leaders. If I do—boooey—I'm gone. I know that quite well. Our people have become so saturated with nonsense and fiction that only the perfectly competent liar gets by."[26]

Corey, as his memoir makes clear, did not believe he was in Europe to serve the Allies. He viewed himself as an American reporter and an outsider, one who was deeply ambivalent about the entry of the United States into the war. Even so, Corey was not known at AEF headquarters as a problem. True, he occasionally challenged some censorship rule or limitation of movement, such as not being able at one time to take his own pictures. But he knew how to trim his copy to pass the censors. In early 1919, when the AEF assessed the work of the various correspondents, it observed, "Mr. Corey, has written personal stories for his syndicate which serves a large number of newspapers in the US and in order to obtain material he made almost daily trips to the front. His work has been very valuable in giving the people the personal side of the story."[27]

In the sole postwar magazine article in which Corey seems to have mentioned his war experience, "Welcome to the Next War," Corey offered a different self-assessment. In the next conflict, he said, "My own part, I trust, would be that of censor—censor and liar. I would not try to be an honest reporter again. The other war knocked that honest nonsense out of me."[28]

In its focus on the suppression of information, Corey's memoir is a companion to another memoir in this book series, *Ed Kennedy's War: V-E Day, Censorship, and the Associated Press*. Kennedy, who headed AP operations in Europe during World War II, fought censorship during the entire war and ultimately was fired for it. His firing offense was to violate an embargo on reporting the German surrender, which he had witnessed with other journalists in a small nighttime ceremony at Reims. He broke the embargo on the grounds, first, that he had heard news of it on a German radio and the restriction on reporting was then moot; second, that, in any case, the war was over so censorship rules no longer applied; and finally that he suspected the embargo was not placed for security reasons, as was supposed to be the case, but for political reasons (the Russians wanted to stage their own surrender ceremony). At first the AP celebrated the scoop. Then management knuckled under to government protests and recalled Kennedy.

Corey's most memorable "transgression" was to venture into Germany at the end of the war with four colleagues.[29] They were not the only ones to go across the lines. A handful of reporters made similar trips after the Armistice was signed. The Allies were not keen for these trips to be made, as they did not want to build up support for the ravaged German population.[30] They found it difficult to stop independent reporters from traveling, but AEF-accredited correspondents were easy to control. They could not cross into Germany without the military's permission, and the AEF would not give it. As punishment for violating this rule, the AEF killed the reporters' stories. In Corey's case, this amounted to seventeen dispatches.

Corey tells the story of the so-called "runaway correspondents" at the end of the memoir, and we provide a postscript on this significant event. Suffice it to say here, the correspondents' stories constituted significant news by describing the hardships encountered by the Germans after the war and the likely consequences of the treaty that would be imposed on them. In 1931, Corey wrote of the effects of reparations on the defeated nation: "German youth says, in effect: 'We cannot make a decent living before we are forty; we cannot get married and settle down; we are paying for something of which we don't know a thing, a war, let alone any talk of war guilt. What is the use of living? We might as well get up and fight the devil!'"[31]

Note on Our Editing Process

Corey's manuscript was a rough first draft, and we approached it as such. We changed the title from the bland *Perfectly Irresponsible* to *Herbert Corey's Great War: A Memoir of World War I by the American Reporter Who Saw It All*, which at least has the virtue of telling something of its contents at a glance. We also annotated the memoir, as some of the characters or events Corey references might be unfamiliar to readers, as some of them were to us; there were still some names or references we could not figure out.

Corey frequently repeated anecdotes, and the writing, even allowing for his arch voice, was sometimes slack and needed to be tightened. He also tended to rail too often against the same things—perfidious Allied propaganda and the thirst for ribbons or awards. Also we excised some of his repetitive and misogynistic takes on the role of American female volunteers in Paris. The latter comments, it should be noted, are sharply at odds with his affectionate partnership with his wife, Carolyn. She was an independent woman who joined him in Europe, but was often on her own due to his constant travel. She helped care for American and French soldiers and refugees, and eventually wrote articles of her own for the likes of *National Geographic*.[32]

There were chapters at the end of the book that dealt with his prewar journalism career and seemed irrelevant to a war memoir, so we cut them as well. The memoir's conclusion on the runaway reporters is not in the original manuscript. We took it from his other memoir, titled "Unpublished Autobiography." It seemed a more fitting end to Corey's war memoir.

All of our edits are silent, which is to say we do not use ellipses to note deleted words or brackets for words that were inserted. Corey's unedited typescript, along with the "Unpublished Autobiography," is among his papers at the Library of Congress and can be reviewed in its original form there. We want to acknowledge the unstinting help given by staff at the library's Manuscript Division and the assistance of Jennifer Tellman, a doctoral student at LSU, who meticulously transcribed Corey's tattered, jumbled manuscript and located relevant newspaper articles. Renee Pierce, in the Manship School and always an important help, assisted with document retrieval.

Herbert Corey died of a heart attack in Washington on December 28, 1954. Half an hour before he was stricken, he was in touch with an old friend from the war, Junius Wood of the *Chicago Daily News*, whose chafing over censorship filled the AEF's files. Corey thanked Wood for a homemade pipe cleaner. Corey said he had enjoyed "his first good pipe smoke in weeks."[33]

We hope *Herbert Corey's Great War* will reestablish his name in the annals of American war reporting.

Notes

1. This is from a press-ready reprint of a *Kansas City Star* story, undated and apparently prepared by Associated Newspapers. It is in box 5, Papers of Herbert Corey, Manuscript Division, Library of Congress, hereafter referred to as HC. The title of his column, "New York Day by Day," was a common trope. Frederic William Wile, mentioned in this book, wrote "Germany Day by Day." *Chicago Daily News* reporter Ben Hecht's wrote "One Thousand and One Afternoons in Chicago." And as Corey mentions, O. O. McIntyre appropriated his "New York Day by Day" title when Corey went to war.

2. Herbert Corey, "O. Henry's Lost Masterpieces: I've hoped they were not his very best," chapter in "Unpublished Autobiography," HC.

3. Herbert Corey, "The Fat Dukes of Clydesdale," chapter in "Unpublished Autobiography." For more background on Corey's earlier career in Ohio, see his chapter "Editors Were Wilder Then."

4. John Maxwell Hamilton, *Journalism's Roving Eye: A History of American Foreign Reporting* (Baton Rouge: Louisiana State Univ. Press, 2009), 224–29.

5. Nathan A. Haverstock, *Fifty Years at the Front: The Life of War Correspondent Frederick Palmer* (Washington, D.C.: Brassey's, 1996), xiii.

6. Oliver Gramling, *AP: The Story of News* (New York: Farrar and Rinehart, 1940), 236.

7. Corey, "The Fat Dukes of Clydesdale."

8. Arthur E. Hartsell to Colonel Aristide Moreno, "Memorandum," March 3, 1919, box 6132, entry 228, American Expeditionary Forces, Record Group 120, National Archives and Records Administration, hereafter referred to as AEF.

9. Corey's name also does not appear in John Hohenberg's *Foreign Correspondence*, Michael Emery's *On the Front Lines*, Joseph J. Matthews's *Reporting the Wars*, or (to the author's chagrin) *Journalism's Roving Eye*. In his five volumes of history on foreign correspondents, Robert W. Desmond mentions Corey in one book, focusing in one graph on his unauthorized trip to Germany after the war.

10. James W. Castellan, Ron van Doppeen, and Cooper C. Graham, *American Cinematographers in the Great War, 1914–1918* (Herts, UK: John Libbey, 2014), 100.

11. "Foreign Correspondents of American Newspapers," June 17, 1918, box 6111, entry 222, AEF.

12. "Foreign Correspondents of American Newspapers." Jason Roger's fascinating book *Newspaper Building* describes the Associated Newspapers (New York: Harper, 1918), 68 and passim.

13. "Herbert Corey Tells of Visit to Germany after Armistice," *Editor & Publisher*, April 3, 1919, 20. In fact, Corey did give some lectures on the war when he was home on leave.

14. This is in an unidentified newspaper clipping, n.d., in box 5, HC.

15. Sloane Gordon, "Herbert Corey, The Anecdote Man," *Pearson's Magazine*, April 1915, 441.

16. Corey's story of the first American assault is in typescript, n.d., box 9, HC.

17. This is from a *Cincinnati Times* story, n.d., box 9, HC.

18. Herbert Corey to mother, August 24, 1918, box 3, HC.

19. Herbert Corey, "On the Monastir Road," *National Geographic Magazine*, May 1917, 385.

20. Herbert Corey, "The Serbian Tragedy as I Saw It," *Harper's Monthly*, August 1917, 327–28.

21. *United States Army in the World War, 1917–1919*, vol. 13 (Washington, DC: Center of Military History, 1991), 86.

22. Herbert Corey to his mother, n.d., box 2, HC.

23. Herbert Corey, typescript of his story, n.d., box 6, HC.

24. John Maxwell Hamilton, *Manipulating the Masses: Woodrow Wilson and the Birth of American Propaganda* (Baton Rouge: Louisiana State Univ. Press, 2020), chapter 1.

25. Herbert Corey to his mother, February 21, 1918, box 3, HC.

26. Herbert Corey to Henry Suydam, November 14, 1917, box 6147, entry 229, AEF. This letter ended up in the AEF files, and yet Corey does not seem to have been chastised for it.

27. Hartsell to Moreno, "Memorandum."

28. Herbert Corey, "Welcome to the Next War," *Outlook and Independent*, September 16, 1931, 81.

29. Emmet Crozier, who gives more attention to Corey than anyone else, dedicated his book to Corey and the four "runaway reporters." *American Reporters on the Western Front 1914–1918* (New York: Oxford Univ. Press, 1959).

30. The desire to suppress the German point of view was so strong that the Versailles Treaty, which came later, explicitly placed a three-month moratorium forbidding the Germans from sending political news from Berlin and Hanover.

31. Corey, "Welcome to the Next War," 83.

32. Corey's wife sometimes used the names Carol and Carrie.

33. Obituary, *Washington Post,* December 29, 1954. Corey wrote perceptively of Wood, who was a superb foreign correspondent, in "About Junius B. Wood," typescript, n.d., box 9, HC.

Herbert Corey's
GREAT WAR

1

Three things in my life I regret. Once I hit a mule over the eyes. She was a nice little mule and meant no harm and I was tired and wet and lost my temper. It was a rotten thing to do. Once Dan Edwards telephoned my hotel room to ask if he might come up.[1] I said, "No." A party was going on in my room and the party was drunk and Dan was drunk. But I was a pretty poor fish to bar my door to the gamest man who fought in the war. Once I bought a house. That was a piece of foolishness. What do I want with a house? Except for these things I've behaved pretty well. I've had a grand time.

The best time of all was during the war. I did not write a book about it while it was going on, for I was too busy enjoying it. Too lazy, too, perhaps. When the daily stint of copy had been turned off, the young man's fancy lightly turned to thoughts of a drink on a café terrace or a restaurant with a tasty poulet à la maison—or the next day's work and a long, freezing ride over dark roads to some other point which would shortly have hell shelled out of it. Civilization was putting on the gaudiest show since the days of Genghis Khan, and I did not propose to miss any more of it than I had to. Perhaps I am not very serious minded. The war seemed to me then and still seems to me mostly foolishness.

Lord knows I had all the chance in the world to write books about it. For the five years from 1914 to 1919 I had a roaming commission in Europe for the Associated Newspapers of New York City. My only responsibility was to get a story in the mail each day. I saw something of every belligerent nation ex-

---

1. Daniel R. Edwards, a graduate of the Columbia University School of Journalism, joined the U.S. Army on April 6, 1917, the day the United States entered the war. He was awarded the Medal of Honor, the Distinguished Service Cross, and the Silver Star, making him one of the most decorated soldiers in the conflict.

cept, I think, Romania. I saw most of the statesmen of the day and liked our own statesmen the least. Any sane man—I thought that I was sane—could see that the smartest thing the United States could do was to keep out of the war. I mean just that. The smartest. Nations have no right to go noble. American editors sold us on the war because their business managers wanted good stories so they could get more circulation.

The only bad moment I had during the war was when Colonel Hamilton Smith and Colonel Clark Elliott and most of the 26th Regiment were wiped out at Soissons. I loved them like brothers and I cried like a child.

I had no more fraternal feeling for our Gallant Allies than I have for the Solomon Islanders. They were trying too hard to trim us. I wanted to boot the Red Cross nurses and the YMCA girls and the dancing units out of France. They were the most noisome nuisances I have ever seen. Only the Salvation Army made good. I thought the Germans would have whipped the whey out of the French if we had not come in. They would not have licked the British, however. In the end the British would have either out-fought or out-traded them.

It was evident that I could not have written a book about the war in this tone while the war was on. I would have landed in Leavenworth in an Oregon boot.[2] Nor did I want to write this kind of book about it after we went in. Then it was up to me to boost the war effort. I did boost, too, except on one occasion. The essentially fat-headed General Staff of the American Expeditionary Forces had ordered that the 42nd Division make a practice march of one hundred miles in the middle of the winter of 1917–18. The division was lousy. I mean lousy. It had no delousers. It lacked good, thick, woolen underclothes. Some of the men had not yet received service shoes and left bloody marks on the hard ice of the French roads. Their overcoats were the shoddy, paper-thin affairs that go-getting manufacturers were then turning out. Douglas MacArthur was chief of staff of the division.[3] He said to me:

"You damned cowardly correspondents do not dare tell the truth about this thing that those patent leather sons of bitches at GHQ ordered us to do."

---

2. The Oregon Boot, created by the warden of the Oregon State Penitentiary, was a cruel device that encircled a prisoner's ankle with a strap that looped around the sole of the shoe. It weighed as much as twenty-five pounds and often caused serious injury to prisoners' legs.

3. This is Douglas MacArthur, who went on to command Allied forces in the Pacific in World War II, administered the Allied occupation of Japan afterward, and commanded United Nations forces during the Korean War.

"I'm not afraid," I said. "But what's the use? The censor will not let it through."

"You're afraid to write it."

"I'll write it if you'll stand by it."

MacArthur stood by it, all right. There isn't any run in him. He used to go over the top every time he got the chance—often having only a swagger stick in his hand—just for exercise. But the story did not get through. When I put on a show at the censor's office I was told that GHQ had stopped it.

"Old General So-and-so is chief of ordnance," GHQ had said. "That story would grieve him."

I am not using the old general's name here. My slant on that situation has changed. It was not his fault that American soldiers in France had joke blankets and dissolving shoes and cotton underwear in a climate that would put chilblains on a Siberian tiger. For two years the greatest war in history had been going on. Anyone with the mental capacity of a barn owl could see that we would be tipped into it for one side or the other. Or against both. Our newspapers and our professors—especially, Dear God, the professors—and our old ladies and our politicians had been busy trying to get us into it.[4] We made no pretense of preparation for what must almost certainly come. No. It would not be fair to blame the old general. But at the time I did blame him.

It was sometime in 1915 that E. Alexander Powell and I were living in the Hôtel de Crillon in Paris, along with M. Henri, the manager, a doubtful but extremely good-looking lady, two or three waiters, and a bartender.[5] There may have been other residents but I do not recall them. France was busily trying to make herself fit for fighting. Guests and servants were scarce. William Jennings Bryan had uttered that immortal prophecy that if we were forced to go to war "a million men would spring to arms overnight."[6] Powell

---

4. Corey is referring to the many university professors who became propagandists. Universities organized themselves to promote the war effort, including by preparing prowar materials. Woodrow Wilson's Committee on Public Information had an entire division that enlisted scholars in the creation of propaganda, much of it tendentious and emotional, rather than factual.

5. Powell covered the war for the *New York World*. Like Corey, he reported from many different fronts. When the United States entered the fighting, he was commissioned as an officer in military intelligence and the next year was wounded.

6. Bryan, a pacifist-minded former presidential candidate, resigned as secretary of state in 1915. He thought the president had pursued a policy toward the war that was not truly neutral. But like many who opposed the war, he had changed his mind by 1917.

and I ran into U.S. Ambassador Sharp in the hall. Sharp was a stove manufacturer from Ohio who had been in Congress and had given some money to Bryan's campaign fund.[7] He was a fat joke. Powell and I snarled Bryan's hooey at him, and he went right into his loyal routine.

"Maybe they'll spring to arms," I said, "but how about springing to shoes or overcoats or rifles or—"

Sharp stopped me. He said that I was disloyal. Powell asked him how many portable army stoves he, as a stove manufacturer, could promise the army that would spring to arms overnight. Sharp said he could supply the army with all the stoves it needed. We both laughed.

"You insult the flag of your nation," said Sharp, waddling away. No. It would not be fair to blame that poor old general back in Washington because the 42nd Division's cooties ate holes in the beams of the huts in which its men were billeted. I thought then and I still think that if we had known the truth and all the truth we would never have gone to war. I think that if the censorship had been limited to the expurgation of lies we would have had a decently equipped army in France months earlier and the more blatant follies of the more bladder-headed staff officers would have been prevented.

If I am writing about the war, it is because the time may have come when people will read the truth about it. One man's truth about it, I mean. What is truth to me would not make truth to Sir Philip Gibbs, for instance.[8] There are many who believe that we did not go in early enough and that we should forgive the Allies all the money they will never pay us anyhow for saving them. I believe that if we as a people had had the sense that God gave geese we would be a good many billions of dollars—and a lot of arms and legs—better off, and the rest of the world no worse off. It wasn't our fight anyhow. The only promise to be made in advance about this book is that it will be sordid and frank. If I find myself going high-minded, I'll tear up the copy and go

---

7. William Graves Sharp, an attorney, manufacturer, and three-term congressman, was ambassador to France from 1914 to 1917.

8. Philip Armand Hamilton Gibbs covered the war for the *Daily Telegraph* and *Daily Chronicle*. He was one of only five accredited correspondents to the British Army. He dismissed concerns about the obligation to submit to heavy censorship, saying in a postwar memoir, "There was no need of censorship of our dispatches. We were our own censors." After hearing Gibbs in late 1917 describe what he really saw at the front, Prime Minister David Lloyd George commented, "If people really knew, the war would be stopped tomorrow. But of course they don't know and they can't know." Gibbs was knighted toward the end of the war.

fishing. I might lie a little, of course. I got into a terrible habit of lying during those years when we were all noble. But I'll do my best. If there may seem to be too many capital I's in it, the defense must be that it is being written about a person in whom the author is intensely interested.

This rambling first chapter is, perhaps, the proper place for a tribute to Heywood Broun, socialist and columnist. It—the tribute—is made up partly of roses and mostly of poison ivy. Broun told the truth, or some of the truth, in a book about the AEF in the first days of the organization in France. To do so he violated his oath as an accredited correspondent and might have been kicked out of France if he had not left voluntarily. This is unlikely, of course. The AEF did not kick correspondents very far during the war. I rated being tossed out myself two years later but was not. That story will wait.[9]

It may be that my feeling against Broun was purely personal. He was a poser in a big way, being especially given to spotlighting his sartorial sloppiness, and at the time I resented this. Many an officer who had never heard of the correspondent of the *Tribune* would remember him forever after seeing him in his regalia. Broun wore his hair in a large, black bunch like Lord Byron's, which stuck out from beneath his cap in a frowsy halo, and he preferred to loosen a few buttons of his blouse and unbuckle his Sam Browne belt when in public. This might have been dismissed as the protest of a great soul against the shackles of a uniform, but his treatment of his leggings seemed to me evidence of a form of dementia. I was then and am now simple and ingenuous and as anxious to be of service as was little Marcel, who clowned it in the old Hippodrome when New York was still a town worth living in and when Frank Ward O'Malley and Irvin Cobb and a score of other regular men sat nightly in Jack's.[10]

"Heywood," I said out of the side of my mouth one day, "Heywood, you've got your leggings on wrong." I wanted to spare him. It seemed to me that he would be bitterly humiliated if his mistake were to be noticed by

---

9. In fact, Broun's credentials were revoked when he returned home and wrote about the war for his newspaper, the *New York Tribune*. His book—really books—came later. He wrote two of them, *The A.E.F.: With General Pershing and the American Forces* and *Our Army at the Front*. Neither of them was very critical, apart from his distaste for censorship. In the first of these two books, he wrote, "The newspaper stories about our troops in France on their tremendous errand should ring like the chronicle of an old crusade, but it is hard for the chronicler to bring a tingle when he must write or cable 'Richard the deleted hearted'" (122).

10. O'Malley and Cobb were known for their humorous reporting.

some thousands of men and officers who were trying to keep themselves clean and decent looking under a handicap of mud and shoddy clothing. His right leg legging was on his left leg and his left legging on his right leg, and each bulged wide between ankle and knee and a large puff of white underpants protruded through the gap. Broun glared at me angrily. I do not recall that he made any reply whatever. His sensitive ego was too greatly bruised, perhaps, and it became immediately apparent to me that the leggings were a part of Broun's personal show.

He continued to wear his leggings wrong side to, and I brooded heavily over this evidence of weakness in a man whose professional work I had long admired even though I disagreed with it. Some nights later the argument at the dinner table in the correspondents' mess rose to unusual heights. I presume that a certain latitude of expression is permitted in the refectories of Yale and at socialist gatherings, and when Broun and Lincoln Eyre, who represented the *New York World*, had a difference of opinion, Broun called Eyre a liar. Perhaps the fighting word was not used. I am not certain. In any case, the two men leaped up—Broun tall and bulky and Byronesque and unbuttoned and Eyre equally tall and forty pounds lighter—and Eyre socked him. Broun went down and stayed down until Eyre had been secured. One of Broun's friends explained that Broun's heart is bad. I do not precisely know what he meant by this.[11]

In any case, Broun's book about the defects of the AEF was true in large part and had a good sale, because it was one of the first, and may have been inspired by pure patriotism. I could not have written anything in the tone at that time, for I had promised to submit every word I wrote to the censor, and I still attached some value to my oath. In any event, I would not have written anything of the sort, for fear of being kicked out of the war, and I would not have that happen for anything in the world. I point with pride to the fact that I did not violate my own oath until after the Armistice, and then only in an effort to help restore American independence and throw a little sand in the smoothly running gears of our allies.

In 1914 I began covering the war in Europe in precisely the spirit of an American reporter covering a fire. That was the way I had been trained to do

---

11. Lincoln Eyre was one of those few who came, as Corey did, in 1914 and stayed to the end. He was considered an outstanding journalist. He died in 1928, in Berlin, where he was the *New York Times* bureau chief. His wife was the German film star Dina Gralle.

things. As correspondent or copy-handler I had covered several large-scale disasters—the sinking of the *Slocum* and the Iroquois fire and the wreck of the *Titanic*—and in none of them had it ever occurred to me to kick the slate out of the Fire Demon or dig up the history of navel architecture.[12] My job was simply to write a piece each day about some phase of the great spectacle as I saw it. Later on, the professors and the old ladies were worked up by the propaganda of the Allies and a combined shortage and misuse of German propaganda, and the American temper went heavily pro-Allies and I went with it. But at the outset I was just a reporter.

"There will be a war in Europe," said the proprietor of a little restaurant on Oxford Road to us that day in 1914 on which the Grand Duke was assassinated at Sarajevo.

"What sheer nonsense," I responded.

My wife and I were in London on a vacation. For years I had been writing the "New York Day by Day" column for the *Cincinnati Times-Star*. New York columnist O. O. McIntyre swiped the title during the war, when I was not using it. I do not blame him. In 1910 or thereabouts the Associated Newspapers took me over, along with the column, and by 1914 I was completely fed up with it.

The Oxford Road restaurant was operated by a pair of Austrians. They had lived in London so long that they spoke English as the English do, which is quite a feat, and their sons had been educated in England. Nevertheless, they were still Austrian citizens and their sons were enrolled on the Austrian army lists. The last I heard of the pair of likable, industrious, good-tempered little Austrians was that they were behind the barbed wire of an internment camp. Their sons died, I was told, somewhere in the Serbian mud. But when they told us of the war to come, I tried to laugh them out of their worry.

"The world has progressed beyond war," I maintained. "It is preposterous to think that war will come."

I am describing my frame of mind because it is indicative of the temper of the United States at that time, or at least of the western United States, where I belong. All my life I had been filled with hot idealistic air. Ministers and professors had assured their communities that there would be no more

---

12. On June 15, 1904, the *General Slocum* caught fire and sank in the East River near New York City. The Iroquois Theatre refers to a tragic 1903 fire in Chicago that took more than six hundred lives.

war, and the old ladies had bravely risen in public to bear the same testimony in their fine, quavering old voices. The fact that "Trouble in the Balkans" was a Monday morning headline meant nothing to us. There seemed always to be trouble in the Balkans. We were assured, too, that if the statesmen were silly enough to order a war, the bankers would not allow it. Banking was still an honorable profession. At that time bankers were not entering their own homes through the kitchen windows under cover of night.

The Austrian restauranteurs were right, of course, but for a time the United States was able to look on rather impartially. Not many native-born Americans were partisans of either side. We were still a comparatively independent nation and able to remember that European nations had always conducted their affairs with an eye single to their own good. The British fleet stood by us at Manilla during the Spanish-American War, but it is also true that during our civil war Great Britain interfered with the Federal government and the Union cause immensely. France made use of us to worry England during the Revolution and then did her best to set Mexico against us when we were fighting our brothers for our lives.

It is difficult for me even yet to realize that the time was to come when one had almost to swear allegiance to King George to be accepted as a good American and stand with one's hat off when the "Marseillaise" was sung. During the war I paid a visit home, and on the return voyage the Dutch ship on which I sailed was held up by a British warship at the mouth of New York harbor. I could see New York's towers through the sea mist and even hear New York's bells. But the British blockade was complete. A tired little midshipman climbed the Jacob's ladder, followed by a sour boat crew.

"Line up," the British midshipman ordered.

For hours Americans stood in line, waiting for a chance to persuade him that if we were permitted to go to Europe we would be tireless lovers of the Allies. Between times we looked over our shoulders at the Woolworth tower and Governor's Island and old Castle Garden and wondered just how much American citizenship is really worth. If that midshipman had decided against us he might have forced the ship to return to port. For that matter he might have taken the ship. He had the power, and so far as a spineless United States government was concerned, he had the law. Later Republican congressman Martin Madden of Chicago got these facts and made a speech in the House. He was one of the powers in the House, too, but nothing happened. Except, as I recall, some other congressman said that Madden was not a good American. But I could not foresee these things when I sat in the little restaurant on the Oxford Road and told a man who knew what he was talking about that the world had grown too sensible to go to war. I wish I had a record of that talk. I'd like to have another good blush.

2

I shall never learn to love the British government. Any British government. It is too smart for the unsophisticated American. But I have a real liking for almost every Briton I know. They are good sportsmen.

Over here, though, we have a different idea of what is implied in the phrase "good sportsmen." We think a good sportsman should lose with a handshake and a smile. The British think a good sportsman should fight until he cannot stand up. When he loses a decision, he bites the victor on the heel.

In 1914 the British showed the world what propaganda can do. The Germans had the desire but not the skill. A German's idea of propaganda is either to buy or bully the other fellow. A French propagandist stands at the salute and repeats "Vive la France" a great number of times. The Britisher buys a drink, smiles lazily, and contributes his idea of what the situation should be in a leisurely way. He may be compelled to take a few liberties with the facts, but he gets there. He cuddled us into a fight with which we had no more to do than with the fashion in undergarments in Turkey and made us like it. I wish I could hope our own people will do better in the next war, but they will not. If the British are with us, they will get us all heated up and we will insist on picking up the check. If they are against us, we're sunk. If we had only known it, the whole propaganda machinery was already visible in the early days of 1914. The British propagandists threw together a crude, creaking, disjointed device and made it work until it could be bettered. We stood goggle-eyed, seeing every move of the nimble British fingers, and never catching a glimpse of the rubber pea. My admiration is practically unbounded for the men who handled the operation. Britons never will be slaves while they have their press agents.

The extraordinary thing to me about the propaganda of the early days is that Americans were by no means the favorite sons of London. We were, not to put too fine a point on it, the damnedest nuisances ever imposed on any nation in the act of going to war. Great Britain was not prepared to fight, as everyone now knows. For years her statesmen had depended on their ability to wheedle or bully their way out of any situation. Overnight the pin was pulled out of the grenade and the nation found itself shot onto an explosive dump-heap. At the same moment Americans came lolloping in from the continent, tongues out like beagles. Not an American landed in England at that time who was not convinced that his hasty retreat across the channel was the saddest case on record and that something should be done about it.

"Why don't you go to the American embassy?" I asked a few hundred complaining compatriots at this time.

"God damn the American embassy" they replied with unanimity and fervor. "We've been there."

So far as I know, Ambassador Page did not move his little finger to convenience his constituents at this time.[1] In this he lived up to the best traditions of American diplomats in Europe, with the exception of James W. Gerard, the ambassador to Germany.[2] It seemed to me Gerard felt a real responsibility for Americans in Germany. Elsewhere our diplomats were too busy with their gilt and tinsel to fret about their countrymen. This may, perhaps, be merely an ill-tempered expression of distaste for them. I am still unable to determine any incident of the war which gave me more acute pain than the spectacle of strutting, pompous little Van Dyke, warming the bottom of his little breeches before the fire on a raw day and thereby shutting all others away from it while he delivered himself of a fulsome paean to the Allied cause. All he said may have been true. It should not have been said by a diplomat from a neutral country.[3]

---

1. Walter Hines Page, a journalist and book publisher, was a devoted supporter of Great Britain during his tenure as ambassador there, from 1913 to 1918. The British reciprocated with a memorial to him in Westminster Abbey after his death in 1918.

2. Gerard, a lawyer and civic reformer, was ambassador to Germany from 1913 to 1917. He wrote *My Four Years in Germany* (1917) and *Face to Face with Kaiserism* (1918). *My Four Years in Germany* was filmed in 1918.

3. Henry Jackson Van Dyke was an educator, writer, clergyman, and diplomat. President Wilson appointed him minister to the Netherlands and Luxembourg in 1913. Contrary to what Corey says, he is remembered by some for protecting Americans in Europe.

Not only were Americans running all over London during those early days, getting in everyone's way, but American correspondents could be found in almost every seam. Some of them had never been in England before, and wrote funny stories about the Beefeaters. Some of them had gold expense money and lived at the Savoy bar, and still others had come prepared to go to the front immediately and simply refused to take no for an answer. My sympathies were largely with the Londoners. The pre-war American had been pretty badly spoiled by politicians and professors and ministers, and if he did not get what he wanted his big blue eyes would fill with tears.

What London thought of us was expressed by an Englishwoman at the Palladium one night.

Frederick Roy Martin of the Associated Press and I had taken our charming wives to the music hall. During the evening a sketch was presented, the scene of which was laid in New York. The hero was English, of course, and at a dramatic moment he shook his finger at the commissioner of police, who seemed to have been modelled on George S. Dougherty, once of the Pinks.[4]

"You defy me," shouted the finger-shaking hero, "an' I'll take your blinking town apart."

There was a portentous rustle of Liberty's heaviest silks behind us and we turned to look into the sunken eyes of an English lady. A duchess, probably. Her face was long and savage, like that of a bad horse.

"Spoken," said she, "like a true born English gentleman."

The evening was ruined. We could not keep from giggling in our underbred American way, and we were afraid that if we yielded to the temptation she would rise with a shout of King and Country and bang our heads together. I know what the rest of the audience would have done, too. They would have looked on stonily and little jets of vocal steam would have risen here and there.

"Serve the blinking bounders bally well right!"

It was during this early period that I saw Herbert Hoover for the first time. London was being drowned in frightened, moneyless, bewildered Americans, and Ambassador Page was as much use to them as a wooden leg in a swamp. The embassy staff did what they could, but that was little, and in any event Page kept its members hopping with messages to dukes and whatnots. The injured Americans were about ready to kick in the embassy door

---

4. Dougherty was a member of the Pinkerton Detective Agency. He is credited with introducing fingerprinting to police forces.

when Hoover took over. I had never heard of him before—no one seemed to know anything about him—but the big room in which the Americans had been doing their shouting suddenly seemed to calm. My only recollection is that of a composed man at a desk, telling someone else what to do. He seemed entirely unworried. Presently everyone else was unworried, too.

If I claim a little credit for showing up the British censorship early in 1914, it must be understood that there is no hero blood in me at all. The facts are simply that I had uncovered a good story. Every other reporter in London knew it as well or better than I did, but none of them could write it. Imagine a well-paid correspondent for an American paper, wallowing in gold expenses, hobnobbing occasionally with lords and earls, cabling a story which might have been run under some head such as this: "British Censor Forging Dispatches to America."

That correspondent would either have been deported on the first boat, or he would have been made useless to his paper by the methods in which the British are adept. No American newspaper business manager would underwrite reportorial courage of that sort. A business manager is definite in his conviction that a reporter's job is to get news that will sell his papers, and that his job is certainly not to get into trouble because of his candor. But this time I was free to act. My job was a roving one, anyhow. The actual news out of London was being served to the Associated Newspapers by other means. If Great Britain wanted to bounce me, I felt fairly certain that I could land safely in Germany on the second bounce. Therefore, I wrote a story which the *New York Globe* headed: "Corey Charges British Censor is Forging Dispatches"

What the censors had actually been doing had either been to cut out words and sentences from dispatches in such a fashion that the entire meaning was altered—and always to the disadvantage of the enemy—or to insert words and sentences to the same end. This, of course, is forgery. In 1914 my story informed the United States for the first time that John Bull would deal from the bottom of the pack. Sir Gilbert Parker sent me a note:[5] "Come in and take tea with me this afternoon."[6]

---

5. Sir Gilbert Parker, a Canadian novelist well known in the United States, was married to a wealthy American and held a seat in Parliament. In the first years of the war, Parker was responsible for propagandizing Americans in hopes of encouraging the United States to join the Allies. Based near Victoria Station, Parker's staff grew from nine to fifty-four and amassed a mailing list of thirteen thousand prominent Americans. His program was done quietly so as to avoid criticism of open propaganda, which was in sharp contrast with the way the Germans operated—to their great disadvantage.

6. Corey had, indeed, stirred up a lot of furor. The *New York Evening Post* reported that

Parker's note flattered me immensely. He was the chief of the section devoted to American propaganda, but I thought of him only as a novelist whose stories I admired. I got into my newly purchased morning coat and high hat and swathed my ankles in spats and bore down on him. This was a new uniform to the American correspondents, and we did not suffer it gladly, but it somehow seemed essential. When I entered Parker's office the eminent novelist was as pleasant as a scorpion. He introduced me to the gentleman who was later to become Lord Buckmaster.[7] Then he ostentatiously locked the door.

"What do you mean by charging that the British censor has forged dispatches to American newspapers?" he shouted. "Where is your proof?"

I was on the spot. I would not give the names of my informants, and unless I gave them the names I stood convicted of a peculiarly mean brand of lie. I would cheerfully have clouted Parker over the head with a chair, but Buckmaster intervened. "Let us talk this over quietly," he said in his pleasant voice.

"You have the proof under your own hands," was my reply. The anger aroused by Parker died at once. "Every dispatch that has been sent is under lock and key in your own office. Examine them and see whether any words or sentences have been written in, in such a way as to change the entire meaning."

Parker sputtered again. Buckmaster sipped his tea.

"You must be sure of your ground," he said with a keen glance at me.

I was more sure than I dared tell him. One of the greatest news-gathering organizations had sent duplicates of every dispatch to New York by mail and every change made by the censors had been noted and a brief prepared setting forth what had been done. Perhaps every other news-gathering organization had done the same thing. Buckmaster considered the situation quietly for a time, and then he nodded.

Corey, in a letter, had "flatly [made] the charge that dispatches have been altered for the purpose of hiding the truth and blackening the enemy's character, and winning the aid of public opinion in America for the Allies." This became a story in the *Times of London*. Corey responded that he did not recall that statement, but "I did charge that dispatches telling of German atrocities were permitted to go through unaltered, and that the sentences in other dispatches in which credit was given to the Germans for courtesy and kindness had been deleted. I abide by that statement." The *Times of London* ran the *New York Evening Post* story on October 26, 1914, and Corey's response the next day.

7. Stanley Buckmaster, 1st Viscount Buckmaster, was a British lawyer and Liberal Party politician. He served for a time as director of the British Press Bureau.

"I suspect that Mr. Corey is right. Some things were said in the House of Commons a day or two ago which seems to sustain him. I shall take steps at once to end a situation which could soon become dangerous and is now intolerable."

My belief is that forgery was abandoned as a weapon in the censor's office from that day. But the printing of wholly untrue propaganda did not stop, of course. To be frank about it, the English were right in this. They were fighting for their national existence and they were the first of the great nations to recognize that newspapers are more valuable than big guns. A few days later, Jack Spurgeon, then the head of the *New York World*'s London bureau, met me at Brown's hotel. He had been told on what seemed to be impeccable authority of the arrival in London of a Belgian child whose arms had been lopped off by the German soldiery.

"It came to me from the authority of eyewitnesses," said he. He named the men. Everyone seemed to be truthful. Unfortunately, the eyewitness stories had been filtered to him through another man, the father of the surgeon who had cared for the child.

"That seems good enough."

"Not good enough for me," said Spurgeon. "I have never before had what seems to be so perfectly authenticated a story of outrage presented to me, but I have investigated scores of similar stories and not one stood up. I'm going to do the same with this one."

One of his best men spent a week on it and completely failed to get the needed proof. Yet every one of the original witnesses insisted that the story was true. Not one had actually seen the child, but in the excitement of the time had repeated the tale as one in their own knowledge. That there were outrages is certain, but I do not believe that they were committed against women and children. The Germans practiced "frightfulness" as a means of making war and had no hesitation in shooting down civilians to overawe a captured town.[8]

---

8. The German military pursued a harsh policy of "*schrecklichkeit*" ("Frightfulness") against civilians who mounted resistance after their military forces had been defeated. Innocent civilians were abused, but British propagandists exaggerated this to create an image of the Germans as utter barbarians.

Corey had the courage to call attention to these exaggerations, which were made famous in a commission headed by former ambassador to Washington Viscount Bryce. A typescript of

When the United States went to war in 1917, Americans believed these stories of maimed babies. Presently more money was needed and the Fourth Victory Loan was launched. The Newspaper Enterprise Association (NEA) cabled its correspondent in France.

"Get fifty children who have been maimed by the Germans. Arrange to bring them to the United States with their parents or other guardians. We will pay all expenses and salaries if need be."

The plan was to make a countrywide tour with them.

Cal Lyon was a correspondent and my close associate.[9] I'd be afraid to say how many thousands of miles we rode together in Army Cadillacs. Lyon more or less believed the stories of mutilation and outrage, and called on the American army's G2 for aid in mobilizing the proof.

"We haven't any mutilated people," said the G2 officers, grinning. "What's more, we do not believe there are any or ever have been. Those yarns were just propaganda. But we'll give you a letter to the British information service."

The British laughed at Lyon and sent him on to the French authorities. The French listened gravely but admitted that they had no victims, had never had any victims, did not believe there ever had been any, and suggested that the stories had served their purpose and might now be forgotten. La Belle Amerique was now in the war thigh deep and throwing money at it with

---

a story Corey wrote on the subject is worth quoting from. This story also contained the charge that British censors inserted bogus information in American journalists' dispatches.

> It is not my intention to deny that atrocities have been committed. But it is frankly admitted by the very men engaged upon this [British] report that many of the stories printed here are incapable of verification, and others have been wildly exaggerated....
>
> In reading reports of German atrocities a certain conservatism should be displayed. It is to be remembered that no impartial report has as yet been permitted by the British War Office. Correspondents are not permitted anywhere near the scene of operations.

The extent to which Corey's story was published by the papers he served is not clear. The story can be found in box 9, HC.

9. Lyon represented the Newspaper Enterprise Association, which was organized by E. W. Scripps. Scripps newspapers shared costs and content for the NEA as well as United Press, which Scripps also owned. Scripps heavily supported the war. The NEA provided prowar editorials and emotional features to the same end. Just before the United States entered the war, Lyon embedded himself with the navy to write about the great opportunities that existed to serve the country.

both hands. Why bother about mutilated people? But Lyon insisted and the French reluctantly sent him on to the Belgians.

"But you will not find any victims," the Belgians said.

The Belgians were inclined to be peevish, as I remember the story that Lyon told. They admitted they had no victims—never had had any—and what about it, anyhow? It was a grave disappointment to the NEA and to Lyon, personally, who had envisioned a triumphal tour of the United States in which he would spend most of his time under a spotlight before a weeping audience, with a small, mutilated baby under each arm. He said that he had seriously considered stealing a couple of children and mutilating them himself. But I do not believe this.

The extraordinary fact about this early days propaganda—as I began to say some paragraphs to the rear—is that Americans were anything but the pets of London at the time. They were in the way and were made to feel it, and they responded with loud and public damnation of their hosts. It would seem that in this atmosphere of mutual dislike the fact would have been recognized that propaganda was making fools of us, but so far as I know, it never was. The reason must be that the Americans who had been chased out of Europe hated the Europeans more bitterly than they did the islanders. Many of them even today recall the goodbye stories told them by German hotel keepers.

"Ged oud," they said in their painfully acquired English. "Pig-dogs."

The United States was still neutral at the time. One morning I was awakened by the telephone and stood barefoot on the tiled floor of the coldest flat on Albemarle Street to hear Fred Grundy's voice over the wire. He was then the resident correspondent of the old *New York Sun*.

"Hello, Corey. I thought you were in Aldershot."

Aldershot was a military prison where Germans were being interned behind barbed wire fences. I rubbed the sleep out of my eyes.

"I've just received a cable from the *Sun* stating that you are a prisoner in Aldershot and that questions have been asked in Congress."

"Someone's kidding you. Goodnight."

Some days before I had visited the internment camp at Aldershot and had written a story about it. It was a good story, too. The sight of the poor German devils behind the wire, living in holes grubbed in the ground, was just as emotionally provoking to me then as the sight of English prisoners behind the wires in German internment camps proved to be some months later. Ranked outside the wires were handsome cars filled with good-looking men and women, wrapped in furs, who had driven down to see the sight. The British would not have bothered about the story but that it had been ginned up into a provocation in New York.

George Sylvester Viereck was then editing *Die Vaterland,* a magazine of German propaganda, and he had sandwiched slices of my story between slices of a story of his own, filled with grief and vitriol, forgotten all about quotation marks, and charged the whole mess to me.[10] The British correspondents in New York were cooperating actively with the propagandists in London. It was their job to spot any American correspondent in England who was not properly sympathetic to the cause of the Allies and have him either booted out or muzzled. They probably cabled:

"Corey's out again. Charges that etc., etc...."

In an exchange of cables with the Associated Newspapers in New York one of my sentences had been misinterpreted and it was hastily assumed that I was in Aldershot along with the Germans.[11] The U.S. Senate took the matter up manfully, and there is no doubt that I would have been properly championed by that body if there had been any need of championing. In the end it developed that my standing with the British War Office was not injured. Still later the incident helped me to get into Germany. I was not at all sore at the British—though considerably agitated by Mr. George Sylvester Viereck—but the Germans assumed that I was about ready to go goose-stepping. Maybe I helped them think so.

---

10. George Sylvester Viereck was born in Munich in 1884 and brought to New York twelve years later. He claimed his father was the illegitimate offspring of Kaiser Wilhelm I. Viereck's early success at poetry led the *Saturday Evening Post* to write, "Not in a decade, perhaps, has any young person been so unanimously accused of being a genius." In 1912, he worked in Theodore Roosevelt's presidential campaign. Ready to do his part for Germany in 1914, he started his weekly, which was heavily subsidized by the Germans. *The Fatherland* inveighed against American press bias. By October 1917 *The Fatherland* had a circulation of one hundred thousand. He went to prison for his pro-German activities in World War II.

11. Corey's cable, which was misinterpreted, read, in part, "In Aldershot prison. Letter follows." Corey's bosses assumed that he was arrested because of stories he had written from Berlin, which were viewed as sympathetic to the Germans. This is reprised in H. H. McClure, the syndicate's chief executive, to "Managing Editors" (editors to whom McClure appealed for help in springing Corey from his supposed cell at Aldershot), box 5, HC.

3

As a member of a rival concern, I am somewhat annoyed by the neat efficiency with which Great Britain went to war. We tackled the job in a bigger and gaudier way when our time came, and were handicapped by crackpot dames, blabber-mouthed congressmen, and the need to give three cheers whenever we sighted our faces over the back bar. Our innate national idiocy rose to the top like cream. In 1917 a man connected with our national plan to put a million airplanes in the wind by sunset talked with me.

"It will be the most superb production program," he said.

His eyes shone like a cat's in the dark. I broke in:

"Perhaps you do not understand one of the lessons taught by this war," I said gently. I wanted to bat him over the head with a bottle. "Fashions in fighting planes change almost hourly. The man with the newest and fastest can drive his enemy out of the air. Mass production of the sort you speak of would be a burnt offering of pigeons. The British, the French, the Germans keep their air fleets mobile. If Von Hassenpfeffer knocks off a few Allies in the morning with his new fighter, he is brought down in the afternoon by Lord Breadpudding's newer fighter."

The man just shook his head at me. The system was all wrong, he said. We would show 'em how to handle a war. The funny part of it is that we did, in the end. But if we had had to last the distance the English lasted, we would have had one devil of a time. For one thing we labored under a heavy she-handicap. Friends told me of the numerous and mostly useless dames in breeches who strutted around American streets during our early period of preparation. I saw them in France a little later. Everyone—or almost everyone—knows that if the ladies had kept their pretty legs out of khaki, the United States would have been better off mentally, financially, and morally. They were a complicated and unmitigated nuisance. Old John Bull did not fool with them the way we did.

"Who are they?" I asked Bob Parr in Salonica one day. He was the liaison officer between what was left of the sturdy little Serb army and the British supply trains. The place was Flaco's Cafe, where everyone drank brandy and coffee at intervals when in Salonica. The "they" were a group of young women in the uniform of the British WAACS. I may be in error about the WAAC part of it. The uniform was British in any case. They were knocking off large goblets of whiskey and water and were smoking pipes.

"But..."

My American morals were being pretty badly shocked. I had a certain knowledge of the Facts of Life, of course, but like most other Americans of my previous and somewhat prudish generation I did a lot of pretending. My British friend was practical, as are most of our British friends. He could not for the life of him see upon what my finicking objections were based. "They" could drive ambulances and trucks and do other hard work, he observed. It would be a hell of a note if the possession of bad habits were to be equivalent to a guarantee of non-participation.

"That little Canadian blonde," said he, "brought her wagon in last night through more fire than most of our generals have ever heard of. What if she does smoke a pipe?"

If we had found ourselves in Great Britain's fix in 1914, we would have started in by filling Buckingham Palace with Girl Scouts in uniforms designed to display the slenderness of the leg. Then we would have drained the Serpentine to make a running track for about-to-be retired majors of the regular army and have built a new and finer Buckingham on the site of the Marble Arch, which would be removed to Wandsworth Common. These things could all be excused by the theory that after the war ended the labor displacement could be cushioned by hiring men to pull everything down again. Even today I occasionally see handsome residences, complete with everything including sewing rooms and nurseries, which were built by our government for someone during the war.

Great Britain does not coddle its women. Persons who have been fooled by novels of English country life may believe that an English gentleman almost never sits down except when a handsome damsel squats on his knee, but my observation runs counter to this theory. Women in Great Britain are the weaker and louder sex. They make a good deal of noise outside of public houses, and nature's foolishness with the clavicle makes it impossible for them to break even with their men in hand-to-hand combat. The Briton takes a proper advantage of this handicap. His women do as much rough work as he does, and there is, perhaps, no place on earth where chivalry is deader than in the British Isles. They sing a song about Cupid—"the cute little charmer who sits up aloft"—and I'll tell you why he sits up aloft. It is the only place he is safe.

Therefore when Great Britain put its women to work during the war they worked. They did not go for the buggy ride, as did ours. This tendency toward extreme practicality was noted as soon as the world began to throw its fit. All the London papers began to talk mournfully of the national habit of muddling through, the implication being that England would only muddle through after having made every possible mistake.

The French hated the English for the part forced upon them in 1914 and 1915. I expect they will continue to hate the English, for it would be a dangerous thing if these old neighbors really understood and trusted each other. As long as England does all the understanding and none of the trusting everything will go along all right, for England will produce a new trick whenever one is needed and dazzle France out of her inclination toward trouble. But in 1914 and 1915 England made France hold the line, because that was the only thing to do. Meanwhile the raw English boys were being hammered into good soldiery. And were they hammered! An English sergeant has no loving kindness at all in his make-up. But when he turns out a recruit, he is the finished article.

One night I occupied the first-class carriage from Salisbury Plains with an enormous Canadian lieutenant in kilts.

"You're an American," he announced. "It's a good thing for you that you are not an Englishman. I'll twist off the head of the first English . . ."

The Canadian was drunk and bloodshot. The door of the carriage opened and three British officers stepped in. It was a rainy night and Salisbury Plains were deep in mud, but the three were clean and polished. The Canadian said:

"Get out, you English . . ."

They withdrew in perfect order. The Canadian gave me his name, which is associated with big money in Canada, and stated that he hoped to kill him a couple of English before he went to France. He was in deadly earnest about it, too, even if he were somewhat drunken. The incident would not be worth repeating, except that it displayed the poise of the upper class Englishman at this time. An American officer would—most of them would—have called the guard. A fine youngster's life might have been ruined because of a moment of bad temper and drink. The English trio pretended that it had never happened.

The nation was being compelled to compromise with expediency, and it did so with immense success. The amount of money that was not being wasted simply appalled me, as an American. A hut on Salisbury Plains was just a hut. It was not a mansion. Girl drivers of lorries slept in their seats when they got the chance. No one suggested building steam-heated dormitories for them. The British military ankle, swathed in its wrappings, is as shapeless as a sack of hay. But it is as warm and dry as conditions permit. The British uniform had evolved through generations toward comfort and has the good looks of fitness. Some thin-necked general must have designed the American uniform of the day, with its silly clerical collar. It may be that shells were not produced as rapidly as desired in 1915. But no money was thrown away in the production. Yet all the time the British kept up their bleat of inefficiency. Of muddling through. I have said before that they are too smart for us—or for anyone. They can lick anyone who will listen to them.

"I think I'll try to get into Germany," I said to Frederick Palmer one day.

"I'll go with you," said Palmer.[1]

Maybe it was the other way around. I have no wish to take credit for the thought. Every correspondent had it, anyway, but not many of them were footloose. Palmer had a commission from *Collier's Weekly* and had filled his rooms on Albemarle street with old saddles and tents, under the impression that as soon as Lord Kitchener found out he was in town he would be sent to the front.[2] Several other correspondents lived in the same house. Samuel G. Blythe and I shared quarters there for the sake of coffee until my wife joined me.[3] Blythe and I loathed with a frantic loathing the muddy mess that the En-

---

1. As noted in the introduction, Palmer was one of the greatest war correspondents of his time. His first war had been Greco-Turkish War of 1897. He wrote about his trip to Germany in his book on the first year of the war, *My Year of the Great War*. He mentions Corey in the book when recounting the trip.

2. Horatio Herbert Kitchener, 1st Earl Kitchener, was a British army general. He was the secretary of state for war in the Great War.

3. Blythe, once the Washington bureau chief for the *New York World*, wrote for the *Saturday Evening Post*.

glish believe to be coffee. They are the worst cooks in the world—everyone knows that—not having progressed beyond the ability that most savages have to roast meat and boil cabbage. They are at their worst with a coffee pot, although no city buys better coffee in the bean than comes to London.

Most of us had discovered that the British had no thought whatever of permitting neutral correspondents to go into the field with their troops. Their leaders had a very well-defined plan to make use of the newspapers. Already they had covered most of the news channels and the Germans were finding increasing difficulty in getting their side of the case before the world. This was added to by the basic peevishness of the German character. I believe they are the strongest nation in Europe today and that they will probably wind up top dog after the next series of wars has been fought. But German manners are always bad, and the German always whimpers if he does not get his way. He whimpered in 1914. No one cared. The English had already established him before the world as the archetype of brute.

Palmer, almost alone of the Americans, had not been able to abandon his dream of being a war correspondent on a white horse. He pestered Whitehall by day and Downing Street by night. The idea of visiting Germany probably appealed to him as a good way to link the British to him in friendship and certainly appealed to the British. Our going was facilitated so far as that could be done. Travel between the belligerent countries was not restricted then, so far as neutrals were concerned. It was in the station at Amsterdam, I think, that I saw a huge, wordy person in a silk hat. He seemed to be a reception committee for a group of Germans. Someone named him: "Hendrik Van Loon."[4]

I was told that Van Loon's activities were being watched by the British Secret Service, but if that was true it is certainly unimportant. Everyone's activities were watched by the Secret Service. The Service knew all and saw all. Once, in Paris, the Prince of Wales and the officer attached to his person escaped espionage, as they thought, and went in search of light and laughter. They saw no one they knew. They saw no one who could by any possibility know them. They were back in quarters at a proper hour, giggling over their

---

4. Hendrik Willem van Loon, a Dutch-American, was a veteran Associated Press correspondent. Before the war he had been posted to Warsaw, St. Petersburg, and London. He accompanied the German army's invasion of Belgium at the start of the war. He also was a historian and children's book author.

exploit. Just as they were turning in there came a tap on the door. There stood good old Secret Service himself.

"Beg your pawrdon, m'lord," said he. "But y'r l'rdship left your 'andkerchief on the piano."

Our experience in Germany is another illustration of the fact that two men simply cannot see the same thing alike. Neither Palmer nor I spoke more German than "bier" and "bitte" and "noch eins." We got to Berlin because so many people who spoke English were willing to be nice to Americans—people who might have pull and in any case tipped well. We shared the same huge apartment in the hotel, saw the same people, heard the same stories, returned on the same train. By that time, we hated each other bitterly, the enforced companionship generating murder in our hearts.

Palmer wrote a story for *Collier's* under the title "The City of Unshed Tears." To hear him tell it, Berlin was just about ready to fall down and die. He saw nothing but fright and discouragement and lack of organization and fear on every side. I do not know how much of this Palmer really thought he saw and how much of it was written to the order of the day. I had seen precisely the same things and heard the same stories and had come to the conclusion that Germany was sorry it ever happened and that it did not happen with the consent of the middle classes, and that if the Germans could get out gracefully they would be glad. But that they were sure of eventual victory, and if they were not resigned to the inevitable losses, they had at least made up their minds to stand them.

Palmer's story was a tremendous hit in London, naturally enough. That was the stuff to give the troops. Germany was scared almost to the point of quitting. One more wallop to the button and she would take the count. The acid comment was made by an English correspondent in New York that although I had seen the same things the veteran war correspondent had seen, I had drawn entirely different conclusions from them. I was identified as the savage American who had found interned Germans not living in luxury in Aldershot and had told tales about the censors and their forgeries. Buckmaster wrote me a note: "Come in and see me some day. How about today, for tea?"

A British government note is an awe-inspiring thing, and I say this as one who has had several of them. They are hand-written, probably with quill pens, on hand-made paper that is stiff enough to use for lining a prairie shack. They have crowns and things spattered about them appropriately, and are delivered by a commissionaire—"humpbacked with medals" as our doughboys used to say. I turned up to see Buckmaster with my heart so high in my throat that it looked like a goiter. It seemed probable that for telling the fact that Germany was not badly frightened—no worse than any other of the fighting nations—I would be ridden out on a rail. Buckmaster said that he was interested.

"You did not agree at all with Mr. Palmer?"

That opening would start the valves popping in any correspondent. I believed that my story was the right one—I still believe it—and that Palmer's was all wrong. I began to unbraid and revel. There were three or four other officers in the room, and they were as interested as Buckmaster. We drank tea until the Oolong ran out of our ears, and they asked questions and I answered them. I was not a military expert, but I was observing, as any reporter is bound to, and no Englishman had yet been able to get into Berlin and out again. They wanted to know precisely the things I had to tell them, and I wanted to tell them these things to prove that my story was true. I had forgotten all about the possibility of being deported. Pride of authorship was at its worst with me.

"Thank you," said Buckmaster at last. "You have been of tremendous service to us."

The other officers thanked me likewise. Ever since then I have wondered—not very heavily—whether I played precisely square with the Germans in telling the things that I had seen. But it seems to me I have a clean bill of health. No obligation of secrecy had been imposed, and I only wrote what I saw and heard. The information the English secured was a legitimate byproduct of my newspaper stories.

About this time I grew very tired of England. A war correspondent who went to war on the Strand and fought his greatest battles in the Savoy bar seemed a joke. Later I discovered that most war correspondents are jokes, anyhow. We are necessary jokes, perhaps, but as long as the censor writes the music to which we pipe we are essentially funny. So I gave France a try for the second time.

Early in August 1914, I had trotted across the channel, filled with the laudable ambition of going at once to the front, and the French had knocked that ambition into a cocked hat. No one was at all sympathetic, but everyone was more kindly and polite than now seems possible. The officers to whom I carried my desire combed their fingers through their whiskers and eyed me thoughtfully and said "ah" in a variety of intonations. In desperation and ignorance, I made two or three tries off my own bat. I had no knowledge whatever of French—bains were pronounced by me just as bains are spelled—and not a very clear idea where the fighting was going on. Consequently, I bounced hard several times. I was arrested and chased back to Paris, and that is all that happened. It must be that the angelic purity of my soul was written clear on my forehead, for no one suggested seriously that I was an "espion" and due for a wall early some summer morning. They merely gave me the bum's rush. The fact that I was able to buy railroad tickets and blunder even a little way toward the front is a further evidence of the utter confusion of the day.

On one occasion Percy Noel of the *Chicago Daily News* and I made about the same trip at about the same time although not in company. The line bulged that day and the train on which I found myself was re-routed all over France, or so it seemed to me, to escape capture. Everywhere the same scenes were repeated. Women, frightened, despairing, saying desperate goodbyes to their men. Old men and boys, wearing thin civilian shoes and the quaint blue and red of the old French uniforms, stumbling clumsily through their drills by the roadside. Cattle being driven into safe territory. On that occasion I wrote the same kind of a story Palmer later wrote about Berlin. It was a land of unshed tears to me. Percy could not see anything but hope and cheer and a fierce desire to get to grips with the invader. It was more evidence that two men cannot see the same thing alike.

Shortly before the Grand Duke had been given his eternal passport at Sarajevo, my wife and I had visited Paris and stopped at the Hotel Continental on the Rue Rivoli. Among the many delightful memories of the visit one remained of the clerk in the reception hall. He was a tall, slender, frockcoated man with a black fan of silky beard. As visitors from a smooth-shaven country, that beard enchanted us and we made unnecessary calls upon him for the aesthetic pleasure of seeing it spread and quiver and throb as its owner caracolled through the English language. The hotel was then chockablock with guests of the true continental sort, ranging from obvious but extremely good-looking adventuresses to Eastern potentates and Americans who were all believed to be rich. On the mantel in our apartment was a gray marble clock, and on the morning of our arrival a workman appeared to wind it. Inquiry revealed that a gray marble clock stood on every marble mantel in the hotel and that the sole duty of the workman was to wind and keep them in order.

On the night of my return to the Continental from London I was the only guest in that vast hotel. The man with the beard was the only hotel attaché in sight. The gray marble clock on my mantel was ticking away. The thought of innumerable mantels on each of which stood a ticking clock in that empty hotel kept me awake that night. As we would say nowadays, I had the jitters.

4

At this time the French and English were busily engaged in calling the Germans cowards. This may have been good propaganda—it cheered up a lot of people—but it did not seem sensible to me. Precisely how the armies of the Allies could go on being pushed backward by cowards I could not understand, and the men who were actually doing the fighting used to get red in the neck when they spoke of the civilian so-and-sos who were blackguarding mighty good fighting men. Charley Sweeney came in from the front one day to have some shrapnel removed and told me of a German charge.

"I watched 'em, God Damn 'em," said he, "and cried."

Sweeney is one of the most remarkable fighting men I ever met. He began his life as the son of a lumberman on the Pacific Coast, but after getting a good look at the comparative sizes of redwood trees and axes decided to be a soldier. He was considered a topnotch cadet at West Point until he got mixed up in a hazing episode. I have forgotten precisely what happened but Sweeney was expelled.

"You may stay if you will give the names of the other men," said his superiors.

"Go to hell," said Sweeney, or words to that effect.

So he fought around in little South American wars for a time, getting a good idea of what happens when a Colt .45 hits a man on the breastbone, and when the big show hustled off to Paris he joined the Foreign Legion. He had a liking for Paris anyhow, for it was his habit to repair to that capital to blow off steam when he had accumulated a stake. He finished his first day of fighting as a private in the rear rank with thirty-five pounds of souvenirs in his pack. That night his mates swiped all the valuable souvenirs and Sweeney threw the rest away. He was to become a colonel in the Legion in the end, which was the highest rank ever attained by an American in that outfit. The higher ranks are properly reserved for Frenchmen, who may be presumed to be loyal.

"The Germans seemed all to be young to me that day," he said. "Just kids. They came in green wave after green wave, singing songs about home and mother, and we cut them down with our machine guns until at last the French soldiers got up from their pits and waved to them. 'Go back,' they cried. 'For the sake of God—go back.'

"But they came on until the dead lay in windrows. It was the finest example of pure courage I have ever seen."

Time out for another little story about Sweeney: When the United States went to war Sweeney went patriotic and after some negotiation was permitted to resign from the Legion and return to the United States to offer his services to our army. The French let him go very reluctantly, for he is a great fighting man. When Sweeney reached Washington our totally green General Staff was engaged in making an army out of totally green men. They did not propose to have a skilled man like Sweeney showing them up. Charley Sweeney was put to digging trenches around Washington, one of the favorite means of training in those days. By and by, he got back to the Legion and we lost him. The last I heard of him he was on his way to Manchukuo to get a little action.[1]

My stories from France did not please the French any more than my stories from England had pleased the English, but for a different reason. I was tremendously sorry for and sympathetic with the French, and said so. Maybe I thrummed too persistently on this string, for what the French wanted written were stories of their successes. After the Marne there was a long time when they had had no successes. It became apparent that no one wanted the war reported as an American wanted to report it, and I went to Germany. Looking back, it seems almost impossible that a neutral correspondent should be permitted to hop across the frontier lines as we all did in those days. But the rules of war had not yet been formulated. In Berlin I found Raymond Swing and Oswald Schuette of the *Chicago Daily News* and Cyril Brown of the *New York Times*.

"We will take you to the War Office and introduce you," they said.

That story can wait on Cyril Brown. He is now the contact man between one of the great moving picture concerns and the celebrities of the

---

1. Corey misremembers this. Sweeney served with the AEF. After the war, he fought with the Polish against the Soviets..

day. When Al Smith talks from the Empire State building's tower or Franklin Roosevelt says "Mai Frands," Cyril Brown's slim figure and aquiline face may be discovered in the background of the picture by those who know him. At that time, he was one of the most annoying puzzles of the war to the Germans. Nothing was verboten to him. When he was told it was verboten he went and did it, being aided in the doing by his enormous fluency in German and the most extraordinary gall on record. The Eastern Front was absolutely closed to correspondents, except the hand-fed German correspondents. Therefore, Brown appeared on the Eastern Front. "We will raus mit you as soon as we get time," he was told.

But he was an American and therefore had to be treated with some consideration, for the Germans had sense enough to know that friendly treatment in the American papers was desirable, even if they did not have sense enough to know how to get it. Brown was put up at the staff headquarters of a German general who was a lover of chess. Not one of his staff officers could play and Brown was a dab at the game. He was permitted to stay, on condition that each night he played chess with the general. Like Heywood Broun, Brown knew the value of stage management, and his costume for going to war consisted of a long, black overcoat with a dogskin collar like those that ham actors used to wear, a black derby hat fitted well down over the ears, a long umbrella, and a cigar. He was just tall enough so that the top of his derby hat showed over the lip of the German trenches, and whenever he took the air the Russians went after it. They thought, and not unnaturally, that some new infernal device had been invented by the Germans and shelled the trenches in hysteria. A prisoner told the story one day and Brown was forbidden to walk abroad. But the chess-playing general continued to favor him.

"We will take you on a staff ride," said he one day.

Brown did not know what a staff ride was. He had never been on a horse. But he was boosted on a charger, complete with black hat and umbrella, and told to ride alongside an orderly at the extreme end of the procession, which was the only place for a civilian. The ride began at a walk and that was all right. Presently the general began to trot his horse. Behind the general were forty officers of varying ranks, each in his proper place. Each began to trot his horse. Civilian Brown's horse began to trot. Brown clutched his umbrella.

"Stop," he said presently to the horse. "Desist—what do you say to a horse?"

His horse was a spirited animal and found that he was not under control. He began to gallop. The orderly began to gallop after him in order to catch Brown and the horse. The officer next ahead could not permit himself to be preceded by a mere civilian and he began to gallop. So did the next officer ahead and the next officer ahead. The general looked over his shoulder and saw his staff galloping after him. If he had restrained his steed his staff officers would have taken precedence, and that would not do, so he began to gallop. Brown's horse was fresh and excited and settled down to run. So did the forty other horses ahead of him, urged on by annoyed staff officers who saw their places in the procession threatened. The general was fat and irascible. He set in his spurs and rode harder than ever. The Russians came out of their foxholes and observed the spectacle in dumb amazement. A General Staff, covered with medals, was being driven like sheep by an odd person in a derby hat, waving an umbrella. Brown's horse passed officer after officer. He passed the general.

"Catch the verdommt schweinehund," yelled the general.

The forty officers set themselves to run Brown down and capture him. All the time they were getting nearer and nearer the Russian lines. They were so close they could almost hear the Russians scratching themselves. At last an encircling movement was successful and Brown was caught and his horse's reins taken over by the orderly, and when Brown got back to camp he was deported to Berlin. It would not be fair to drop Brown from this narrative as a serio-comic character, however. Later he made his way not once but twice to General Headquarters, at a time when Colonel Nicolai, head of the German Secret Service, was sure that every hole had been stopped. Brown would not tell how he got in until he was given the story that he went for. That's Brown.

Oswald Schuette of the *Chicago Daily News* was another striking character. After the war ended and radio became a popular thing, it occurred to Schuette that the big radio concerns were making life miserable for the small independent manufacturers. That was enough for him, for he is a born crusader. Show him a situation that needs righting and he promptly sets about righting it. He organized the independent radio manufacturers—few of whom had any money to speak of—and began to harpoon Owen Young of the Radio Corporation and Walter Gifford of the AT&T and the other multis of the trust. It is too long a story to tell here, and, anyhow, Schuette was given an entire chapter in a book not long ago and that is enough for any man, but it may be briefly summarized.[2]

---

2. The *Chicago Daily News* corps of foreign correspondents was superb. This was thanks to the vision of the newspaper's owner, Victor Lawson, who at the turn of the century saw the need for first-class reporting of the world by American reporters. *The New York Times* and others relied heavily on foreign journalists for their overseas news even after World War I.

One by one Schuette's independents either sold out or went broke. He fought on. His salary was not paid. He ceased to get any expense money. He dipped into his savings and fought on. In 1932 he forced the U.S. Department of Justice to recognize that his contentions were well founded and that in any case he could not be stopped from telling his story, and in the end a compromise was reached by which it is my impression that Schuette won every essential thing that he had been fighting for. The victory was complete. Young and Gifford in effect assented to his terms. The only flaw in his happiness was that by this time there were no independents left.

Raymond Swing, also of the *Chicago Daily News*, was one of the American correspondents who continued to remember throughout the war that he was an American. Not that he was not sympathetic with the Germans among whom he worked at this time. I defy anyone not to be sympathetic with the people of a nation—any nation—who were suffering as were the people of all the belligerents if he lived and worked with them. Swing did his best to present the facts of the case to the United States, as those facts were seen in Germany, but he never became a propagandist for Germany.

Swing had Schuette and Brown introduce me to the German War Office and nothing happened. Not even any promises were made. The German propaganda at this time was in the bullying stage, plus much futile dabbling in politics. I was taken one day to see Sir Roger Casement in the hope that I might write a piece touting his plans for Ireland.[3] He seemed to me a likable old man, sick in bed in an uncomfortable German chamber, with all the sincerity of the slightly cracked. No doubt he forfeited his life when he played the part he did in the Irish rebellion of 1916. He offered no regrets, as I recall, when he was shot in The Tower. But I do not believe that in the United States we would have shot a lunatic.

At this time we were selling shells and supplies to the Allies, and the Germans were making a tremendous fuss about it. It did no good to retort that in other wars Germany had done precisely what we were doing. The only result would be that the German end of the argument became abusive and scurrilous. It was because of this national trait that I left Germany in a huff some months later, although Germany did not seem to worry about

---

3. Roger Casement was a diplomat and Irish nationalist. Casement was a human rights activist. After his retirement from government service in 1913, he threw himself into Irish republicanism and sought help from the German military. He was arrested, convicted, and executed for high treason by the British.

my departure. At that time there were seven American military observers in Germany, headed by the fine soldier Joseph E. Kuhn.[4] They were treated with plenty of German good manners—no one has more good manners than a hochwelgeboren German—but no friendship. At last, it was indicated to them that they might go for a visit to General von Hindenburg on the Eastern Front.[5]

Von Hindenburg was then, as he is now, the idol of the German people. His wooden statue was the one thing that every visitor to Berlin wished to see, and stories of the fine old man were being told everywhere. One of them, I remember, gave the reason for his enforced retirement before the war. It was the kaiser's habit to lead personally one of the armies in the sham battle which wound up each year's military maneuvers, and it was the habit of the general commanding the other army to permit his forces to be soundly licked, no matter what pains were necessary to uphold the theory that the kaiser was a great strategist. This duty fell to Von Hindenburg on one occasion, but the kaiser discovered that his victory had an annoying shallowness. He was not a fool. Whatever else one may say of the old ruler, he was not a fool. He called Von Hindenburg.

"What would have happened if this had been war?"

"I would have driven Your Majesty's forces into the German Sea," said the soldier.

He was banished to the eastern swamps, where he laid the way for his future victories. Naturally the American officers were more than delighted at the opportunity to see and talk with the man who is still considered an authentic military hero of the war. They were escorted to the town in which Von Hindenburg had his headquarters. On the appointed morning they were taken to his tent.

"One moment, gentlemen," said their escorting officer.

He disappeared in the tent. The Americans stood waiting. Time went on. More time went on. They heard the sound of voices and crashing German laughter within. More time went on. Presently they discovered something. Other German officers were taking occasion to stroll by and grin at them. In

---

4. Major General Kuhn had been an observer of the Japanese army during the Russo-Japanese War, and of Germany's army early in World War I. After the United States entered, he commanded the 79th Division, and then the IX Corps.

5. General Paul von Hindenburg commanded the Imperial German Army during World War I. He was president of Germany from 1925 until his death in 1934.

the end the Americans turned on their heels and returned to their quarters, convinced that they had been deliberately affronted. Their escorting officer was offhand about it when he was asked for an explanation.

"That Field Marshall," said he, "would not consent to receive officers of the nation which is providing shells by which our good German lads are being killed."

The American military mission went home as soon as might be after that affair. At the time I tried to get my credentials as a correspondent, the bitterness toward the United States had not fully developed, however, although the Germans were edging toward it. For three weeks I sat in the Adlon, hoping for permission to go somewhere, and calling on "The Prush" each day.[6] "The Prush" had been nicknamed by Cyril Brown. He was a short, square, gruff Prussian captain, whose contempt for all civilians was marked and who regarded all newspapermen as pig-dogs. This is the attitude of the German military caste and the American navy at all times. One day I blew up:

"I want you to listen to me," I said to The Prush.

He harrumphed and scowled as I spoke.

"You Germans are the most condemned jackasses I have ever known. You bellyache that you are not getting fair play in the American press. You say that we print English lies...."

"Maybe they are lies. Maybe not. That has nothing to do with the case. You say we do not print your side of the story. What do you want us to do? Print these longwinded pieces you hand out to us? They are not worth printing. The only thing American correspondents here want is news.

"If you had common sense you would understand that the way to get what you want in the American press is to let us go somewhere and get what we want. There is not an American reporter here in Berlin who did not come originally with friendly feelings for you. There is not one who is friendly toward you today. Why should any of us be friendly? How can you be friendly to a nation of fatheads?"

This is likely not a verbatim report, but it cuts close to it. I began by being coldly dignified and wound up beating on the desk and squawking like a parrot. The thought of my wrongs overcame me. Here I was, a reporter, gold money in his pocket, with new clothes and field glasses, in the only practically calm area in Europe and unable to get out of it. In the west the battle lines

6. The Adlon was a famous Berlin hotel frequently used by correspondents.

were popping with big guns day and night. In the east the Russian armies—we still believed in the Russian armies in those days—were engaged in a stupendous struggle with the Germans. I sat in the Adlon bar morning after morning, with the other correspondents, and in the afternoon sat in the Adlon lounge and watched be-medaled officers being purred over by pretty women while I drank tea. It is no wonder that my language was not parliamentary.

"What are you going to do about it, Herr Corey?" asked The Prush with a grin.

"I'll tell you what I'm going to do about it. I'm going back to France and I'm going to do my damnedest to help the French cause. And I'm going to start tomorrow."

Late that night I was asleep in my room in the Adlon. A large and impressive chamber, with massive furniture and a bathroom big enough to exercise a horse in. I had packed my bags, taken my final drink, said goodbye to my friends, and cursed Germany for what I assumed was the last time. There came a thundering knock on the door. There stood an orderly with a note.

"At eight o'clock tomorrow morning you will leave for the Eastern Front. Be ready at seven o'clock for your conducting officer."

We did not leave just at eight o'clock, for I recall that I managed to wangle enough time to buy a fur-lined overcoat of field-gray, in which I looked like a meek German general, except that there is no such thing. Then began weeks of riding in open cars through eastern Germany and along the Russian frontier. Snow was everywhere. The iron-hard snow that squeaks like a rat under wheels, and over which a wind blew that stiffened my face into an iron mask, no matter how I tried to protect it. My conducting officer was a delightfully intelligent little chap who had been a professor in one of the army schools. He was slender as a wraith and his uniform fitted as though he had been poured into it. He had no overcoat.

There appeared to be a cult of hardiness among the younger officers. A fat old general might swathe himself in furs if he wished, but at the time the young men were determined to show themselves above any care for the shivering flesh. There was a rumor that they wore chamois skin underclothes over silk, but there were no indications of such soft luxury on my little conductor. Only when we were well away from any superior officer did he step out of his Spartan pose and pull on a thin raincoat as a windbreaker. I do not know how much of a fighting man he might have been, but at standing cold he was a hero.

5

Life, as Mr. Raymond Hitchcock used to sing, is a funny proposition after all.[1] Shortly after the visit to the Eastern Front, Edward Fox of the *New York Sun* and I committed practically the same offense against the Allies. We tried to inform the United States what was going on in Germany. It ruined Fox. I am not sure that it did not kill him in the end. I got away with my sin because I switched in time. Von Hindenburg deliberately insulted General Kuhn and the American military observers, and I lost my temper and went to France. Therefore, the Allied propagandists stopped shooting at me. Poor Ed Fox was still a target.

"You will now go out and witness a battle, Herr Corey," said my conducting officer one morning.

So we started for the battle. The conducting officer had seen battles before and was not so very hot about taking a low caste civilian—and an American civilian at that—into another one. I had never been able to get into a battle and looked forward to a big treat. Ed Fox had another conducting officer and another car and perhaps went by another road. At all events our large machine, with an orderly seated by the side of the driver and the conducting officer sitting by the pig-dog, tore up the Grodno turnpike right plum into the middle of the largest celebration I had ever seen. The German army under General Von Marwitz was going forward at a lope, and the Russians were putting up a fine rearguard action.[2] After a time we came in sight of a great, square house by the side of the turnpike, which was as straight as a gun bar-

---

1. Hitchcock was an American actor on stage and in films and a Broadway stage producer. "Life's a Funny Proposition After All" is a song by George M. Cohan, who often sang it himself.

2. Georg von der Marwitz was a Prussian cavalry general who commanded several German armies on both the Eastern and Western Fronts.

rel. There were no trees around it, but at one side was a range of one-story outhouses.

"Someone is watching us," I said to my conductor with a giggle. I was nervous but not frightened. One is never frightened the first time under fire. Through the door of one of the outhouses peered a white face. It was strikingly canted to one side, as though its owner was sheltering his body behind the door casing. Hours afterward we tore down that road as though the devil were after us, which in effect he was. The white face still peered through the open door. It was the face of a woman who had been hanged.

We chased the battle that banged on ahead of us. The bodies of the dead lay everywhere in the woods on either side. The boots had been stripped from the feet of the Russian dead by the thrifty Germans. Presently shells began to pop near us and rifle bullets whined uneasily. The conductor barked:

"Halt!"

The car slid on the snow when the brakes were applied. The conductor said that we had gone far enough and would go back. In my complete ignorance of war, I protested. I had not seen nearly enough. Then I committed the unforgivable sin.

"I am not afraid," I said.

The conductor took this as an affront, although it was not so intended, and we went on until even my dim wits perceived that we were getting too much of a good thing. But I did not have the moral courage to back down and we went on some more. Finally, the conductor elaborately apologized for ordering the driver to turn the car around and return. He was responsible for the equipment, he said. The next day the returns began to come in. The Tenth Russian Army had been well smashed. We watched something like 140,000 prisoners drift toward the rear in separate, orderly groups. I do not know what the total bag was. Heaven only knows how many guns had been captured, and Russian generals were at six for a penny. Seven of them, very glum, were brought in a single taxicab which had been commandeered. The Germans said the hairiest was a Grand Duke, but furnished no name. The excitement went to my head and I wired a brief story to the Associated Newspapers, although spot news was not my job.

Henry J. Wright was then the editor of the old *New York Globe*. He was a straight man and an able journalist and inclined to the cause of the Allies, for he was English born. The Allied news services had put an entirely different complexion on the battle, distorting the fact that the Tenth Russian Army was knocked to bits, and Wright not unnaturally preferred the Allied story. He cabled the War Office at London for a statement and the War Office—of course—replied that the Russians had been practically victorious and that the stories sent out by Corey and Fox were examples of German propaganda.

At this distance it is possible to be philosophic about this denial. It was essential to the Allies that they win the support of the United States. How essential it was even the Allies might not have known at the time. Events were to show that if we had not come in when we did they would have been thoroughly licked—although England would have made a dogfight out of it—and that they could not have stayed in as long as they did if they had not been able to borrow the money which later they were to refuse to pay back. A greater effort, perhaps, was being made at this time to swamp and submerge the American mentality in Allied propaganda than to meet the Germans in the field. The capture of the United States was actually more necessary to them.

But when Fox and I learned that we had been discredited by the English in the eyes of our own people, we blew up. Fox went back to Berlin and wrote a frankly pro-German book, in which he told what he had seen during our trip to the Eastern Front. I was too busy gaping around Germany and the Western Front to follow his example, but it had become apparent that unless the United States had both sides of the question put before it, whatever judgement our people ultimately arrived at would be biased and ill-informed. I do not mean to suggest that our final action should not have been taken. We were unquestionably justified in declaring war on Germany. We would also have been justified in declaring war on the Allies. It was six of one and half a dozen of the other.

Raymond Swing was a great friend of an American-born countess in Berlin. She was a meek, likeable little woman who had been a belle at one time but had been having her clothes made in Berlin. She was, of course, a rich woman by German standards, but had gone over completely to her husband's people. Her vast apartment was filled with clumsy pieces of German art, and one occasionally met at her teas high-born hausfrauen who were likewise clumsy. The American countess and her German friends had set up a fine resentment in my breast against all things German by the crudity of their patriotism. One of them lifted her glass to me one day with a toast:

"Gott Strafe England!"

I was willing to strafe England a little bit, but not to call on God to help me, and was very considerably embarrassed. But when I returned from the

Eastern Front, having witnessed my first battle and seen with my own eyes that the Russians had been superbly licked, to find that my story had been disavowed by the New York Globe on the authority of the British propaganda office, I strafed with the best of them.

One day the countess said: "You luff Chermany?"

She had actually begun to talk English with an accent, so great was her devotion.

"No. I do not love Germany. Not any more than I do England. But I think it is important that the United States should have both sides on which to form a judgement. My letters from home state that our people are going heavily pro-Allies. The German side should be more efficiently presented to the United States."

"Vill you say this to one of our great Cherman chenerals?"

"No. Any general would want to set up an institution of propaganda. I only want to see the news of the day given fairly to the United States."

In the end I wrote her a letter, in which the suggestion was made that a German news bureau be set up in New York, under the direction of competent New York newspaper men, and that American reporters be brought to Germany to furnish the news—American style. The propagandists should be ordered to let them alone, and they should be given access to everything and be given interviews with everyone of importance, from the kaiser down. Precisely this sort of thing was even then being done by Karl von Wiegand, to the delight of the United Press, which employed him, and the frothing fury of the English.[3]

"Don't try to give away this German news," I recommended. "American newspapers don't like handouts. Make them pay for it, but make the news good enough and real enough so they will be glad to pay."

Nothing came of the suggestion, of course. Months later Dr. Albert's papers were stolen in New York, and I read in the World that among them was a typewritten document in which this plan for an American news bureau was outlined and "which showed an understanding of American psychology and newspaper practices far beyond the comprehension of the savage German diplomat." This quotation is from memory and is not precise. In reading the World's story I could recognize some of the sentences of my letter to the

---

3. The German-born Wiegand worked for UP until 1917, when he joined the Hearst newspapers. He was considered sympathetic to the Germans.

countess. There is no doubt that she had worked it over for presentation to some high-born general, and if it had been accepted it is possible the part we were later to play might have been modified. My complaint is not with the part we played, but that we were so played upon by the propagandists of the Allies. It is possible, of course, that if we had known all about everything we might have been as hostile to the Allies as we were to the Germans. And that *would* have been a mess.[4]

As soon as Ed Fox's book appeared, the English sharpshooters began work on him.[5] The charge was immediately made that he had been bought by the Germans. It is my conviction that not one of the American correspondents on either side of the battle line ever got a penny from any one of the belligerents. I knew most, if not all, of the active correspondents, and I believe them to be honest men. I do not now resent the charge against Fox, even if it were not true. In modern war it is essential to weaken the enemy by any means at hand, and if the destruction of the correspondent's reputation seems advisable, that reputation will be destroyed by the propagandists as impersonally as their brethren in the field will shell an old woman's cot. I see it that way now; I did not see it that way then.

In 1917 Ed Fox volunteered for the American army and was sent to an officers' training camp. Someone dug up the story that he had been in German pay. Perhaps it had been added to. I do not know. I do not know that it was not true. At all events Fox's commission was taken away from him. Shortly afterward he died. The operators had begun their work on me but then they laid off. It would not be good sense to discredit a friend. But they did not have time to stop a story in—I think—the *London Times* that I had been carrying information across the lines, hidden in an intricate code worked into the tartan cover of my hot water bag. It was a swell story and I appreciated it, even if I did not have a hot water bag. But when I proved to be as friendly to

---

4. "Dr. Albert's papers" were notorious. On a Saturday afternoon in July 1915, Heinrich Albert, a German spy and propagandist in the United States, boarded a New York City train. In his hand was a briefcase full of papers marked "*streng vertraulich*"—"strictly private." He did not realize he had reached his stop until the train was about to leave. Albert bolted from the car, leaving his portfolio behind. By the time he realized his mistake, the Secret Service agent shadowing him had run off with his papers. These ended up in the office of Treasury Secretary William Gibbs McAdoo, the agent's boss. McAdoo leaked them to the *New York World* on the condition that it tell no one from where they came. The *World* splashed the contents of Albert's briefcase across its pages for five days starting on a Sunday in mid-August.

5. The book was titled *Wilhelm Hohenzollern and Company* (1917).

the French people as I had been to the German people, the sniping stopped. Not once during the war did I write about responsibility for the war. I do not know which side was responsible. The roots of the thing went back a thousand years. By and by, another war will come along, for Germany will inevitably try to tear down the Treaty of Versailles. Which side will then be responsible—the side which wrote the treaty or the side that signed it under the gun?

No one was more bitterly attacked by the Allied propagandists than Karl Von Wiegand, and quite right they were. He was worth more than a park of field artillery to Germany. Von Wiegand's history is a romance in petto. He was born in California, if I am not mistaken, had worked on American newspapers all his life without great success, and had somehow wandered into Berlin some years before the war and set up as a sort of penny-a-liner for the old *New York Sun*. He was poor as Job's turkey, for it was understood that he was only being paid $15 a week. That was all that Berlin news was worth to the old *Sun*, which was deep in the red. After the war began, Roy Howard of the United Press took Von Wiegand over at a small advance in pay.

"I am not making enough money," Von Wiegand said to me on one occasion. "I must ask Mr. Howard for more. But I am afraid he will fire me."

It was a fine practical joke, it seemed to me, to urge Von Wiegand to ask for more pay. Howard and I were reporters on rival papers at one time in Cincinnati, and enough of the old comradeship remained to convince me that it would be very funny to help Von Wiegand dig into Roy's pocket. It was a tightly closed pocket in those days, for the UP was just beginning to get ahead, and every nickel had to double as two bits. The cost of furnishing a war service was tremendous, the returns were only beginning to come in, and the rival Associated Press had a war chest larger than the much publicized chest at Spandau.

"He can't fire you," I said. "Make him pay. Make him pay plenty. But ask for a little at a time."

In the end Von Wiegand worked his salary up to $85 a week, with an occasional 10 or 15 cents for expenses. He was the poor relation among the correspondents in Berlin, and rarely appeared at the Adlon bar for the very good reason that he had no money to spend. This compelled him to work very hard, to keep his mind off his troubles, and the fact should be borne in mind by all business managers who are trying to keep down reportorial salaries. Von Wiegand had a way of disappearing from sight for a week or so and re-appearing with an interview which was the most sizzling sort of hot stuff. His little chat with the crown prince is an instance. One day Karl came in to see me at the Adlon.

"I want your advice," said he. "The *New York World* has offered me more money, and Mr. Howard is coming over from London to see me."

"Won't he meet the raise?"

Mr. Howard would not. He is several times a millionaire now and the UP is a great organization, but it is possible that he actually could not pay any more to Karl at that time. Roy Howard can coax birds out of bushes if the birds will listen to him, and Von Wiegand knew it. He wanted the additional salary the *World* offered, but he knew that Howard would bear down on him. "Just one big family. All poor boys together. One for all, all for one."

He might not have the moral courage to take the offer of the *World*. So I did my best to boost his morale and left him fearful but determined. Perhaps the convincing argument was that the cost of a trip from London to Berlin and return would be enough to keep Von Wiegand in sausages for months. Some time later Von Wiegand went to the Hearst papers, which thereby secured the services of an ace, so far as Germany was concerned. He was probably thoroughly pro-German in all European matters by then, but was almost certainly a good American. After all, a man who was as unfairly attacked as Von Wiegand was by the English could hardly be expected to kiss and make up overnight.

Frederic William Wile, now the political commentator on one of the national radio chains, did not have so pleasant an experience. Wile is American born and had made a great hit with Lord Northcliffe some years before the war. Northcliffe sent him to Berlin to represent the *Daily Mail* of London. He is possessed of a perfectly hellish energy, is a thorough-going reporter, and played the *Mail*'s hand to perfection. He had lived at the Adlon for years, and Louis Adlon was his warm personal friend.[6]

---

6. Wile was an Indiana Hoosier of German-American stock. He started overseas with the *Chicago Daily News* and later became the Berlin correspondent for Lord Northcliffe's *London Daily Mail*. When the war started in 1914, the Germans ransacked Wile's office and expelled him. Back in London, Northcliffe gave Wile a column, "Germany Day by Day," in which the reporter made British propaganda out of German propaganda by combing the German press to report on how it portrayed the war "with clumsy fabrications." Although Wile was a highly respected journalist, one of the first to go into radio after the war, his pro-Allies enthusiasm carried him away during the fighting. Although he claimed his experience in Germany trained him "to read

When war was declared Wile discovered to his surprise that the Berliners and especially the Adloners hated him with a complete hatred. He was known to almost everyone, and the *Mail* was an especially sharp thorn in the German flesh. He was obliged to get out of Berlin in two days, and unless the story told was untrue, the servants of the Adlon threw things at him when he left. The story probably is true. The Adlon bartender was known to every American in the city. He spoke good English, mixed American drinks, and was regarded by most of them as a friend. One night he departed from the strict level of bartending ethics and got very drunk. Where upon—whurroo!

He declared a private war on all Americans in sound of his voice. It did not end until a correspondent whacked him over the head with a chair. The next morning, he was on duty again. Pleasant as ever.

---

between the lines of German papers," he gave credence to one of the more outrageous pieces of war propaganda, that the Germans rendered the bodies of dead soldiers for oil, fertilizer, and pig fodder.

6

The United States played Frankie to the European Johnnies during the Great War.[1] They done us wrong. As one of the injured people, however, I am compelled to admit that the Europeans were not greatly to blame. Perhaps there has never been in history an instance of a great nation—or at least of a large number of people living inside the same ring fence—being so completely dominated by the spoken, crooned, bleated, and intoned word of other nations, each of which had a selfish interest to serve. The cream puff spinal processes of the Americans at home were matched by the marshmallow vertebrae of the Americans in Europe.

I would not go so far as to say that there was not one loyal, straight-up, independent American resident on the continent or in England. I know better. Half a dozen of my friends in Paris, for instance—maybe more—are as good Americans as can be. I will not give their names, because the fact has been buttered over with French sympathies until it is hardly suspected, and if they were accused even at this late day they might not be admitted to French homes. With the exception of a small group of correspondents, army and navy men and career diplomats, the fact is as stated.

Any American who lived in Germany cheered der kaiser in his sleep even though the kaiser thought of the goosestep as the poetry of motion. Any Americans—exceptions noted—who lived in France sang themselves to sleep with the "Marseillaise" and did penance on the Place de la Concorde because we had not taken over France's job of defending herself. Any American who lived in London in private sorrowed because he could not wear a monocle with conviction, and if he had been living there any length of time he threw away his sock suspenders as a gesture of amity.

---

1. "Frankie and Johnny" is a song about true love gone off the rails. When Johnny cheats on Frankie, she shoots him.

A striking fact was that the expatriates were oblivious of blood lines. Americans whose forebears had probably hidden under bushes during the Wars of the Roses could be depended on to adore Germany if they lived there, and an American whose family had been German since the Teutons stopped cutting their meat with sharp stones would drool over La Belle France if his home were in Paris. The classified exceptions noted—correspondents, army and navy men, and career diplomats—were good Americans for professional reasons. The small groups of real American residents kept quiet about their shame.

All correspondents have no more bowels of compassion than brass monkeys. They have been trained first to find the story. They can and do produce moving documents about murderers, thieves, and prostitutes, their personal tongues in their personal cheeks all the time. Their one loyalty is to their papers. If their own country gets in the way of this loyalty, it is too bad for the country—and except for this, they were loyal. In 1918, American correspondents up from the front in Paris used to meet with practical unanimity at Ciro's or in the Hotel Daunou. Both establishments found with regularity among their guests very pretty girls, and the American correspondents knew every one of them.

"The American correspondents have been warned to stay away from these places," I was told by an officer of the French secret service. "They meet many spies there. They might be indiscreet."

The warning was passed on, but the correspondents went right on going to Ciro's. They all said they get lots of material there. This was probably true. An unmarried correspondent is more useful than a married correspondent. A married correspondent is more useful than a married correspondent who has become a father, at least until the smell of sour clothes drives the father out of the house. Aid could be found at Ciro's and the Hotel Daunou for all three classes. To each according to its ability. Army and navy men have been invariably loyal, so far as my knowledge goes, from their regulation heels to the summit of their sometimes O.D.[2] heads.

And career diplomats? It is a journalistic habit to shoot shots at the spatted sons of the State Department. Some of them, it is true, are all moldy because their guardians left them out in the rain too long. But for the most part they are intelligent and industrious and manage to get a good deal done. I

---

2. Olive drab, the color of military uniforms.

have suspected some of the more completely goose-faced among them of being decoys for their wiser brethren, and people who think of them as typical of the State Department are often badly fooled by the hidden sportsmen. My impression is that the men of the consular service are just a shade wiser if not as rich as the State Department men. But the diplomats by appointment—oy, oy, oy! Soch a beesnees!

My own explanation of this lack of national character among Americans at this period is that life had been coming so easy for us ever since the Civil War that we had gotten into the habit of fooling around with the uplift. Once, for my numerous sins, I went on a lecture tour, and the chairman of the evening invariably opened proceedings on a high spiritual level and always stated that I had a "message." Bless us and keep us! I had no message. What I wanted to tell them was that Europe was in one hell of a state and that if Europe blew up—as there was a strong probability that Europe would blow up—fragments of Uncle Sam might be found in the goulash. My audience wanted sweetness and light. I was all for ipecac and they called for chocolate soda.

All this—I think—was the result of decades of prosperity. We had ceased to be citizens and had become evangelists and sweet singers. Ever since I can remember, my home, my town, my state and nation has been drenched in saccharine oratory. Not only had we become our brother's keeper, but we were determined to keep him better than he had ever hoped to be kept. There probably isn't an old lady in the United States, bless every one of them, with willpower enough to stand erect in the presence of an audience who has not at some time quavered about our national duty to someone or other. Missionaries have kept Chinese Christians in rice for a century. And as for professors—Dear God! I do not know the precise number of colleges in the land, but it seems to me that a majority of all the faculty members are at all times engaged in giving high-minded and absolutely irrational advice. In consequence of these things we had lost much of our national spirit. All flags looked alike to us.

No one need bother to accuse me of a profound anti-European complex. I admit it. As a matter of course my prejudice against our late allies is greater than against our late enemies because the Allies did more things to us and did them harder. The Germans would have done them—and worse, perhaps—if they had had the chance. But a kindly nature arranged that Germany could not materially injure us until after we stopped fighting her, whereas there has been no closed season with our allies. But if I am prejudiced, I am, I trust, also fair. The Allies did precisely right in cuddling and cheating and finally abusing us as they did. Why shouldn't they? We loved to be cuddled and abused.

In Germany I learned for the first time precisely what breed of bird is a war correspondent. In France and England I had not been bothered by the censorship. My letters were dropped in the mail and in every instance, so far as I know, reached New York without having been opened.[3] The two countries had too many other things to do and too few men to do them with, and their censorship was practically confined to continental mail. But I was in Germany distinctly on sufferance. If I could not prove myself to be an asset the exit out would be opened to me. No one used harsh words, of course, but the understanding was precise.

Therefore, I made myself agreeable and so did every other American correspondent in Germany. Likewise, so did every correspondent in France or Italy or England. It is impossible for a person of sensibilities and imagination not to share to some extent the sorrows and fears of the people at war with whom he is domiciled. In Germany I told of the courage and determination of the people, just as I told the same things of the peoples of France and England. The little old mother who hobbled by the side of her son marching to war on Unter den Linden, tears in her eyes and a proud smile on her lips, was as pathetic a figure to me as the black-clad mothers of France or the red-faced cockney women who, as they marched, joked with their men who were about to die. I did not write about the rights and wrongs of the conflict because I did not know them. During the war I had a talk with Jean Jusserand, the French ambassador in Washington.

"Germany made an unprovoked assault on us," he asserted passionately.

"Germany certainly began the war. But would you say that no provocation had been given? Germany and France have been fighting each other for a thousand years. There were hundreds of provocations on either side."

"Oh, well," said Jusserand, "if you are going to go back into history."

Between times I met the Americans domiciled in Berlin. Without remembered exception—the correspondents and the diplomats and the army and navy being always barred from this generalization—they were not only

---

3. This may not have been true. The British censors often opened correspondents' mail and passed the interesting bits to their superiors.

pro-German but anti-American. They asked why the United States sold shells to the Allies. They refused to accept the obvious answer that business is business. They defended the opening submarine campaign. They God-strafed England with fine éclat. I acquired a comprehensive and acrid peeve at my fellow countrymen, and especially fellow countrymen who spoke with queer accents but had passports and visas and were engaged in various underhanded businesses. Names might be mentioned, but to what good? I could not give them all, and the Americans who were living in France and England were equally noisome.

This being the case, and I think my statement will be accepted by every American who knew the facts, it is no wonder that the Germans were deceived about the American temper. They listened to Americans goddamning their country and to their assurances that we would never fight against Germany and to their completely idiotic declarations that the United States could be made to pay a ransom after the war. I have heard Americans say all of these things in Berlin. Bernstorff and Boy-Ed fiddled around with their ideas of a Mexican offensive on our southern border and with a revolt of German citizens in the northwest, and the Berlin Americans said they were quite all right.[4]

It is probable that if the Americans in Berlin had been good, two-fisted, scrappy specimens, Germany would not have given the provocation which eventually led us to go to war. The efforts of our government to keep us out were misconstrued because of their gray ape chattering. We were in the hands of professors and politicians and pacifists, and we made no preparations against the possibility that we might be forced in, and that silly blindness was accepted as proof of our cowardice and emphasized by the resident

---

4. Count Johann Heinrich von Bernstorff was the German ambassador to Washington. The son of a one-time Royal Prussian foreign minister, he spent ten boyhood years in Britain when his father was ambassador to the Court of St. James and married a German American. While in Washington, he had as a mistress Cissy Paterson, whose family owned the *Chicago Tribune*. When posted in Washington in 1908, he was given ample funds "to inform the American public about the peaceful and friendly intentions of German foreign policy."

Naval attaché Captain Karl Boy-Ed was attached to Bernstorff's embassy. Boy-Ed had been an effective propagandist in Germany for naval expansion. Seeking to disrupt production and shipping that benefitted the Allies, he and other agents provoked strikes, crafted financial deals to corner the market on strategic materials, and planted bombs. He was expelled from the United States after the publication in 1915 of sensational news stories in the American press based on secret documents that had been obtained by the British.

Americans. Not only the Germans, but all European nations are unable to understand a people given to half-witted oratory about the blessings of peace when the fighting is actually going on. Henry Ford's peace ship confirmed all of Europe in the belief that our brains have been replaced by honey.[5] The correspondents did not feel it a part of their duty to set the Germans right. They were in Germany on a job.

Henry Suydam of the *Brooklyn Eagle* and Oswald Schuette of the *Chicago Daily News* and Arthur Ruhl, then of *Collier's*, and Cyril Brown and I were once taken on a tour of Belgium. We were all clamoring for a sight of the front. Instead of which we were shown the palace of Leopold at Laaken, in which the old king entertained his royal guests, and which contained two bathtubs and five copies of the Temptation of St. Anthony. We also saw many bell towers and city halls, until the tour became a joke and we proposed a series under the title "Romping through Starving Belgium." Ruhl almost blew up with indignation at this bad humor. How that boy can hate! It was proposed that we go see the battlefield of Waterloo.

"To hell," said Messrs. Brown and Corey, "with the battlefield of Waterloo. Show us a battlefield more up to date."

On the fateful morning we refused to leave the breakfast table. "The Prush" sent in orderlies and finally came himself, red-faced and barking in Prussian fashion, and was rebuffed hard. Nothing like this rebellion had ever happened in Germany. Not even Maximilian Harden was more incomprehensible to the military mind than correspondents who would not do what they were told to do.[6] He could not go to Waterloo without us, and he dared not put us under arrest, and in the end we won our point and in consequence stood well with The Prush ever after. If the resident Americans had stood up for their country, they would not have earned the contempt of the Germans, as they assuredly did earn it.

So far as I could see, "Jimmy" Gerard, a former judge, was a regular ambassador. He had a fight a day with the German Foreign Office over something or other and held up his end as high as they held their ends. Once they tried to humiliate him by permitting him to wait in the foreign minister's

---

5. Ford's peace ship was the ocean liner *Oscar II*, on which he carried prominent peace activists as well as himself to Europe in early 1915 to mediate an end to the war. It failed.

6. Harden was a German journalist who wrote in favor of the war and annexation of much of Europe, Africa, and Asia.

anteroom. Judge Jimmy stamped out. Presently a Foreign Office servant waited on him to say that the foreign minister was now able to receive him.

"Fine," said Gerard. "Tell him I'm here. He can drop in to see me at any time. I'll not keep him waiting—as he kept me."

A higher official came to scowl at Gerard. The foreign minister, he said, never called on ambassadors. It was the part of the ambassador to do the calling.

"I have called," said Gerard, grinning a savage little grin. "It's up to him to return the call."

"The foreign minister cannot do that," said the official.

"That's all right," and Gerard. "I've called. It's a show-down."

So-o, as Ed Wynn would put it, the foreign minister called. Gerard's independence was resented by the Germans, who could not get used to his stiff-back.[7] But the real howling was done by the resident Americans. They just laid right down and cried. They were so ashamed, they said. Gerard did not, so far as I know, take any part in the diplomacy of the day except an American part. If there was another working ambassador of whom that could be said, I would like to have his name. Certainly Herrick and Sharp were as unneutral as possible, and so were the Pages at Rome and London, and so was Henry Van Dyke in Holland.[8] The only other ranking diplomat who stayed American I can call to mind at the moment was in Romania. One of the stories about him is a classic. An equerry called one day with an invitation to take tea with the queen. The diplomat met him in short sleeves at the door.

"I'm damned sorry," he said, "but I just can't do it. You go back and tell the queen I'm hanging my pictures."

And he was a Romanian by birth, I believe. It was not nice, perhaps, and it put a hole in court etiquette, but the Romanians rather liked him for it. He was more their idea of what an American should be than were the Americans they were daily meeting.

When the German high command did get through its numerous heads that the American correspondents wanted news and not argument about the holy German cause, it proved to be far more efficient in the matter of propaganda than were either the French or English military leaders. The brains

---

7. Ed Wynn was an American comedian.

8. Myron Herrick preceded William Graves Sharp as ambassador to France and was reappointed to that post in 1921. Thomas Nelson Page was ambassador to Italy.

of the Allies seemed to be retained in civilian service, for the most part, and correspondents were taken on jaunts to the less active parts of the front. No tinge of complaint enters into this statement, for I think I was favored beyond the average. But the real hot propaganda was done by hand-holders and titled speakers and ladies and editors, and it did the job. Neutral correspondents were classed by the Allied generals as nuisances in the forward zone. The Germans knew better.

No correspondent who really wanted to see what was going on at the front had reason to complain in Germany, once the initial resistance of the General Staff was broken down. Various of the colony were taken to every field of war and shown everything and permitted to write with far greater freedom than the Allies ever gave us. It may be true that in the early days of the war the Germans had more to write about. Their various services functioned perfectly, and it was never hard to find some place where a German success might be shown. The drawback from the German side was that it was increasingly difficult to get the copy out, while the Allies had no trouble at all. It is my belief, though, that if the Germans had had the same free access to the American press that was possessed by the Allies, the American decision on entering the war might have been different. It is not conceivable that we would have espoused the German cause—especially as the Germans were as offensive as they knew how to be. But we might have huddled into a determined and well defended neutrality. Which, for the Allies, would have been just as bad.

Now that it is all over, too, it is worth saying that the Germans proved themselves to be as good sports as were the Allies. My firm conviction, in fact, is the difference between them in courage and patriotism and intelligence and sportsmanship isn't the value of a plugged nickel. The early German leadership was better and the early German organization was superb, but that was due only to the fact that the Germans had been at the job longer. So far as decency—even liking—for the enemy, one was as good as the other. I remember a German officer who had been in that bloody fight at Neuve Chapelle in which thousands of English lives were sacrificed. "Because their fine, brave, foolish officers did not know their business," he said.

Told me with tears running down his cheeks of the incredible courage of the British yeomanry.

"They didn't have a chance," he cried. "They knew it. They must have known it. They marched forward knowing they were about to die. Even if they had taken the position it would have been valueless to them. Their officers must have known that. The soldiers must have been able to see that for themselves. But they could not be stopped until they were dead."

I wrote a story about it at the time, and it eventually was published in the *London Times*, with a characteristically journalese sneer attached. But then it was widely known on both sides during the war that the civilians were a poor lot. That was an article of soldier faith.

7

I left Germany because of the manner in which all Americans were being treated and more especially the manner in which the officers of our military mission were treated. It had encouraged a furor Americana in me. At Aix la Chapelle our party of correspondents was seated at a table in the railway restaurant, perfectly quiet and inoffensive, enjoying beer and whatever German delicacy may have been put before us, when a young man came over.

"I lived for most of my life in New York," he said. "I worked for so-and-so."

"What are you doing here?"

"I am with the German secret service."

We made him welcome at the table. There was the possibility of extracting some news from a secret service man who carried a banner. But he had hardly gobbled his first glass of beer when he began deliberately insulting us and insulting the United States. It was apparent that he had joined us for that sole purpose and felt himself sage. Not only were we Americans but we were correspondents, which is still lower. Ordinarily I was able to sit by and hear my country abused without a tremor. I had had plenty of practice. But on this occasion I put on a regular George M. Cohan show and cussed and snorted until the secret service man tucked his tail and ran.[1]

Numerous such experiences confirmed me in the belief that Germans have very bad manners, taken en masse. They have a tremendous manner, mind you. No one can bow from the belly and click heels with the overwhelming authority of a German. The officer caste wears monocles and give the general effect of a lion tamer sitting in a cage under a spotlight with the

---

1. Cohan was an entertainer, playwright, and composer who came to be known as "the Father of Broadway." Cohan was the author of the wartime song "Over There," with its famous refrain, "the Yanks are coming."

big cats. All that is manner. They have no manners, which is a different thing. Manner is training. Manners are the product of a good heart and kindness. Or so it seemed to me. My German acquaintances would listen to good music with tears in their eyes. They were moved to the bottom of their souls, apparently. I said of them many times: "What good, simple, emotional, kindhearted people they are." The next day that judgement would be reversed.

In the War Office a fine young officer had a desk at which he apparently had little to do. Because he had been an attaché in Washington at one time and talked far better English than I do we became great friends. He was a count—or something of the sort—and a member of Berlin's best society. In time we grew so intimate that he told me of his experiences in the early days of the war. He had accompanied one of the first columns into Belgium and had been revolted by the savagery of the invaders.

One of the reasons why the United States was drawn into the war later on was, of course, the policy of "frightfulness" with which Germany began. Wholesale execution of civilians was a commonplace. The least offense on the part of the civilian population was punished by the execution of a platoon of poor, helpless devils who had been taken as hostages for the good behavior of their village. This fact—and it was a fact—made possible the wild stories told by the English and French of the mutilation of women and children, and those wild stories helped form the American attitude later. The "frightfulness" which had actually occurred was almost forgotten in the superior horror of the stories of outrages which did not occur.

My young friend the count had asked to be given a desk job in Berlin, where he might be spared these savageries at first hand. No one doubted his courage. He had given evidence of that. But this puling sentimentality was not understandable by the good, simple, emotional people I had seen crying into their beer at the strains of a waltz. Everyone I knew who knew the count said that he was crazy. It was very sad, they all agreed. He was a fine young man—ach so—and a member of a great family. But madder than a garden full of March hares. It was this revelation of the essential barbarism of the German people, as well as their bad manners in general, that drove me away.

I had a lot to learn in those days about what was real.

Mind you, I am not decrying war. I think it is swell. I think we shall always have wars and that if this new technocracy continues to whoop up production as it has been whooping it up, then war will be the only way in which the population of earth can be cut down to a practical and profitable limit.

I spent five years in Europe during the war and I would give a promissory note for a leg to be paid six years from today if I could have five more years like them. But when the count and I sat shuddering while he told me of his dashes through burning villages, his car bouncing over the bodies that littered the street, the crying women in the doorways, the blood and flames and misery everywhere, I blamed the Germans. No other people, it seemed to me, could do such things.

Later I revised my views. Tom Johnson of the *New York Sun* rode with me one day in 1918, during the fighting on the Marne.[2] We got into the headquarters of the 3rd Division and there heard the story of the sergeant named Brown. I do not vouch for its truthfulness. We did not check up on it, for we could not print it in any case. We were still the bright young Galahads, over in Europe on some imperfectly explained but humane mission, and nothing like the story of the sergeant named Brown would pass the censor. But here it is, as the officers at HQ told it—laughing:

"Brown came in with forty prisoners a little while ago. He had two machine gunners with him. The prisoners had been picked up in the bend of the Marne."

The bend of the Marne was an area roughly four miles by five, as I recall it. The Americans had jammed through the German lines in the bend that morning, and the more or less quadrangular area had become a no man's land, in which brisk fighting continued between roaming bodies of troops. Brown had been in the front of the advance and had been sent back with a body of prisoners, much against his will. As he marched through the disputed ground American officers spotted him with his convoy and added more prisoners to his bag. On arrival at HQ he was called to account.

"You have papers for two hundred and forty-three prisoners" said HQ, "and you only turned in forty. What happened to the rest of 'em? Did they get away?"

"Hell, no," said Sergeant Brown. "But it got a little hard when there was

---

2. Johnson was a longtime *Sun* reporter. In one episode involving Corey, he and Junius Wood of the *Chicago Daily News* were blocked from sending stories on severe supply shortages. General Pershing called them in and said they were correct but that he was concerned about being held responsible for criticism of the Quartermaster Corps and embarkation authorities. The general cabled the War Department to authorize release of the stories. This was turned down. After the war, Johnson wrote the book *Without Censor: New Light on Our Greatest World War Battles*.

so many of 'em, and so I just turned on the mill and cut the bunch down to a size I could handle."

Which recalls the story of my good friend Casey Jones, who specialized in No Man's Land with the 1st Division until someone shot him through the stomach. Casey is one of the best. He plays a little poker, shoots some dice, likes whisky, Virginia ham, politics, and soldier stories. He is adored by a lovely wife. He is no more profane than a canary and would get out of bed at midnight and go into a blizzard without pulling on his pants if a friend called him.

Casey was one of the between-the-wires specialists in the 26th and at dawn one morning led his squad and six German prisoners toward the American trenches. The Germans knew the wire better than Casey did and went through a hole he did not know existed and began to run toward their own trenches. They were separated from the American by four feet in distance and an impenetrable band of wire.

"Halt," called Casey Jones. They did not halt.

"I had to kill 'em," said Casey.

Pretty tough biscuit for a kindly American, to be forced to shoot six presumably decent Germans at a range of four feet. The Germans had grinned at him mockingly from the other side of the band of wire. Maybe they, too, had heard that Americans were soft. Then Casey crawled through the hole in the wire and took their properties out of their pockets—a newly dead man is appallingly warm and flexible—and went back home to turn the stuff into Intelligence. I was frisky that day and tried to kid him, but Casey didn't take it kindly.

"Hell of a note," I said, "to kill six strong, healthy guys just because you lost your temper when they played a little trick on you."

Casey's voice was throaty.

"Pop," he said. (Those who knew me in the 26th called me "Pop.") "Pop, I give you my word that never in my life have I killed a man in anger."

Casey Jones patiently explained to me what I knew very well all the time: if they had gotten back to the German lines they might have done us harm. No doubt they had picked up some information in their night in No Man's Land. It was his duty to prevent that.

Nowadays I am not so certain that the Germans were not right when they maintained that my friend the Count was crazy. War produces odd changes in humanity. One night, three years later, I took shelter from the storm in a cavern at Cheppy, which the Americans were using as a dressing station. As I talked with the officer commanding, three stalwart boys from Iowa came in and saluted.

"Sir," said the spokesman, "we would like to go back to our outfit."

They had come in some hours earlier with a message.

"No use," said the O.C. "I've had word about your outfit since you left them. It's wiped out. Not a man left."

The three Iowa boys stood there.

"Sir," said the spokesman, "we've heard that. But we want to go back to 'em."

They did not rant about revenge or anything of the sort. The three merely wanted to go back to their buddies. Die with them if necessary. Just three ordinary, commonplace, Iowa farm boys. The O.C. nodded.

"Go if you like," said he.

In the main part of the cavern were a score or more of cots covered with gray German blankets. Not long before, the station had been taken from the Germans. On one of the cots was a nude and middle-aged German who had been shot through the bowels and was in agony. His head bald with that obscene baldness only possible to a true Prussian skull, round and high and knobby. On the peak of it was a little gray forage cap. In the cavern were two or three American women. Two nurses, as I remember, and a Salvation Army woman. When the agony from his wound overcame the German, he would squirm to a half sitting posture and began to babble and pray in his own language. His forage cap would fall off. He would stop his babbling and paw around in the gray blanket to find it, and cock it back on his head.

"Ach, Gott," he cried. "Ach, mutter!"

Then his cap would fall off again and he would begin to scratch around for it, and the American women and men in the cavern would laugh. It seems incredible now, but we all laughed together. It was damnably funny. War certainly does do things to you. But three years earlier, in 1915, while I was still in Germany, I did not understand these things. I left for France convinced not only that the Germans had the manners of small pigs but that they were a race of bloodthirsty savages at the bottom. I maintain my position as to their manners, but I do not think they are any more savage than the rest of us.

In any case, my position as correspondent in Germany was becoming hard to maintain because of the growing feeling at home against the Germans. The day-by-day story of the actual military operations was covered by other correspondents, and in my mail letters I was forced to confine myself to human interest stuff. One of the stories aroused particular anger among the Allies, who protested vigorously against the publication of material designed to show the undoubted superiority in morale and material then possessed by their foes. No one bothers about consistency in war. At one moment the Allied spokesman would point out this German superiority as the result of long preparation—which it was—and therefore proof of a German plan continued through years to attack at the first opportunity and obtain their objectives before Europe could rally against them—which it may well have been. At the next moment, the Allied spokesmen would demand that American reporters who told of this German superiority be immediately shushed.

The story was told me by a Baltic baron who was my conducting officer on one trip. During his period of study as a staff officer before the war the student officers had been taken to the Black Forest. On what was presumed to be their graduation night—American terms are being used—a tremendous banquet was given at the old schloss which had been used as headquarters by the older members of the staff. Wine flowed in a continuous torrent. The officers were constant in their attention to the juniors. Each drank with each junior in turn, and a German drink is not mere sipping. Bottoms up was the rule.

"I was very drunk," said the Baltic baron.

Toward the end of the evening the General Commanding stood up at the end of the table.

"He was very drunk," said the Baltic baron.

The General Commanding gave a number of toasts to the royal family and the solar system and the Mysteries of Udolfo, and each toast was swallowed to the last drop. Then the General Commanding, holding on to the table, shouted the terms of a military problem.

"Do not take notes," he ordered.

The student officers listened with their young souls in their glazing eyes. Some devilry was being prepared for them, they knew. When the General Commanding concluded stating the problem, he said:

"Your horses are at the door. Go. Work out this problem."

Whereupon he sat down. The drunken young staff found their horses held by their orderlies in the castle courtyard. Rain was falling with that sour determination noticeable at midnight in Germany. They mounted and rode into it, trying to remember the terms of the problem which had just been stated. Their business was to make a reconnaissance, observe the terrain, check in at control stations, and get back to the schloss at a pre-determined hour and write out their reports.

"I did it," said the Baltic baron triumphantly. "We all did it. Some not so gut as others—ach, vass—but all did it."

"And what was the big idea?" I asked, mystified. It sounded Bedlamite to me. But the Baltic baron explained that a German staff officer could not stay on the staff unless he proved himself fully capable. Many a time in war or during a social evening it might be his duty to become very drunk indeed. He might upon occasion get drunk purely for the pleasure of it. But if he could not get very drunk and still retain control of all his faculties, including his memory, then he was not fit for staff work and would be sent back to the troops.

My impression is that training of this sort produced an excellent staff. Certainly a better staff at the beginning of the war than anything the Allies had to offer. German staff officers were always and capably on the job. Germany's initial failure to win the objectives for which she had planned was due—as it seemed to a civilian who knows nothing whatever about war—to the fact that the French made up with an ability to improvise when they were in a hole for the organization they lacked and by the stubborn refusal of the British to admit themselves licked. During the first battle of the Marne, the Germans marched farther and faster than any other troops—barring some of the foot cavalry of our own Confederacy—had ever marched in the face of an enemy. They stopped mostly because they were so infernally tired that they could not lift one leg in front of the other and attack a tired enemy which was able to hold on because it could lie down.

8

Perhaps I was in error when I declared, a few pages to the rear, that the Germans have the worst possible manners. Come to think of it, no nation likes the manners of any other nation. The Austrians said Germans were pigs, and the Germans thought of the Austrians as saloon-keepers and cage-livers. The British have a stupid arrogance that would irritate the statue of General Sherman on the plaza at Central Park. They are not only sure they are all right, but they are confident that everyone else is all wrong. Once I rode from Holyhead to London in a compartment with an officer of the Guards. He was young, good looking, entertaining, and quite as intelligent as the average officer in the Guards. He said:

"There are some things about you Americans that are positively revolting."

We had had a spot or two by this time. I said that I knew a lot of revolting things that had perhaps not occurred to him and that I would be glad to tell him, but I wanted him to speak first.

"Englishmen who have gone to America and have made money return to this country," he said, "and are insufferable. Your man Carnegie, for instance."

My reply that he seemed to be complaining of Englishmen, after all, and that the fact they could come to the United States and make so much money that they were able to return to their natal villages and swank a bit is a proof of the superior advantages of the United States merely irritated him.

"Over here we keep such rotters in their place," he said.

"Except when they marry into your aristocracy," I said.

"My word," he said, staring at me. "My word."

So another friendship was broken.

American soldiers billeted with the British invariably hated their neighbors more than the Germans. The British returned the hate. They got along together merely because they were compelled to get along together. To this day the average Briton thinks of us as "Colonials," which is a term of reproach submitted to docilely by the Colonials themselves, who are ashamed of their origin, but usually brings on an attack of hollering when used to an American. They can spot us at a vast distance, too. Once I walked in Trafalgar Square, wearing English clothes, English shoes, an English hat, and smoking an English pipe. The old newspaper woman who sat in front of the *Chicago News* building had never seen me before, but when I approached her, she said:

"'Ere you h' are, sir. H' all the H' American pipers."

To all Americans "the French, they are a funny race," and to the French we are "dirty Americans," to be spoken of as such. We think of them as "Frogs," which is all wrong, because a frog is a harmless and generous animal, and their recognition of certain inescapable facts of life seems sheer perversity to us. On their part, they believe that all Americans are sap-headed, in which conviction they have much to support them, and can be swindled without protest, which is not as true as it used to be. Because they are of necessity frugal to the point of stinginess, we think they are of an inferior and rather loathsome order, and they properly despise us for our silly openhandedness. We admire and laugh heartily at their manners, and they would bar us from the country except that they need our money. The rule is without exception, so far as I know, that each nation at its heart distrusts and dislikes every other nation. For all that we try to play tunes on the League of Nation's piccolo.

In certain basic elements all nations are alike, however. The people of Germany did not want to go to war any more than did the people of France or England or Italy, but having gone to war made the best of it bravely and uncomplainingly. Just as they did in the other countries. I said as much to my friend the German baron one night at the Little Black Piglet, which was a restaurant in the rear of the Hotel Adlon in Berlin. Then the baron launched into prophecy. It was not recognized at the time, but he was as true a seer as Isaiah himself. I had remarked that I had been able to find no essential difference in the attitude toward the war of the different peoples.

"They could not help themselves. They are doing the best they can."

"True" said the baron, glumly. "No European nation wanted war. The only nation which will go to war because war is something it wants will be you Americans."

I did not understand him.

"You are being talked into going to war to save the Allies," he said. "Maybe not for a year—two years—but you will go to war for all that. You are a young nation and you do not know how rich you are, and war seems an adventure to you. Presently our blundering diplomats will make the last of their wrong moves and you will come in."

He was right, of course. We were talked into it, and we did go in like a young man going to a show. The process of talking us in, however, displayed the essential differences between the German and the English propaganda. German and Frenchman had the same point of view. They were in trouble, they needed help, we could give it, and for God's Sake why were we wasting so much time? There is no appeal in that to a people who regarded the one as Krauts and the other as Frogs. The English put it to us that our duty was to save our souls alive, and we rose to the fly of duty like a pickerel to a piece of bright tin. But the fact that we did go to war as an adventure is the reason why—in my belief—our soldiers were the most efficient fighting men on the continent when they had grasped the rules of the game. They were incredibly kind, once prisoners had been rounded up and sent to the rear, but until then they killed for the fun of it. When Dan Edwards, tied together with strings and bandages, went AWOL to get food for his outfit and win the most extraordinary breastplate of decorations for personal gallantry ever bestowed on a soldier in the war, he was not moved by any fury against the Germans or any desire to change the map of Europe or save La Belle France. He just went for the ride.

Like all the other nations, too, the Germans thought and spoke of their diplomats as being fish-headed and herring-gutted. It was taken for granted that whatever they did would be wrong. Nor did I find any warmth of respect for the kaiser, although the Germans I met seemed to be fairly loyal to him for what he had done in making a commercial and manufacturing nation out of Germany before the war. It was assumed that he had been plastic in the hands of the General Staff, and when tales were told of his crying and praying because he saw too clearly what was to come they simply evoked laughter. One of the tales I was not permitted to write was of the kaiser's one-man dress parade in his garden.

"We—the General Staff—would not permit moving pictures to be taken of him except as we directed," said my informant. "He would make himself look ridiculous. But a moving picture man managed to get in touch with him one day and obtain his promise to pose on the following morning. We knew of it, of course, but we did not interfere. There was no use of having needless trouble with him."

When the morning came the kaiser marched out into his walled garden, wearing his brightest uniform and all his medals. The movie man was hidden from the staff behind a bush. The kaiser strutted and preened and the movie man ordered him to walk and talk and swing his good arm and put his hand on his sword and do all the other monkey tricks that occur naturally to the mind of a movie man.[1] From time to time the kaiser went into the castle and put on other uniforms and more medals and marched and counter-marched some more. When the fun was over the staff had the movie man arrested and his film developed.

"Ach, Gott, never have I so greatly laughed," said my friend on the General Staff. "We sat in the staff room and watched the kaiser in the film and laughed until our sides hurt. It was, dear Gott, the funniest film I have ever seen."

"What did you do with it?"

"We kept it. If ever the kaiser does not do what we want him to do—see?"

I have never been able to convince myself that the Germans were not acting in accordance with the rules of war—there are no rules of war—when they torpedoed the *Lusitania*, but that is as unpopular a point of view now as it was in 1915. They gave plenty of notice, and those who defied danger with the *Lusitania* can only blame themselves. But no greater mistake could have been made by a nation that was addicted to mistake making, for it made an enemy of the United States. The British did things as savage later—not so long ago a British general turned machine guns on a crowd of Indians attempting to hold a meeting of protest in a public park—but they knew how to make use of the *Lusitania* incident to their advantage. They were similarly indignant when the Germans made their first use of gas. The British had no gas. In the report of the various disarmament conferences which are being currently held in Europe it will be observed that the arms the British wish banned in future fighting are those arms they lack, and those arms which might be most injurious to them. No one can criticize this attitude. It is the duty of every nation, as of every man, to protect itself. But there is no reason why anyone not directly concerned should be fooled by the argument. Nor is this to be taken either as a criticism of the British or of their method. All nations except our own handle their affairs with an eye single to their own advantage and security. When the United States gets old enough to keep its

---

1. Kaiser Wilhelm had a deformed left arm, possibly the result of nerve damage during a breech birth delivery. He blamed the British doctor.

chin dry it will do the same. Until that time we will go stumbling around the world, good natured, generous, and dangerous. We were moved only by holy motives in 1932 when we shook a minatory finger at Japan after her adventure in Manchuria. As an exercise in godliness that was perfectly all right, but as an essay in statesmanship we merely proved once more that we have not fully grown up.

In 1915 I was not grateful to the baron for his prophecy. Few Americans could believe at that time that we could be chatted into buying a share in Europe's war. Certainly no American newspaperman in Europe could believe it. We had been a decent, home-keeping, self-respecting people on the whole, and had been friendly to the fighting nations on both sides. The brawl was tremendously interesting and gave us a good market for our goods and offered further proof of the faith we had been brought up in, that Europe was a bad-tempered, somewhat insane, and extremely dishonest area, peopled by warlords, cannon-fodder, and weakling aristocrats who were occasionally able to marry the less likely of our rich girls. No one could have made us believe that in a little while the test of Americanism would be the measure of our devotion to a foreign flag. It is hard to believe even yet. Not only was the baron a prophet but he was a good storyteller.

That the baron is still alive is one of the miracles with which this incredible war is filled. He is an Alsatian, a high-colored, lusty bachelor, an excellent officer, but somewhat less completely soldier than is the usual German. His French is rather better than his German, although he is German to the last thread. This is one of his tales that I printed at the time:

> "Me," said the baron, "I, I was a fool. The trench was quite deep and I had been sleeping. I was very safe. Then, because I woke up and wished to acquaint myself with the situation, I thrust my head out of a loophole."
>
> A French rifleman was on the lookout for just such an excellent target. His bullet caught the baron almost in the middle of the throat, by the side of that cartilaginous lump known as the Adam's apple. The baron bled a great deal. It was six hours before it was possible to lift him out of the trenches and take him to the rear, for the approach trenches had not been completed. A soldier of his company went with him. There were no ambulances at that moment.
>
> "I have the cart of an excellent peasant," said the soldier. "He could not refuse me. There is a field hospital back here. Let us go."

They wandered on the back trail, the baron lying in the body of the cart, the soldier driving, the peasant walking behind, lifting up his voice in protest. Ten minutes after they had left the illumination of the rockets and the gunfire the night became impossibly dark. The soldier turned down a side road the peasant found for them in the blackness. The baron's clothes began to freeze. By and by they came to the door of a little inn. Over it a small Red Cross sign was tacked. The soldier hammered on the door. A French surgeon came.

"Enter," said he. "I will do what I can."

The baron had begun to drift off into unconsciousness, in spite of the raw cold and the pain. He knew the bleeding must be stopped. So the soldier and the surgeon took him down from the cart, and the kind peasant drove off cursing into the night. In the dingy, candle-lighted common room of the inn they found a dozen soldiers stretched upon the floor. None had been seriously injured. They swore in a dozen tongues.

"There is a better room upstairs," said the surgeon.

The soldier and the surgeon carried him up the dark and winding stairs. It was a dainty woman's room into which he was taken, the baron remembered. He tried to visualize its occupant before he drifted off again. He woke to find himself trying to frame a gallant apology to her for the profanation of her little room. The surgeon and the soldier had removed his clothing and bathed him and dressed the wound. The soft, fragrant linen was inexpressibly comforting to his fevered flesh.

"We are in luck, my captain," said the soldier. "This is not an army hospital. It is but an inn, and this good doctor is doing what he can for the sufferers who come. There are but few, for no one knows."

Time passed. The baron woke to find the surgeon and the soldier bending over him. There was something in their faces that he could not quite fathom. The room was but dimly lighted. His eyes were faint from weakness. By the effort he roused himself to know that the surgeon was begging a favor, most apologetically.

"If you would permit yourself to share a bed with another wounded man," the surgeon said.

The baron was past caring. But his eyes sought the face of the soldier. The soldier nodded. "It is quite all right, my captain," said he.

He does not quite remember what followed. He knows that he was lifted from between those adorably fresh sheets and carried down a hall into a large room—the state apartment of the inn. The great four poster bed with its heavy canopy, and the rich curtains, and the quaint, old-time furniture told as much. Upon the polished table in the center laid the helmet and accouterments of a French cuirassier. His spurred jackboots were limp upon the floor. As the curtains of the bed were parted the baron caught sight of a heavy, strongly marked face upon the pillow—a face with high Gallic cheekbones and dark, expressive eyes and a sweeping mustache. A sheathed sword lay by the side of the man on the bed.

"Welcome, German," said the man in a strong voice. "Are you noble?"

The baron rarely refers to his family. But he has all the pride of birth his Spanish forebears had three centuries ago, when they first won an estate and a title in a little German principality. He roused himself from his lethargy enough to snap an assent.

"Good," said the man in the bed. "I, too, am noble."

The soldier and the surgeon busied themselves in making the pair comfortable. The soldier placed the candle in a corner of the room, so that the baron's memory carried a tale of long, flickering shadows playing on the ceiling and moving as some draught from without stirred the candle flame. The doctor approached the bedside.

"I have done what I could," he said. "Now I must go."

"Goodbye, Pierre," said the other man. "You are always kind."

There came silence in the room. The great bed was very soft and very warm. The baron gave way gratefully to sleep. Once the other man spoke, in a harsh, rough voice that was no longer strong. It seemed hardly more than a whisper to the baron, but that whisper vibrated like a tang of metal through the air.

"At least," said the whispering man, "not alone."

The baron roused himself by an effort. He tried to turn his head, but the stiff bandages about his neck prevented. He could only see the long shadows playing across the checked and yellow ceiling, with its old plaster ornaments. He tried to ask a question, and then a swift conviction of the uselessness of it all came over him and gave himself again to sleep.

"Once, later on, I felt a stir at my side," said the baron. I knew that the man had moved in bed. But I did not waken. Hours afterward, it must have been hours, for the candle had flickered out and the room was quite dark, I woke again. My head was clear, although I was very weak. I lay there in the great bed, groping in my memory for the incidents of the previous day. I remembered the harsh-voiced Frenchman and the shadows against the ceiling. I moved slightly.

"And then I found that one hand was lying at my side and was tightly clasped in the great hand of the Frenchman. He was quite dead. His hand had chilled and stiffened. We laid there, quiet, hand in hand, until my soldier came to say that he had found an ambulance and I was to be taken to our own field hospital.

"The explanation? I have none. But in my own mind I always think of that Frenchman as the man who feared to die alone."

When that story was published in the United States the Associated Newspaper cabled me to go to France. I was quite willing. What with one thing and another I was fed up with the Germans. But I did not know what had happened.

9

When I got back to France I found that I had written myself into a hot spot. A few hundred thousand of my fellow countrymen were sucking the ends of their pencils nightly in the effort to find new ways in which to call me names in letters to the editor. I was supposed to have become thoroughly pro-German, although I thought then and still think that I had merely been reporting the human side of the war as I saw it, as a correspondent from a neutral country should report it. But the sinking of the *Lusitania* put the lid on any chance the Germans might have of getting so much as a pleasant look from us, and the Allied propagandists at home took full advantage of it.

I am repeating myself, but let me say again that they were doing precisely what they should have done. It was their job to get sympathy from the United States which might be imposed on for cash later on, and if they could get that sympathy by barbecuing a correspondent that was quite all right. I did not like it a bit at the time, especially when on reading some of the letters printed in the papers that had been taking my stories. I found what seemed evidence that the chain letter had been used and that there was a striking identity of content between the indignant letters printed in—say—Minneapolis and Des Moines. If this seems unintelligible to the reader, he is hereby informed that the way to get action, pronto, out of a newspaper is to write letters to the editor. The business department reads letters and is more afraid of them than scorpions.

The German Americans did not savvy this strategy. They did not savvy any form of strategy for that matter. They had liked my stuff from Germany, because it told of the more domestic side of the war and of the courage and devotion the Germans showed in common with the other peoples. When my letters from France began to come in, in which I treated the French in precisely that same way, they used to form platoons and call on editors and say to them that I was a schweinehund. Bad, bad business. The man who has been wronged by a newspaper had best keep his mouth shut. In that way he may escape further publicity. If he is bursting with anger he may write a letter. Under no conditions may he call on an editor. An editor is usually a hard-boiled person, who fought his way up and is not averse to taking on a few more scalps if he can keep the business office from knowing anything about it. The German callers found themselves magnificently outbarked. If they had written letters—more letters, that is, than the Allied propagandists—they would have had better luck.

In a drawer in my desk the other day I found the copy of a story written in Germany at that time and never published. It is a perfect example of the kind of thing I was writing, but it reached New York after the American shoulder had turned definitely cold toward Germany, and H. H. McClure, the editor of the Associated Newspapers, did not send it out to the service. If it had been sent out, it either would not have been used or it would have stirred up more and hotter floods of indignation for the unfortunate editors; and McClure very wisely suppressed it. Here it is, and if it contains any argument for the justice of the German cause then I am a German general. But no doubt it might have roused some sympathy for the Germans, and as we had definitely ceased to be a neutral nation by this time, its publication would only have meant more trouble:

> BERLIN—The other fellow who heard the story thinks the true hero is the man who received the Iron Cross. I favor the rogue.
>
> It happened before Namur. The German army had been jamming forward, little by little. The rogue was a Hanoverian cement worker, with the thirst engendered by generations of dust in his throat. Time after time his captain had suspected him of breaches of discipline. He gives it as his conviction that the rogue should have been hanged each day.
>
> "He was a thief," said the captain. "I think he set fire to houses. Many times I punished him."
>
> The day before, the captain had opened the door of the peasant's cottage. Inside was the rogue, with his nose buried in the top drawer of a dresser. In a corner cowered a woman, her hands crossed on her breast. She was too frightened to cry out.
>
> "Beast," said the captain, heartily. So he knocked the rogue down. The rogue got slowly up and stood attention. The captain knocked him down again.

"Tomorrow," said the captain, angrily, "I'll have you lashed to the wheels of a gun carriage. I'll teach you not to steal."

The rogue glowered at him dumbly, but saluted with a brisk snap. Next day the battle opened. It did not seem feasible to lash the rogue to the wheels of a gun carriage. A dozen times that day the captain felt the rogue's eyes on him. It was his duty to lead his men by ten paces when the charge was ordered. The brown line of the distant French trenches was marked by tiny sparkles, where the rifles were speaking. The captain thought most of the rogue, ten paces behind. They came to a potato field.

"On your faces," was the order.

The fire was a bit too hot. So the Germans hugged the ground and waited for it to slacken—or for other orders. The captain scooped out a little hole in the soft earth, and then writhed himself around to regard his men. The rogue's eyes were on him. That did not concern the captain now. The French fire was too heavy. Back of the potato field was a black strip of woodland. If the men could have reached it, they would have been sheltered. But if they had broken, the long German line might have broken with them. The captain felt a touch upon his shoulder. It was his lieutenant. Beads of sweat were starting on his forehead.

"Ten of the men are dead," said the lieutenant. "Will you not give the order to fall back to the wood?"

"No," snapped the captain.

An hour went by. The captain raised his head slightly to look at the enemy. A bullet struck him in the throat. His head fell forward, so that his face was in the soft earth. He cried to the man at his right.

"Quick," said he. "A tourniquet about my left arm. It has been struck by a shell. Stop the bleeding."

But the man at the right could find no wound upon his left arm. Another man writhed his way along the ground to the officer. It was he who found the little hole in the neck, from which a single drop of blood had oozed. They stripped the wounded man. In the small of his back was a blue wound, not so big across as the top of a lead pencil. The flesh had closed on it. A stream of blood, no thicker than a hair, was trickling down. The captain's left side was paralyzed. The lieutenant writhed his way to his side again

"You are dying," said the lieutenant, "Now you will give the order to retreat."

"No," said the captain.

Lying on their sides, two men dug with their hands as terriers do until they had excavated a deeper wallow in which the captain might lie with greater safety. He looked along the line of his men. Twenty were dead. The rogue's eyes were fixed on him; he had crept nearer. A man whose rifle had jammed laid himself upon the ground, so that his body sheltered the captain from the French bullets.

"I am useless," said the man. "But perhaps I can save you in this way."

The noise was continuous. Bullets shrieked overhead, and the heavy thumping of the larger guns made the ground tremble. The captain felt a man crawl by his side. He could not turn his head, and so the man crawled around to the other side, where the captain could see him. It was the rogue.

"Are you thirsty?" asked the rogue.

"Yes," said the captain, indistinctly, because of the paralysis. Suddenly he began to suffer from thirst.

"Damnably," said he.

"So am I," said the rogue.

The French fire grew heavier. The captain felt his head lifted from the earth. He had been thinking of his suffering and of his life cut short—he is but a young man for a captain—and the tears had been running down his face and mingling with the soft soil so that they made a paste. A great, hairy hand appeared before him, and a dirty handkerchief, mired with sweat, wiped the mud of tears from his cheeks.

"Drink," said the rogue.

A big, black canteen was held to his lips. It was a larger canteen than soldiers ordinarily carry. In it was a mixture of many liquors, and it was almost full. "But go light," said the rogue. "It will be hours before we can get out of this place of fools."

The captain looked at the rogue with gratitude. That fiery draught gave him strength. But the rogue misinterpreted the look. He grinned impudently. "All stolen by me," he said.

The lieutenant came to him again. He had flattened himself into the very earth, had the lieutenant. He moved slowly and with infinite care, and was very pale.

"While you yet live," said the lieutenant, "will you not give the order to fall back? Some of us may be saved."

The captain put his right hand upon the shoulder of the rogue, who was lying by his side.

"If the lieutenant comes to me again," said he, "kill him. It is an order."

"It is an order," said the rogue, cheerily. His pinpoint black eyes snapped. The lieutenant began to hitch himself through the soft earth, and pushed with his feet. The captain saw his face. It was the color of fear. His mouth was open and saliva dripped from it.

"A poor soldier," said the rogue, with satisfaction, "a poor soldier."

"Silence," said the captain.

Night came on. Down the line a bugle rang. The captain called to his men. "Six of you," said he, "pick me up and carry me forward when we charge. I will not be left here to die in the dark."

The Germans charged, shouting gutturally as they stumbled over the furrowed ground. The wounded captain was half carried, half dragged into the trenches with his men. The French gave way before them. In the morning the general commanding the division came. He bent over the captain, and as he did the lieutenant stepped forward.

"He should have the Iron Cross," said the lieutenant. "He would not let me retreat. He held the line. If I had run away I should have killed myself in the wood. I know I shall never fear again."

The stretcher bearers came, and the captain was placed upon the canvas. As they were about to lift him the rogue grinned at him. He was in the French trenches, in the midst of a battlefield, barren of all but death and wounds. He shook a gurgling swig from the canteen at the captain's ear.

"It's full again," said the rogue.

In Paris, I found E. Alexander Powell practically alone at the Crillon. Never before in my life did we live in such luxury and it is practically certain that we never will live in such luxury again. The Crillon was then the swankiest hotel in Paris and almost as empty as a drum.

"It's the funniest thing," Powell said. "The French will not let me go to the front."

"They won't let me," I said. "I have just left the War Office en ricochet."

"Then let us unite our forces and see what we can do," said the hopeful Powell.

My case was understandable enough, but Powell's was a mystery to me for months. He had been with the Belgians. Or, rather, he had been living at Brussels, as correspondent for the *New York World*, and dashing out toward the front to get his stuff now and then. Perhaps he had laid on the local color rather thickly. I don't know. The Belgians were very S.O.L.[1] at the time and every one sympathized with them. Powell and I, being naive and unsophisticated, and if he does not like this I bow my head to him in apology, but I maintain that we *were* naive and unsophisticated, assumed that the Allies were all good little pals together, one for all, all for one, and that a kind word said for Belgium was greeted with flag-waving and gun-firing at the Quai d'Orsay. It was not that way at all. The French reasoning was that France was also suffering and that the attention of the world should be centered on her and that every gesture of kindness for Belgium was a gesture that had far better be expended for France. Powell was just as unpopular as I was.

"Have you seen Poncet?" he asked.[2]

"A little black-muzzled man who says he cannot speak English?"

We had both seen him, and M. Poncet had given us the Gallic finger. He would have nothing to do with either of us. Powell could afford to wait, but it was up to me to get some kindly tales of France printed at home very quickly, or I might be out of a job. We hunted up an American colleague.

"I'll try," said he, doubtfully.

Then we had one of the breaks of the game. Poncet was suddenly ordered to get down into his home country and begin doing his military service, and his pleas that he was considerably more valuable as a chief of the press department than as a tired and worried conscript did not get him anywhere. For two weeks or so, or until he could wangle his way out of the ranks and back to the job for which he was fitted, he ported arms patriotically, and during that period his place was filled by M. ———, who had been in the Chinese embassy and also knew New York and the curious ways of Americans.

"I understand," he said to us. "You shall be given the privileges you desire."

We thought there must be a catch in it.

"I think you are quite as friendly to France as you are to Germany," he said to me, "and it would be folly to dismiss a friend."

---

1. S.O.L. (Shit Out of Luck) dates from World War I.
2. André François-Poncet was a politician and diplomat with journalism training. He occasionally had press duties during the war.

When Poncet came back he tried his best to get us out of our somewhat slippery saddle, but by this time both of us had had a chance to write some of the friendly stuff about France that our folks at home wanted and had taken that chance. I am not speaking for Powell, but for myself only when I say that I had just begun to realize what a good thing for the correspondent is the reporting of a modern war, and I did not propose to give it up. As a reporter, too, I had always written what the editor wanted, just as has every other reporter. If Marianne was to be my gal from now on, why, Marianne was to be my gal. I did not quarrel again with the French authorities until an American army was in France, and American soldiers and girls and distinguished visitors were spending money in Paris in large, rectangular bunches. Then I wrote a story one day of the practices prevalent in certain of the Paris department stores of putting one price on goods for Frenchmen and a much higher price for Americans. It was a well-documented tale, too. Presently I got a letter from the Ministry.

"This article seems inspired by a feeling of hostility for France."

It was not hostile at all, I replied. But as an American I did not like to see the shopkeepers rob my fellow countrymen. I had the proof, I said.

"If you persist in this attitude," wrote the Ministry, "it may be that it will be necessary to expel you from France."

"Try and do it," was my reply. "Try and do it. I am an accredited correspondent with the AEF, and if you think you can deport me because I am trying to protect the AEF from your shopkeepers—just try to do it."

Fini, as the doughboys used to say. I heard no more about it.

10

About this time, I discovered that 2 cents worth of ribbon and a 50-cent badge is a form of intoxicant. The man—American, Frenchman, beggarman, thief—who is once decorated is never happy until he is twice decorated. Ribbon hunting became one of the great indoor sports of the war. Decorations are not given blindly, of course, and it is up to the hunter to show that his services are worth the investment. There is a story, for instance, of an officer of the United States army who was at one time in possession of a lot of hospital supplies. One of the Allies needed them.

"I have already received a great many decorations," he is reported to have said. "My services have been greatly appreciated."

The needy ally offered a little decoration. One of the kind that King Albert of Belgium carried with him when he made his visit to the United States after the war. They did not mean anything in particular, but they were just as gaudy as any other decoration. The officer said that he was no longer interested in the little ones. He wanted one with a collar attached.

"But . . ." said the ally, protesting.

"Well?" asked the officer. So he got his decoration, and the ally got his iodine, or whatever it was. They story may not be accurate to the last syllable, but is of interest as a sample of the stories that were told. It might be of interest, sometime, for Congress to appoint a committee to investigate the ribbon situation and discover how many Americans were decorated during the war and for what. Congress has investigated almost everything else, and this suggestion should be good for trips to the capitals of Europe, vin compris. There were, I believe, some thousands of them.[1]

---

1. Corey makes a good point about the lavish handing out of medals. A correspondent wrote after the war, "The French, Italians and Greeks offer the journalists something that they themselves would like to be given—decorations. There are few American newspapermen in

It had been indicated to me in Germany—in a fashion as subtle as a train of freight cars piling up in a cut—that if I were a very good correspondent there was no doubt that the Iron Cross would be conferred on me. No doubt the same suggestion was made to every other correspondent in Germany, and so far as I know not one of them rose to the bait. No such mistake in tactics was made in France. Now and then an American was given the Cross of the Legion of Honor for services rendered to France because the American loved France, and believed her cause immortally right, and worked and pleaded and gave for her in the most unselfish and devoted spirit. Such Americans were honored by the decoration and France was honored in the gift. Each such gift was followed by a determined charge on the Quai d'Orsay by other Americans who wanted ribbons and were willing to qualify in almost any way they could.

No criticism is here implied of the European nations which grant decorations in recognition of civic service. This is a part of the European system, and a most useful part. Man is a parading animal and loves plumes and epaulets and he will do more for ribbons than he will for money or pension. Nor do I believe the American tuft-hunters realized that the services required of them might conceivably do their own country an injury. In order to win the decoration, in fact, it became necessary for them to be sincerely devoted to the country of their temporary adoption. But the effect upon public opinion at home of the constant rhetorical output of some thousands of eloquent, enthusiastic, vigorous ribbon hunters may be imagined.

"They tell me they are going to give me The Cross," she said.

Her identity will be shielded, because I liked her and because it would not be fair play to pick out one among so many and because she meant everything she said about the particular nation which had promised the cross.

"I am going to write a book," she said.

"You should have more than one cross if you write a book. They usually give two crosses when the copy is turned in and two more when it is published." This, it seemed to me, was pretty good kidding.

"Oh," said she. "Is that so? I did not know that."

Paris who haven't at least one of the little ribbons Frenchmen wear in their buttonholes." The correspondent noted that the decorations helped win over the reporters and at the same time were "an actual boon in gaining entré" to news sources.

Her large and handsome eyes were filled with pain at the thought that the particular nation had attempted to shortchange her. In time she wrote the book. Her adventures at the front were handsomely told, although it was reported then that they had consisted entirely of long automobile rides and pleasant dinners in inns at a safe distance from the battle lines. Long afterward I saw her picture. She was wearing the crosses.

I can report at first hand on the ecstasy created in the breasts of the recipients of orders. Long after the war was over, France awarded me something or other in the Order of Public Instruction—I think that is the name of it—in recognition of my services to France. I had not at any time served France, except when the United States entered the war it became a part of my job to boost the partnership. To the best of my ability I had served the United States only—and myself. I certainly did like my job. During the war, no Frenchman dreamed of giving me any kind of a ribbon whatever. I did not rate any. But when I read the letter in which permission was given me to buy a ribbon, which at a little distance can be mistaken for that of the Legion d'Honneur, and a badge to be worn on the left breast, I fairly palpitated for a time. I did for a fact. Yet the actual rating of the decoration is about equivalent to that of school master in a small Ohio town. Other correspondents were also given this ribbon. They throbbed in unison with me. Funny. The only American who seemed to be averse to getting a decoration was Wild Bill Donovan.[2] Of course, there may have been others.

Colonel Donovan got his cross near Nancy somewhere. He had done something brave and important—I have forgotten precisely what—and two American doughboys had also been picked out for decoration. They had knocked off a few Germans in some night raid, as I remember it, and were still a little uncertain about the legality of their act. The French, and they are a superbly wise people, began to give Americans crosses early in the period of our participation, but at this time no one knew the ritual. A French regiment was drawn up in a hollow square and Donovan and the doughboys were at the center of it. The scene might as well have been that of a military execution.

Ta-ra-ta-ra, the bugles sounded.

---

2. William Donovan commanded the 1st Battalion, 165th Infantry, 42nd Division, during World War I and earned the Medal of Honor for bravery. In World War II, he headed the Office of Strategic Services, the forerunner of the Central Intelligence Agency.

No horn player on earth can get more and better thrills than a French bugler. The chills scampered up and down our backbones. A general or two and a few colonels and a guard of honor marched briskly down one side of the square and up another. Then to the center. Donovan was called out. He stood there, awkward, embarrassed, evidently somewhat puzzled by the whole thing. The general who did the conferring made a snappy little speech that goes with the ceremony and pinned the cross on Donovan's breast, and then—smack, smack—kissed him first on one cheek and then on the other. Donovan's eyes were white and his cheeks hollow when he returned to his place in the ranks. I watched him. When he got a chance he worked his handkerchief out surreptitiously and wiped his right cheek. Then he wiped his left.

Somewhere I have a photograph of the two doughboys in the center of the hollow square waiting the approach of the squad which was first to make a speech over them and then hang a cross on them and then kiss them. They were the AEF's two most miserable men.

On one of our joint trips to the neighborhood of the front, Alexander Powell put his foot in it by writing a piece about the Prince of Wales. The facts of the incident are clear enough, but precisely why the British Empire swelled with indignation was then, is now, and ever shall be a mystery to me. The inner explanation, of course, is that in some way Powell had run crosswise of British propaganda, but how he ran crosswise we shall never know. My theory is that the British press department feared that a story about the prince in running pants might check the rising tide of American devotion to their cause. But that remains only a theory. It may be that Americans like their princes better in high hats.

The French had arranged a trip to the English front for us. There were two advantages in this, from their point of view. They got rid of our importunities for a little while, and they annoyed the British, who did not want any correspondents on the premises and especially did not want American correspondents, who might be still disabled by the American point of view. In time we wound up at St. Omer, which was then the British GHQ, and were dumped on the headquarters doorstep and then let alone. Never have I been so severely let alone anywhere. We wandered into the old inn used as HQ, and no one stopped us and no one spoke to us. Slender young officers wearing the most beautifully brown-polished boots I have ever seen, and superbly cut uniforms and the various tags denoting services, hurried in and out and looked at us blankly and said nothing. We clung together sadly because there was nowhere else to cling.

"You're H'americans, aren't you?" asked the MP sergeant at the crossroads.

A battle was thundering not far away and ambulances were jolting in, five or six minutes apart. They were short, canvas covered, double-deckers, and the feet of the wounded on the litters wobbled loosely as the ambulances bounded over the rough road. The MP sergeant was acting as traffic cop and waved the ambulance drivers this way and that automatically, while he eyed us with interest. We were, he said, the first H'americans he had ever seen to be sure of. When we spoke to him he grinned in simple pleasure at the way we did it.

It was he who told us of the Prince of Wales. The prince had been at St. Omer the previous week, he said, and each morning came out in his shorts and ran briskly for half an hour before breakfast. This, it seemed to us, was an admirable thing to do, and beneficial to the digestion. Powell's story about the bare legged prince in shorts, galloping through the French field, was published in the *London Daily Mail*, and was highly unappreciated by the British. It may be that Victorian prudery overcame them, and they felt that royal legs should not be spoken of, but this seems hardly probable. After all, the British approve of brisk outdoor exercises. It may be that candor of the sergeant was unwelcome.

He said the prince "was not a right good runner." But after all, Powell did not quote him.

It may have been on this same trip that Powell and I had one of those adventures which is so pleasing to look back upon and is not at all pleasing at the moment of happening. We had landed in Dunkirk on the morning that the first of the long-range German guns was firing on the town from a distance of twenty miles or so and were billeted at the Hôtel des Arcades on the Place Jean Bart. This was a good old country inn built over cellars that at some time had been the wine vaults of a monastery. I was opening the first reluctant eye when Powell came to my bedside.

"Get up," he said, "Don't you hear the guns? We are ordered to the cellars."

I scrambled into my clothes; in the corridor I paused to lock my door. For what had seemed an interminable time I had been conscious that someone was buzzing for a servant. In the hall I glanced into a half-open door. Within was a middle-aged Englishwoman in a dressing gown and a state of furious indignation. In the corridor stood a frightened chambermaid. The Englishwoman said:

"Why have I been made to wait for my hot water?"

The chambermaid wrung her hands.

"Does not Madame understand that the Germans are firing on the Place Jean Bart and that we may all be killed?"

"And is that," the Englishwoman asked magnificently, "any reason why I should be made to wait for my hot water?"

The cellars did not suit me at all. The entrance was down a narrow, corkscrew stair, and it seemed evident that if a shell should hit the Hôtel des Arcades those in the cellar would stay there until uncovered by archaeologists of the future. So, Powell and I popped out into the bright sunlight, where stood the statute of the Admiral Jean Bart. There came a mean, whistling sound. Later we were to become well acquainted with it, but this was my first experience. Whung! A flyer was overhead and had dropped a bomb on the Place Jean Bart. Messrs. Powell and Corey retreated handsomely to the cellars. Brrrarrrrhh! The solid stone trembled. A shell from the distant gun shook the hotel over us. We returned to the sunlight and the statue of the admiral. And then another bomb dropped near us and we throttled back to the cellars, only to repeat our call on the late admiral a few moments later. Years later the French officer who was conducting us came with his car and bowed blithe greetings.

"This morning," said he, "we shall go . . ."

Whung! Brrrarrrhh!

"After you, Corey," said Powell. "After you, Powell," said Corey. We were dignified and unhurried and maintained the dignity of America and chatted freely as the car left Dunkirk over roads jammed with fleeing peasants, all their belongings in little carts. At the road intersection were huge crucifixes, and men and women had thrown themselves on the ground to pray at the feet of the compassionate Christ. The French officer listened to us for a time and then said with a puzzled air:

"If Messieurs will speak just a little slower? I find it difficult to comprehend. Is it not?"

Even in these days of incredible confusion we lived like fighting cocks whenever we found an inn. There might be only a few dishes, but they were invariably well cooked and well served, and always a bottle of good wine could be found. The Frenchman is a grand fighting man and he gives his gold freely to his country when it is in peril and steps up his accustomed economy in every possible way, but he will not stint his stomach. Throughout the war this remained the case. England was on starvation rations but France always lived well. Later, in Paris, Mrs. Corey became interested in helping the wounded American soldiers—almost from the beginning she had been connected with A Corner of Blighty, which was an English auxiliary on the Place Vendome. Roland Smith, a businessman of New York, sent her a regular monthly check.

"I must have some soft candy for the men in the jaw ward," she said one day.

The jaw ward was that sector of hell in which lived and suffered the men who had sustained injuries to the face. They lived on liquid food only, which they poured into their poor, torn throats from little goose-billed tureens. Ordinary candy was forbidden them, but they longed for sweets as only hurt men can.

"I'll find you plenty," said a French friend.

He came back with pounds of chocolate, a peculiarly French delicacy, light and fluffy and delicious. There was an abundance in France, then and at all times during the war. One only needed to pay the price. But if this reads like a blow below the belt at a devoted people, I shall hasten to say that it is not. My admiration and love for the French is real, although when they try to sob the United States out of things of permanent value, I seek to resist the act while admiring the method.

Everyone knows the French are the only people on earth who know what good cooking really is. If there remain infidels, then I conjure them to go to France and get converted. They have only a few raw materials, by comparison to our own gastronomic opportunities, but they do more with them. Untutored American cooking has not progressed as yet far beyond the boiled dog state, although there are signs of improvement since the AEF came back from France and spoke to its women. Italian cooking is next best to that of the French, and English cooking is merely boiling and roasting. By the providence of Heaven the English like it.

Throughout the war French officials cultivated the conviction among their allies that if the French people were overly stinted at the table French solidarity would go up in smoke. I do not believe this for a minute. During my years in Paris we lived at the Pension Herrenschmidt on the Jouffroy, kept by a fine old lady of eighty-odd years. She had lived through the siege of Paris in 1870 and at times was reduced to eating rats, and assured me confidentially at one time that if it became necessary she could make a rat ragu over which

I would smack my lips. No one can make me believe that a people who were as valiant in other respects would turn yellow if they were made hungry. It is more likely that the French—an eminently practical race—determined that, inasmuch as they were doing most of the dying and suffering, they would at least not do the starving, and so made their allies come through. That national point of view, it seems to me, is worthy of emulation. They never lost sight of their own interests. On the other hand they did their best to make us lose sight of ours.

Stanley Washburn on one occasion accompanied me on a visit to Verdun.[3] This was at the height of the bombardment, and the town was in complete ruins. Only a day or so before a shell had come through one of the ventilators of the citadel and finally settled under the table at which the staff was dining. Fortunately, it did not explode. Outside was the evidence of what was, I presume, the most blood-careless attack and supremely courageous defense in the history of modern war. The great domed roof of the stone citadel rumbled continually at the thunder of the guns. Yet the meal we sat down to with the commander was worthy of the attention of an epicure, and the food of the common soldier was genuinely good. I looked into that matter. It is, perhaps, easier to be a hero on well-cooked food than on goldfish and corn willie.

On our return Washburn and I spent the night at a place that had been well shelled to bits, and I destroyed whatever standing I had ever had with him, if any. Washburn had just returned from a stay in Russia, where he had been representing the *London Times*, and was properly equipped with the brown-polished boots and fur coat of the English war correspondents. But we had waded through mud and slime, and in the morning his boots had shrunken, although the orderlies had restored their glow. He could not pull them on under his own power, and so enlisted the services of the two orderlies. One held his chair and the other pulled at his boots and the floor was polished and the unhappy trio skated about in one of the few comic sketches of the war. Mr. Washburn bit his lip at my laughter. Even our French conducting officer smiled slightly.

3. Stanley Washburn, another colorful correspondent, started out as a foreign correspondent for the *Chicago Daily News* in the early 1900s. He covered the Great War for *Collier's Weekly* and the *London Times*. Lord Northcliffe, proprietor of the *Times*, sent him to Russia in 1914 with instructions to shape positive attitudes toward the Allies. Washburn expanded his brief by advising Tsar Nicholas on Russian opinion as well. In 1917, he served as a military aide to two American diplomatic missions to Russia and was subsequently commissioned a major in the U.S. Army.

11

One advantage of a democratic form of government is that it is not necessary to tell the democrats what is going on. If a question arises it is only necessary to repeat over and over three words—no, four words: "Duty—Humanity—Our Country." The democrats will come along like sheep. In retrospect it hardly seems possible that a large, throbbing land, practically filled with inspired editors and old ladies and professors and a few wage-earners, would bite into such an apple as the Allies offered us, without first determining that there was no worm at the core. But we did bite in. From August 1914 to April 1917, we had been well and copiously fooled.

Timeout while I thrum again on the single string. The Allies were not to be blamed for fooling us. It was their national duty to save themselves by any means possible. When the Germans refused to abandon the use of gas, in response to their tearful outcries, the Allies began contentedly to use gas themselves. If the Allies had told us everything they knew about their own desperate situation, we might—perhaps—have signed up for a war which was to cost us an as yet unknown number of billions of dollars, and lives, and pension plans, and compensation schemes and second-rate congressmen and AEFs. We might have been so high-minded and courageous. On the other hand, we might not. Who can tell?

I landed in New York on April 5, 1917, which was the day we declared war against Germany. Everyone was excited and cheerful. It had been my intention to go straight to Washington and see for myself what was being done, but it happened that the *New York Globe*'s annual dinner was on the fifth, and I was easily persuaded to attend it. The dinner guests included the entire editorial and business and mechanical force. I knew most of them, they were a fine lot of men, and I looked forward to having a good time. By permission

I brought with me as my guest Edgar Brown of the *Chicago Daily News*. Our paths had crossed in Italy, Macedonia, Germany, and France.

"Get up and say something," commanded Henry J. Wright, editor of the *Globe*. He was a fine man, high principled, practical, of Scotch birth, devoted to the Allies, but a good American.

"Let Brown break the ice." Public speaking is like chaff down the back. Annoying but inevitable at threshing time.

Brown broke it all right. An impulse of heavenly candor moved him. He went through the situation in the near East item by item, took up the fix in which the embattled European countries found themselves, and outlined the German plans and told of German successes and of Allied dissension and failures. His conclusion was:

"Today the Allies are licked and broke. The only way they can be saved is through the aid and sacrifice of the United States."

The *Globe* force listened with its collective jaw dropping. It had hoped for a nice, rousing speech of enthusiasm and cheer. The kind of a speech that congressmen almost always deliver in times of stress. Brown was as comforting as a wet rag. They called on me. Recent practice in hypocrisy had formed me into a fairly habitual cheat. Only by the repetition of glad words in which I did not believe had it been possible to stay on in Verona as a war correspondent. Brown's example temporarily pushed me off my pedestal and I followed his truths with truths of my own. When it was all over, Mr. Wright asked: "Are these things really true?"

The editor of a New York paper, in constant touch, presumably, with every source of news, actually did not know how desperate was the state of the Allies in the spring of 1917, when they finally sold us the pup. It must not be understood that the newspapers of the United States did not get and print news from the various seats of war, which was to all intents and purposes accurate. But it was not truthful. If a communique from either side stated that "An operation which has been in progress for several days has finally succeeded in moving the line from Mont Here to Lac de There," that communique was perfectly accurate. But to be entirely truthful it should have continued with the statement that the side issuing the communique had just had all the bark beaten off it between the points named, and that the operation was successful only in that the bedeviled, starved, exhausted soldiery had been able breathlessly to dig in on a new line and hold on until the reserves could be rushed up. It was not possible to keep the United States ignorant of a majority of the physical facts, but the careful censoring and the delaying of the news and the fairly complete control of the sources kept the United States in ignorance of much of the significance. In 1917, conditions in France seemed so desperate that several regiments were on the edge of revolt.

"They will not suffer much longer unless some hope is offered," said a friend who was an officer of artillery in the French army.

"It is not that we have lost courage, but we are a practical people. If we are to be beaten in the end, we had best take our licking now, and get it over with, and hope for better luck next time."

I told my friends of the *New York Globe*—either at the dinner or after the dinner—of these things. For weeks my friend, the artillery officer, had been standing by, ready to turn his guns on the mutinous troops. He grieved over the necessity, for he sympathized with the men who felt that if further suffering were to be useless, the sensible thing to do was to end it. But he would have mowed down the mass as relentlessly as though they were Germans. War is like that. The United States did not know these things. Yet people who do not know us speak of us as a practical people.

American correspondents were not to blame. They did their very damnedest to get the facts across. Their editors edited whatever guts out of their stories the censors had left in, and business managers prodded the editors constantly for more and better pro-Allies stuff. Pro-Allies stuff was popular stuff. Again, I must repeat that this is not being said in criticism. Whatever American journalism may have been in the old days when editors wore high hats, with pistols under the spiked tails of their coats, journalism now has become a big business. W. L. Rogers left the *New York Globe* to establish a weekly paper for the technical instruction of newspapermen in the new factory idea.[1] No business in which so much money is interested can be anything else than practical. It is, however, regrettable that this fact was not more fully recognized in 1917. The factory still had the golden rules of a past day pasted on its office walls.

For reasons of my own I will not use the name of the correspondent, but most newspapermen who were in France at the time will know him. He represented one of the great American papers. I had and have an intense admiration for it. I know of no paper which is more fair, more honest, more painstaking in its search for news, and in his handling of news the correspondent

---

1. This may be the son of Jason Rogers, who was publisher of the *New York Globe*.

had a well-deserved reputation. He has been decorated since then, but even that has not impaired the quality of his Americanism. At the most it has conferred upon him a distinguished admiration toward France. The fight of the Chemin des Dames came on, in which France did not gain a victory. The cost in blood of the operation was extravagant. Behind it was an important story of the French army and parliamentary politics. This correspondent filed the story to his paper.

If that story had been published, at that time, it would have helped to open the eyes of the American public to what was going on. After holding it for some weeks the editors decided against publication. Their reason was a perfectly straightforward and logical one. The sentiment of the United States was wholly with France, and such disclosures might weaken us in the faith and give comfort to those who still were skeptics. The correspondent asked permission to offer it to a weekly magazine that had asked for some of his stuff, and that permission was granted. The weekly magazine published it some weeks later, and the politicians in France who were offended by its disclosures began to raise merry hell. Mark this: The truth of the facts disclosed had never been questioned. The reputations for sanity and generosity of certain politicians was affected. The fuller and more dramatic revelation at the time of writing of the discord in French high politics—already well known to those Americans who followed such things—might have been a warning to the United States. The upshot was that the correspondent lost his job with the daily paper. Then he went with the weekly magazine. Eventually he lost his job with the weekly. I do not know why, but I presume that the editors grew tired of having the French diplomatic corps dance around in the outer office every time one of his stories was published. He stayed on in France, and more eventually still he was decorated and has lived happily ever after.

Other, older, wiser nations have presumably known how to guard themselves against the danger of such failures in information by employing trained and disciplined diplomats. I think that poor old Ambassador Sharp in Paris knew that a war was going on—in fact, I know he knew that a war was going on because of an incident in which I was involved. I had been in Switzerland, and while there heard some interesting stories about the activities of an American temporarily resident in Paris. He was accused of being a fairly successful spy. Such stories were always of interest but were always received with decorum and reserve. Outside of the cheese business, the principal occupation of Switzerland at that time was the harboring of spies. The republic could not do anything about it, except bounce those spies who did their spying too publicly, and everyone knew that if all the spies habitually resident were to climb Mont Blanc on a given day the ice cap would be obliterated, and no one cared greatly. The arrangement was convenient to both sides. On my return to Paris I mentioned the story to a member of the American embassy staff. In my folly, I thought that information of that sort might be interesting and perhaps important. Sharp sent for me.

"Where did you get this information?" he asked. "Give me the names of your informants."

"Nothing doing. I'll tell you all I know of the story but I will not tell you where I got it."

"If I hear of you repeating this, I shall have you deported," said he.

"Well," I said, "I will be damned!"

Here I was, prepped to get a lot of gratitude and I got this. The rest of the conversation need not be repeated. Sharp is dead and in his way was a good man and a kind man, who should never have been an ambassador. If he had ever functioned as an ambassador, the diplomatic corps of Paris would have had his eyeteeth. But, of course, he did not. From time to time Colonel Edward M. House came to Paris and straightened out the tangles, and the rest of the work was done from Washington.[2] House knew what was going on, of course, everywhere—and he kept President Wilson informed. But it was no part of the business of either man to tell what they knew to the editors of the United States, except occasionally to keep them straight.

Shortly after my return from Germany in 1915, I had wearied of conditions in France. I had written myself out on heroism and courage, and no operations were going on that the French wished me to see, and in any case I could only have written a synthetic version—in which, I say again, they were perfectly right—and my studies of the Parisian restaurants had convinced me that they would be open to the hungry and thirsty for a long time to come. So I went to Rome to see what was going on. Ambassador Thomas Nelson Page received me kindly. He was at that moment filled with rage.

"An American correspondent came in to see me this morning," he said. "I was ashamed of him as an American and I told him so."

"What was the matter?"

---

2. Colonel House, as he styled himself, was President Wilson's backstage adviser and personal envoy during the war.

"He had just returned from Germany," said Ambassador Page, "and told me a lot of nonsense about the Germans. He said they still hope to win the war, and that they have been successful in most of the fighting, and that their organization is superb."

He paused to swallow some of his anger.

"All this, of course, is untrue," he said. "I do not understand how this man dared tell me such things."

All these things, of course, were true at that time. The Germans in 1915 confidently expected to win the war. They had every reason to think they would win it. They were sorry, I think, that they had ever gotten into it, for the resistance they encountered had been alarmingly stiff, but they were sure of victory in the end. They would have won the war if it had not been for the final push given by American troops, which the Germans did not believe would ever be given. Page's attitude was that of every political diplomat we had in Europe. Not one of them—on the Allied side—preserved the attitude proper to diplomacy. No political diplomat ever will.

"Who was this correspondent?" I asked.

"A man named Suydam," said Page. "Henry Suydam. He is representing the *Brooklyn Eagle*."

"He is considered one of the foremost correspondents in Europe," I said.

Page blew up again at what he called Suydam's "unnatural" attitude. Suydam is still with the *Brooklyn Eagle*, as its Washington correspondent, and still regarded as one of the foremost in his profession.[3] Mr. Page had departed so far from what it seems to me should be the attitude of a diplomat that when President Wilson visited Italy after the Armistice he refused to meet him at the frontier and at first made no arrangements to entertain him at the embassy in Rome. Whatever may be said of the wisdom of the course followed by President Wilson, it will hardly be denied that he was animated by a sincere desire to restore order to a disordered world. "Peace without victory." Someday someone in full possession of the facts will be permitted to tell the story of Page's refusal to pay honor to his president on that Italian visit. It will be of interest as a revelation of the manner in which a fine, high-minded, kindly man may be a misfit in a job for which hardboiledness is a

---

3. Suydam's patriotism could scarcely be questioned. He took a leave from professional journalism during the war to head offices in London and Amsterdam for Wilson's propaganda arm, the Committee on Public Information.

requisite. Ambassador Walter Hines Page in London was of the same type. His published letters to President Wilson show a remarkable state of mind, to say the least, in a man holding so important a post.

Suydam and I got together at once and started on a trip to Venice. The Adriatic coast had been closed to foreigners at this time, and we knew the chances were against our getting there, but we thought we would try. It became a humorous and successful excursion, which ended in our arrest and ejection from Italy. At Venice, we had made a most successful coup at the passport gate in the railway station. Some sure-enough spy had just been arrested and the place was humming with excitement. We dawdled about on the outskirts of the crowd, undecided on our course. Suddenly a rift opened in the crowd, and I saw through it that the two carabinieri on guard at the gate had momentarily turned their backs to each other and were telling their friends with many gesticulations the exciting story of the morning. I popped through. As I was getting on the gondola for the Hotel Danieli I heard excited chattering behind me. Then Suydam came, flushed and angry.

"I told them," he said, "that I was with the consul general American—meaning you."

Each carabiniere thought the other had passed me through and Suydam got away with it. For one day and night we saw everything that Venice could offer, and then we were arrested and taken before the Italian port authorities. The navy in every country detests the sister service and vice versa, and the Italian naval officers were no exception. They listened to our tale with glee and had us retell it and stood us lunch and wine and then reluctantly turned us over to the civilian authorities. A certain amount of American shouting got us free, but when we were actually in the train to the French frontier we were hauled out again.

"The story these two assassins tell is a lie," shouted the excited officer who had been in command at the railway station on the previous night. They could not have gotten through my lines. There must be a subterranean passage."

The idea of a subterranean passage through the canals of Venice tickled us for a moment, but the situation became serious. If we were detained while a search was made for the passage we might have stayed in Venice for the duration. Some more American shouting was prescribed, and so we exclaimed that no one could insult us that way and get away with it.

"No man can call me a liar," I yelled.

In point of fact men have called me a liar and gotten away with it. This time the bluff went through, and I demanded that all the American authorities be summoned immediately to court, and the desire of the carabinieri who had wanted to detain us was refused. We left Italy under guard. It had been a pleasant and mildly exciting episode, but the cream of the jest during that trip had been skimmed at Rimini. We had alighted at that little medieval town, determined to visit the Republic of San Marino, the oldest republic and one of the smallest states in the world. It occupies a mountain top and at one time its army had a gun, which was dismantled because each practice shot fell in friendly territory. At Rimini we were arrested, of course.

"But you have no right to arrest us," we protested. "We are the citizens of a neutral state, bound on a visit to another neutral state. An attempt to interfere with us would be a violation of international law."

The matter was taken up very seriously and decided in our favor. Italy and the United States were on the friendliest terms, and it was far from the intention of any Italian to give offense to the great republic of the west.

"It is of a certainty," we were told, "that if our Foreign Department were to take this up with your State Department, the decision would be in your favor. You, as citizens of a neutral country, have every right to visit San Marino, which is also a neutral country. We shall place no obstacles in your way."

Suydam and I began to preen ourselves.

"We will take tomorrow morning's train for San Marino."

"But you do not understand," said the officer-interpreter. "If you were here in Rimini tomorrow morning you should take the train. No one would interfere with you. But you are now in a zone which has been barred to foreigners and we have every right to expel you. So you will take the train for Bologna at six o'clock tonight."

Everyone laughed. It was a simple and good-humored solution to an international question. We dined and wined and visited a monastery and a Roman arch and said goodbye reluctantly. I seem to remember assuring the officer-interpreter that he was a good guy.

12

I have been looking over the originals of the stories written from the various battlefronts during the war—and, not to be untruthful, from the various cafes and hotels which offered inviting fields of exploration—and comparing them with what was left after the censors got through. I am struck by the similarity of the American and the German methods of dealing with the press. The censors of both nations—to generalize from my personal experience—understood the drama of the big show. They liked stories of courage and devotion. They did not shy at pathos or tales of suffering, but they were, and rightly, rigid in their insistence that nothing of military value be written.

But oh, the British and French censors!

They were more practical than the Americans and the Germans. They frankly recognized that the manipulation of fact had become a weapon in war. They insisted that the enemy's acts be painted in blacks and scarlets and that no rascal fought in the Allied ranks. All of the horrors were done by the other fellow. This was good business, of course. When our next war comes on, it is my hope that our own censors will not permit themselves to repeat their errors. In war it does not pay to be fair. No Allied censor, to descend to the particular, would ever have allowed the story of the three tired men to go through. The German censor liked it. "It is true," said he. "That is what war is like." Here it is:

> It was the baron who told this story of the three tired men. He told it one night in the Little Black Piglet in Berlin.
>
> "I got it from their captain in the hospital at Baden," said the baron. "He said he was the Prince of Peace, and that it was his mission to put an end to the war. Poor fellow. It was very sad. He and his company had

been caught in heavy shell fire at the Battle of the Marne, and they died about him in heaps. It turned his brain. He ordered those who were left to throw down their arms and go forward waving green branches.

"Are we not all brothers?" he asked. "Why, then, should we kill each other?"

His men seized him and hurried him to the rear. As soon as possible he was taken to a hospital. The baron said it was very sad. Very sad. Fortunately, he recovered his mind somewhat later and returned to the front. He was killed at Ypres. The baron found him a most entertaining companion in the hospital at Baden. When he did not permit his mind to dwell upon his hallucination he was quite as sane as any man.

"And very truthful," said the baron. "A simple, straightforward fellow who shuddered at cruelty."

The three tired men figured in the incredible march that General Von Kluck's army made toward Paris.[1] That army covered distances daily that no other army, perhaps, has ever dared attempt. At the outset speed seemed the very essence of the attempt, if it was to be successful. The army marched day and night. When a regiment could march no longer it fell out by the side of the road. There the men slept, their open mouths turned toward the dust hidden stars. They lay in heaps as though the machine guns had already swept them. The neverending procession of guns and gray autos and marching men swept by them. Drivers lashed their staggering horses. Men were hysterical with the fatigue and the frightful pressure of the drive. They barked oaths in cracked voices.

"The three men were Social Democrats," said the baron. "But that fact was not significant, except that it drew them together in the march."

Because they thought alike they had exchanged places with other comrades until they were able to march in the same file. It was quite well known to their comrades that they did not approve of the war. They believed it to be a war made by politicians, of which the people had no share. But they proposed to do their duty loyally by the Fatherland.

"It might have been avoided," they said to each other. "But all the

---

1. Alexander Kluck commanded the German First Army's march on Paris at the beginning of the war. His march through Belgium became notorious for the reprisals against civilians. The maneuver conducted in coordination with Karl von Bülow's Second Army to Paris was stopped short of Paris, thus beginning trench warfare.

world has gone mad. Now that the war is on, each German must do his share."

Fresh from the comparative ease of garrison duty, their young muscles well hardened by constant exercise, they bore the initial stages of Von Kluck's drive without complaint. They marched shoulder to shoulder, their faces stolid and expressionless. Now and then they exchanged some trivial comment. Their boots struck heavily upon the road in that characteristic full-foot step of the marching German. It is as unlike the marching step of the Englishman or Frenchman as the German is unlike his antagonists in all other respects. Then came the two climatic days of marching, in which some parts of Von Kluck's army covered forty kilometers on each day.

"I, too, was in that march," said the baron soberly. "I know the agony. I longed for the relief of tears."

It was worse because the supreme effort came at a time when every physical power had been exhausted by the extreme exertions of the days which had preceded it. These men were no longer strong. They reeled as they walked. The eyes of some stared out of their dust masks as though in a sort of catalepsy. Tears trickled from the half-closed eyes of others and made little channels down their cheeks. Some men gave way to a kind of sleep and walked on numbly until a misstep aroused them. Their feet were torn by the marching until their socks were soaked in blood. A frightful agony pervaded every muscle, to give way later to a numbness that was but the opposite pole of pain.

"We drove them," said the baron very soberly. "Oh, it is quite true, all that has been said of us. We drove them on with blows and curses. It was necessary if we were to save the army."

For these days of forty kilometers each came after the drive toward Paris had been stopped. Von Kluck was racing back to the trenches, which had been prepared by his pioneers, eighty kilometers behind his nearest approach to Paris. If he did not reach these trenches safely his army would have been destroyed. The French army was pressing on his heels. The British were still formidable. The orders were that no man—no man—was to be permitted to fall out.

"For if one had stopped to rest then two would have stopped," said the baron. "That would have meant destruction. The task before us was an inhuman one. We could only accomplish it by inhuman means."

The three tired men had done their part as best they could. But they lacked the resistance to fatigue that the farm-reared peasant possesses. One had been a clerk and one a watch maker and one a waiter in a restaurant. They were alike in their indoor origin and in their ideas and at last in their fatigue. For a time they were hypnotized by the surge and movement of the marching men. Thousands and thousands of green-gray uniforms shouldering wearily on. They went through that first day of forty kilometers. Then came an hour's sleep in a field by the roadside, and then their captain roused them again brutally.

"On, on," he cried as though in frenzy. He lashed them with his cane. In their perfect discipline, no less than in their dumb misery, they had no thought of resentment. They marched on that second day until the time came when the clerk could march no farther. His muscles refused to obey the command of his brain. The corporal had been striding by his side, swearing at him, threatening him with the bayonet, but he had finally been emptied of all power.

"Goodbye, my comrades," he muttered to his two companions. "I can march no more."

"We will stay with you," said the two.

The captain—this clean minded young man who shrank from the thought of cruelty—was staggering at the rear of his company, that no straggler might escape from the ranks. The company was at the head of Van Kluck's army. It would not be possible to permit three men to rest by the wayside, a visible temptation to every one of the miserable thousands who were to limp along that road.

"Go on," the captain cried. Striking them with his clubbed sword. "Go on."

"We cannot," they answered drearily.

The captain's eyes fell to the road again. "You know the orders," he said to the corporal. "Be quick."

"Come," said the corporal.

They lurched across the gutter which bordered the road and stood by the stone wall of a park. With one quick movement the corporal threw a cartridge into the chamber of his rifle. The three young men looked at each other in farewell. Drugged and numb by their utter exhaustion, they seemed to have but one thought. That they were to enter into rest. The captain—he who was later to declare himself the Prince of

Peace—stood in the road, looking on at the group. The dense column of marching soldiers passed on endlessly. No one spoke in the ranks now. No one gave even a passing glance to the tragedy that was to be enacted.

"Forgive me, my comrades," said the corporal.

They looked at him dumbly. The watchmaker nodded. The clerk smiled at his fellows.

"Goodbye," said he.

The corporal fired three times. With each shot one of the three crumpled on the dusty grass. They seemed as though lying in slumber. One had pillowed his head upon his comrade's knee. The corporal looked down on them with a twisted, pallid smile. Slowly, as though in thought, he reloaded his rifle.

Then he leaned his breast upon it and fired.

A grim little thing, isn't it? And quite true. I hardly understand now why the German censor permitted it to pass. I know the Allied censors would have stopped it if the tired men had been of their side. I might even have been put under arrest for writing it. It is doubtful if even the most open-minded American censor would have put his ok on that bit of history. It was the understanding at home in the earlier days of our participation that we were fighting a war which was perfectly bloodless. The theory was that American soldiers shared only glory, and never cooties, mud, or vin rouge. I took a picture of the first funeral in the 166th Regiment, AEF, and when the censor got through with me, was my face red? That sort of thing, he pointed out, would dishearten the folks at home.

13

Gordon Gordon-Smith and I were the mavericks of Macedonia.[1] Or perhaps it might be better to say the Ishmaels. Every man's hand was against us, except that of the Serbs, and they did not count. It was merely their country. Gordon-Smith had for years been one of the experts on Middle Europe under Gordon Bennett at the *Paris Herald*. Then Old Man Bennett shifted gears one night, for no known cause, and Gordon-Smith was out with a handsome bonus in the wide, wide world. He found a place with the *Manchester Guardian*. That automatically made him almost an enemy. The *Manchester Guardian* was one of the few papers left in Great Britain for which the thinking was done entirely in its own editorial offices. No pre-digested ideas in bottles were ever left at its door by an interested government. Being a large, handsome newspaper, staffed by men who were gentle and kindly as kittens and dearly loved a good scrap, the *Guardian* was able to preserve a fairly independent course. It was wholly loyal during the war, but it was not blind.

In Macedonia, the Allied Powers were engaged in a petty game of politics. There it first began to dawn on my innocent American mind that the war was being conducted for some other reasons than the defense of small nations. France and England planned to make a profit out of it, so did Germany also. Those interested in finding out just what Near Eastern profits were to be pouched in case of Allied success are invited to make a study of

---

1. The fighting in the Balkans began when Austria-Hungary attacked Serbia. Other belligerents from the Central and Allied Powers joined in the conflict in the coming months. Serbia was ground zero for the Great War due to the assassination of Archduke Franz Ferdinand by a Serb nationalist in Sarajevo in 1914. Gordon-Smith was a correspondent for many British news organizations as well as the *New York Herald*. It was not uncommon for British correspondents simultaneously to hold government jobs. As noted in the introduction, Corey was with the defeated Serbian forces in the winter of 1916–1917.

the question, or get in touch with Gordon-Smith, who is now attached to the Jugo-Slav legation in Washington. In order that the beans should not be spilled, the Allied Powers had closed Macedonia to all correspondents except the hand-picked, and they were sending very carefully composed and censored reports.

Gordon-Smith and I managed to get through the cordon for different reasons. He had been in the Great Retreat with the Serbian army, which was beyond any question the most heroic feat of arms of the war. The defense of Verdun was superb, but, after all, the embattled French had a friendly country to fall back on. The Serbs made their way through snow-laden mountains, in the dead of winter, with no supplies to speak of, no organization, encumbered by most of the Serbian schoolboys of military age, who had been gathered up to save them from Austrian conscription, and with a well-armed and well-fed army on their heels. The percentage of loss to the whole number engaged was incredible and unmatched during the war. Not much has been heard about it since. Not much will ever be heard about it until the exigencies of high politics calls for publicized pity and admiration for the Serbs.

If Gordon-Smith had been merely a correspondent for the *Manchester Guardian*, he would not have been permitted to stay in Macedonia. He barely managed to anyway. But he had attached himself to the Serb headquarters and was regarded by them as the mouthpiece through which contact could be maintained with the world. The French and English headquarters could not well expel him without losing face, for the *Manchester Guardian* would have been terribly vocal over such an outrage. I was an American, the newspaper I represented might be roused to anger if one of their correspondents were thrown out of Macedonia for reasons of politics which did not at all correspond to the beautiful things the Allies—and the Germans—were saying of themselves in print, and in any case it was assumed that I would not stay very long. Richard Harding Davis and a band of hardy followers had just seen the Macedonia war front through the windows of the Hotel Olympos and had happily returned to civilization. This is not intended as a nasty crack at Davis. He was one of the best. In Salonica he was helpless. Politics tied his hands and feet.[2]

---

2. As noted in the introduction, Davis was, indeed, "one of the best." No American correspondent cut such a dashing figure as the square-jawed Davis or had such a commanding byline.

"Do not report to the French or English headquarters," I had been warned by Emily Simmonds, a Red Cross nurse attached to the Serbians.

Someday I would like to tell her story. Miss Simmonds was one of the great women of the war and all the greater, to me, because she was not hunting headlines. A Londoner, born in 1914 she met Miss ———, the daughter of an English county family, and they started out to do their bit for their country.[3] Miss ——— came of a family of sportsmen. Guns and horses had been more in her line than dances and dresses. She had just returned from a big game hunt, on which she had blown almost all that was left of her inheritance, when she met Miss Simmonds. The pair started for the war.

They were unable to get on one of the nursing units in England and, being impatient, went to France. There they were likewise rebuffed. No one had time to talk to them and check up on their qualifications. It was easier and more practical to take the native-born material. Somehow the two girls got through to Serbia, and there went through the Great Retreat and the typhus epidemic which followed. A great American surgeon was one of the heroes of the fight with the plague; Dr. Ryan will never be forgotten by the Serbs. Only a little while ago they placed a decoration on his grave in Pennsylvania. It was rarely that Miss Simmonds could be induced to tell of the typhus fight. One tale I remember:

"I tore open the man's shirt," she said, "He was lying unconscious with a score of others in an unheated railway station.

"Why," I said. "Look! He is wearing a red undershirt.

"It was the first red undershirt I had seen among the hundreds of sick. Then I looked again. It was not an undershirt at all. It was a blanket of typhus lice, moving upon his bleeding breast."

Another:

"We had our temporary hospital in a railway station. The dying men laid on the floor. We had almost no medicines and no comforts. The most we could do was to give them water when they moaned. The dead were stacked in the station yard, to freeze stiff. Like cordwood."

My first meeting with Miss ——— came some months later. She had abandoned nursing for the more active practices of arms. At first she was merely a private in the Serbian army, wearing the same clothes, toting the

---

3. The unnamed woman here is almost certainly Flora Sandes. Sandes, a Yorkshire-born nurse who enlisted in the Serbian army, rose to the rank of captain.

same packs, as the stiff old veterans of the Great Retreat. Then some officer noted that her practice in big game hunting had made her a most useful guerrilla. She knew how to lay ambushes and trail enemies, and she had a sportsman's eye for the lay of the country. When I first met her she was lying on a pallet of blankets at the Serbian front, so full of shrapnel that she rattled, but still able to hold her company together. The stiff old veterans adored her. She was a captain at this time.

Miss Simmonds knew what she was about when she warned me to keep away from the French and English headquarters and make my play with the Serbs. Some months later, Mr. Kohl, then the American consul at Salonica, and one of the finest of the too rarely appreciated consular service, asked me to meet a large British general at dinner. Kohl was a friendly sort. His idea was that I would be aided by acquaintance with the general. In point of fact, my presence in Salonica had not previously been brought to the general's attention, and he was surprised, and he was not pleased, and he cross-examined me throughout the evening as though he were Max Steuer himself.[4] Shortly afterward my troubles began. I was not rooted out of Macedonia, but I was not so interested with it, and it did not seem worthwhile to stay.

At this time the poor old Serbs were doing what fighting was being done. Not much was said of this in the French and British papers. If the Serbs won a small victory against their old foes the Bulgarians it became "an Allied advance." If they were checked or driven back regrets were expressed for "the defense of our gallant Allies, the Serbians." The Serbs had their straightforward peasant souls in the war. The country they were fighting over was Old Serbia, taken from them centuries before, and remembered in song and tradition. They proposed to take it back at any cost. Their immediate opponents were the Bulgarians, with whom a feud has always existed, and who are as good fighting men as the Serbs themselves. The Allies were engaged in watching each other, for neither Frenchman nor Briton wished his partner to obtain anything that could be translated into tangible benefits at the end of the war. They were opposed in a fairly friendly way by the Turkish lines, as neither felt any furiously warlike impulse. Now and then some of them would get leave to come into Salonica to make whoopee. The poor old Serbs and their enemies the Bulgarians were left in the field to fight alone.

---

4. Steuer, a Slovakia-born American lawyer, was known for vigorous cross-examination of witnesses.

"The war could be ended in Macedonia," Gordon-Smith declared. He was eventually sent on to London to make this representation on behalf of the Serbs. No one wanted to end the war in Macedonia. Politics.

"We could have won the war in Macedonia," Gordon-Smith declares today. Give him full credit. He has not changed his mind. He discoursed over the radio on the political reasons why the war was not ended in Macedonia until as a nation we fell for crooners in 1930 or thereabouts. By this time the war was an old, old story. Only the debts remain as bright and new as ever. We were accustomed to see Alexander of Serbia ride around town in his second-hand Ford. He was a nice young fellow, near enough his peasant forebears to be a first-rate fighting man, and inclined to be a good deal of a nuisance in Macedonia. He could not be argued out of a fixed belief that the Serbs should get something out of their toil and bloodshed and seemed actually to resent the Allied idea that they were engaged in a somewhat difficult form of business. In the end the Serbs got cheated, of course. The city of Salonica was given to the Greeks for political reasons and only a little lane was left through which the Serbs might have access to the sea. It is true that Salonica had once been a Greek city. There is still an altar to be seen from which St. Paul preached to the sinners. But the Greeks did not deliver the goods during the war and the Serbs did. It probably does not make any difference. One of these days the Balkans will blow up again. The new-laid Jugo-Slavia is bursting at every seam right now.

It is probable that Americans will always disagree more violently with the English than with any other people, and in the end patch up a satisfactory working understanding. Our men in France fought with the Britishers billeted alongside them, but if need come, the Yanks and the Tommies did their united best to lick any non-English speaking opposition. The British politician is, in my humble opinion, the slickest article in the known world, but the individual Englishman is apt to be a good sport. In Salonica someone gave me a card to the Officers' Club—which had once been the club in which the Young Turks hatched their successful rebellion against Abdul Hamid—and I dropped in one day for a highball. No one looked at me or spoke to me for a time, which is good club usage. Then an officer came over.

"Why are you Americans not doing your part?" he asked.

I do not know whether he intended deliberately to be offensive, or whether it was merely the characteristic bluntness of the Briton. At all events I went oratorial without warning. I had been hearing the same question for two years and was heartily tired of it. Like most Americans, I had regarded the Balkans merely as the place from which the Monday morning headlines had been coming for years and had not expected to have forefingers shaken at me.

"You do not understand," I said feverishly. "Your newspapers have never presented the truth to you. You do not know what the American attitude is, or why it is. The one thing you want to do is to make use of us in some way."

"Really?" Type will not convey the mingled curiosity and contempt expressed in that single word, combined with the arrogance the islander feels for all Colonials and outlanders.

"Listen." I delivered an impassioned talk, going into details of history and bloodstreams and politics and the manifold offenses committed against us by the Allies as well as by the Central Powers.

"By Jove," said my interlocutor. "Interesting, what? Do you mind repeating what you have just said to some pals of mine?"

Being still warm, I expressed my willingness, and we went to dinner in a private room with a dozen or so other officers. The incident has just this importance. When the evening ended everyone expressed his pleasure at having heard the American point of view for the first time and conceded that we were justified in maintaining it. Once more did I come to a realization that there is no one more open-minded and fair than the Englishman, when he is shown the other side of the case in which he is interested. World politics being what it is, he is not always shown the other side. Neither are Americans. Nor the people of any other nation.

If I bring Ralph Estep's name in at this point, it is for two reasons, either of which is persuasive to me. The first is to make clear the feeling against roaming American correspondents in British headquarters' circles, and with which I heartily sympathize, after a considerable lapse of time. As a class we were not playing the political game of the Allies, or anyone else, with any enthusiasm. They put up with us because the putting was the lesser of two evils. The second reason is my long-held desire to say something about some unknown American officer for the murders of November 11, 1918, which may perhaps keep him awake at night. Estep was a newspaperman of Detroit, who had at one time been the chief press agent for the Packard Motor Company. He was brilliant, somewhat erratic, and very likeable. One day up country he had missed connections with the Serb convoy on which he should have ridden back toward tents and rations. He was plodding along a mud road in utter dejection, sans company, sans food, sans any dependable knowledge of his whereabouts, and limping because of worn out heels. A large, luxurious, imperial motorcar approached him, throwing up a bow wave of mud. Estep recognized its two occupants. His face lighted up. Here was rescue.

"Hi," he cried, throwing up his hand.

In the car was Admiral Sir Mark Somebody (name temporarily forgotten) who had been in command of the British watch ships when the *Goeben* and her partner the *Breslau* slipped through the Black Sea to comparative but inglorious safety with the Turks. For this feat of arms he had been deprived of his command and sent to Macedonia. An admiral, of course, was as useful in Macedonia as two old ladies in a stokehold. He wore a breastplate of medals and a broad red-face and was reputed to be a fine old gentleman in private life. With him was (name also temporarily forgotten), the correspondent of the *London Daily Mail* in Macedonia, since knighted for his journalistic services, and properly so. If I am not mistaken he made a lecture tour through the United States after the Armistice, during that period in which the Allies were still able to borrow on the cuff in this country. Knowing the value of his services, I think that Great Britain was stingy with him. He should have been made a duke.

"Hi," shouted Estep again.

The wave of mud splashed him in the face. The admiral and the uniformed correspondent glanced at him. One of them said, "One of those American correspondents." This was not an important incident, of course, but it is perhaps significant. Sometime later poor old Estep failed to connect with an expense check and marooned himself in his room in the Hotel Europa until it should arrive. He had gone to Macedonia on an ill-judged freelance expedition at a time when the attention of the world was mostly directed elsewhere. When his hotel bill had mounted to threatening proportions, he went to bed. If he had left his room, even for a minute, the door would have been padlocked against him, but under the Salonica laws he could not be ejected. It may have been a week later when I missed him from our communal midst and investigated. Estep was in bed, pale with starvation, but by this time so angry because no one had been sufficiently interested to look him up that half an hour's argument was required to get him out, even after his bill had been paid.

On November 11, 1918, Ralph Estep was a lieutenant in the Signal Corps in France. He had made something of a name for himself as a frontline photographer, but not enough of a name to suit him. The war had come practically to an end. At eleven o'clock that morning the Armistice was to go into effect. The Germans were sitting out in the sun all along the line, happy to escape from their muddy dugouts and welcome the return of peace. All along the long battle line frantic French soldiers were embracing each other, and tossing their caps in air and crying, "La guerre, c'est fini."

Then some American general ordered one final, farewell charge.

I do not know who ordered that charge. It is now doubtfully possible to forgive it on the theory that blood makes some men mad. The American doughboys looked at each other in consternation when they heard they order.

"Somebody's gone nuts," was their characteristic comment.

But they charged, an idle, murderous, utterly useless, indefensible charge, which has never been explained. The infrequent references to it have been met by blank silence. In New York City my physician and personal friend had been Dr. Leo B. Meyer for years. He had volunteered to go to war as a surgeon. For thirty hours following the charge he stood in blood shoe-sole deep in his first aid station, operating on the men who had taken part. One of the men who died was Ralph Estep. In his camera was the last picture ever taken of American doughboys charging in someone else's war.

And as Long John Silver said, you can lay to that. Unless I am totally mistaken, we have gone out of the Don Quixote business.

It was no part of my work in Macedonia to write about the part that Allied politics was playing in the Near East. The folks at home were not only not interested, but if I had attempted to tell them that the French and English generals in command were engaged in the big game more than in fighting the war I would not have been listened to and might have been recalled.[5] In the meantime, the Serbs were fighting a nice little part-time war, which was just the kind of a war a civilian could understand and even like. Now and then they got together for a big fiesta and had a grand fight and moved the line half an inch on a large-scale map. Between times they carried on a picturesque guerrilla campaign.

---

5. Corey learned later that his stories were not particularly interesting to the American papers he served. In addition, he had the problem of censorship. "If I wrote a story that was worth publishing the censor killed it. The stories he didn't kill were not worth publishing." He did, however, enjoy the assignment, which had the flavor of his outdoors experiences in the West as a young man. "It was an unimportant field of war," he wrote to his mother, "though of intense interest to me for various reasons connected with tents and horses." Corey to mother, April 17 and May 3, 1917, box 2, HC.

"I had to lay on top of the rock all day long," a Serbian commando told us one night in camp.

He had been poking around the Bulgarian line by night. Being in danger of discovery, he had climbed on a high rock in open view in the meadow in which the Bulgarians were encamped. On top of the rock was a hollow, which fairly well sheltered him from observation. As night fell he found to his dismay that a sentry had been stationed at the rock.

"Presently he got tired and leaned against the rock. So I just leaned over and put my knife through his heart."

One night Gordon-Smith and I crawled up to an old barn, in which an advance post had been stationed. It was one of the abominably black, heavy nights common to the Balkans. The light of a candle would have shone as brilliantly in it as that of a star. In the old barn was a squad of Serbian soldiers, buried in musty hay. Somewhere in that impossibly dense darkness a gypsy violently was playing his heart out. Just before dawn we crawled back toward a more complete safety and possible hot food. It had been one of the great nights of our lives. That day we squatted behind rocks while the Bulgarians tried to burst shells in air just over us and so rip our unprotected hinder ends into steaks. That was also unforgettable.

But these simple pleasures could not continue. It appeared to the English and the French that we might be arousing too much sympathy for the Serbs—or might, alternately, have too much to say about the politics of the Macedonian adventure. Enough was being hinted at even in English papers at the time to reveal the fact that it was not merely the winning of the war but the division of spoils after the war that was in the minds of the politicians of both nations. Gordon-Smith went to London to present the pleas of the Serbs that a real push be made in Macedonia, and so cut the tail off the German snake. A French officer greeted me cheerily one day on my return to Salonica from the Serbian front. "You will not be permitted to return to the Serbs," he said, "Orders."

That was all right. I wanted to go to Paris anyhow. Mrs. Corey had been on a seven months' tour of Italy, in company with Miss Alice Rohe, who has been one of Italy's interpreters in American magazines of recent years, and I thought we might make a visit to the United States. It had become evident that the continued appeals for aid and rescue had worn down the American resistance. It still seemed madness that we would buy shares in other folks' war, but extremely likely that we would do that very thing.

French press credentials allowing Corey to visit the front.
(Library of Congress)

Corey using binoculars to look out from a fortified trench. Undated.
(Library of Congress)

Corey pictured in the uniform of a correspondent accredited to the American Expeditionary Forces. Correspondents wore officers' uniforms with an armband such as Corey's, with a "C" on it. Undated.
(Library of Congress)

Gen. John G. Pershing with his chief of staff, Lt. Gen. James G. Harbord. Harbord's signed note to Corey is barely visible at the bottom of the photo.
(Library of Congress)

Corey in uniform, probably in Paris. Undated.
(Library of Congress)

Corey photographed these battle-weary troops taking a break.
(Library of Congress)

Soldiers lying on stretchers in the street. Undated.
(Library of Congress)

Undated portrait of Corey.
(Library of Congress)

Corey smoking in the company of an American AEF officer outside what is probably a French country house. Undated.
(Library of Congress)

A group of soldiers wearing gas masks pose for the camera in a village. Undated. (Library of Congress)

14

This chapter is really the prelude to chapter 15. It may help the reader to understand why the English and the French did not believe in 1917 that Americans had any stamina as a nation. They accepted many individual Americans, who had fought in their ranks, or forgotten their duties as diplomats and become propagandists for the Allied cause, or had contributed in goods or words. But they did not think that as a people we had any fighting blood. Something of that misconception was due to President Wilson's unfortunate "too proud to fight" speech.[1] They misrepresented that phrase to us constantly as a part of the effort to get us to a boiling-over point. Part of the misconception—if you leave it to me—was occasioned by our pop-eyed ignorance of what was going on. Americans came to England and France, men and women, rich and poor, blind as little dogs about what war really is. They were excited about many things that had not taken place, although the propagandists said they had. They seemed not to realize that the whole trick in war is to kill the other fellow before he kills you. Yet the stories which follow, and scores of others like them, had been published in our papers. This one was written while I was with the German army.

---

1. Wilson gave the speech on May 10, 1915, three days after the Germans sank the *Lusitania*. He said, "The example of America must be a special example. The example of America must be the example not merely of peace because it will not fight, but of peace because peace is the healing and elevating influence of the world and strife is not. There is such a thing as a man being too proud to fight. There is such a thing as a nation being so right that it does not need to convince others by force that it is right." Wilson was annoyed at himself for making the remark, off the cuff, for it seemed to be a call for out-and-out pacifism, which he did not mean. He wanted to suggest the need to stay calm in emergency.

Somehow war has never seemed quite so grim a business—quite so desperate and hard and unfeeling—as when I read a placard that was posted on the walls of Lille.

"Two English aviators are supposed to be concealed somewhere in this town.

"Those having knowledge of their whereabouts are required at once to notify the military authorities.

"The death penalty may be imposed in case of violation of this order."

There you are. That's war. I have given a very free translation of that poster, but it is sufficiently accurate. It epitomizes the spirit of war. It is a game scored on points. If the English aviators got away, presumably with fresh knowledge of the disposition of the German troops within the town, they would score a point. It was the business of the Germans to score a point by capturing the English aviators. If any civilians were caught in the interlocking meshes of this game:

"The death penalty may be imposed."

It was an interesting story, that of the aviators. We shall never know how it ended. The morning we left Lille the captive balloon was gleaming like a swollen and unnatural pearl in the early sunlight, high over the town. The people were standing about in silent, unsmiling, perfectly self-possessed groups, and reading the poster. We walked down the main street, between hillocks of stone and mortar that had been handsome stores and banks previous to the bombardment of October. In front of the untouched railroad station—it's labelled a "bahnhof" now—little shivering boys sold us postcards of Lille as it used to be, when the tourists still came. Our train ran quite on time through a green and empty countryside. Only here and there one saw men or women or cattle. Three times shrapnel broke high above us in the neighborhood of Courtrai. Someone—nationality unknown—was searching the skies for an aviator. We could not find his machine. We only saw the shrapnel clouds.

"They were very brave men, these English," said the officer of the German General Staff who accompanied us. "Perhaps they will get away."

There was a note in his voice—the tributes of one brave man to another—that seemed to hint that he hoped they would get away. They had been pestering about Lille for some time. Presumably each visit added a trifle to the stock of information the English had about the Germans in Lille. Sometimes they visited Lille at night. It is an unpleasant thing to lie in bed and listen to the nasty snarl of the flyer, loose somewhere in the dark above. Sometimes one bomb will wreck a town.

"The two English flyers," said our officer, "dropped bombs on the church of St. Martin d'Equerme. The church was made caput. But they did not intend to do so."

Early in the war the fashion was set of making a frightful uproar whenever a church was damaged. The truth is, of course, that neither side injured a church except for military reasons. (That holds good for the great cathedral at Rheims.) Both used steeples for observation points. Armies always will do that very thing. Both sides shelled observers out of church steeples, to the certain injury of the steeple, whenever they caught the glint of the glasses. Armies always will do that very thing, too. But there was a good deal of hypocritical nonsense written on both sides about the soldiers who did these things. It came as a surprise to hear the German soldier say that the English aviators had not intended to drop bombs on the church of St. Martin d'Equerme. It would have been so easy to say the other thing.

"Something went wrong with their machine and they were forced to come down. They had to get rid of the bombs before they landed. They did not know they were dropping them on the church."

They came down all right—there in the midst of Lille, a French town held by German soldiers—in the darkness. Next day their battered machine was found. To get away they must have performed a very miracle of evasion. One cannot move after dark in Lille except within a radius of a few blocks. Sentinels are on the street corners. The man or woman who walks at night must have an "ausweis" or pass of a sort that satisfies. Unrestricted movement is not permitted the civilians in any captured town. It would be a temptation to disorder.

There was this point in their favor. They had but to open a door—to tap on any window pane behind which a dim light gleamed—and they would find friends. Lille is courtesy itself to the invaders. The few men who are left perform their duties well, and the women who have taken the place of the men who have gone are solicitous in their anxiety that the casual visitor shall be made comfortable. But Lille does not smile. She has bowed to the inevitable, but if she dared she would rebel. The day we left the two English aviators were likely hidden safely in some cellar. Some Frenchman or Frenchwoman will risk life a dozen times in the effort to smuggle them out. It is a pity we cannot know the end of the story.

All taken towns are dark at night, but while we were there Lille was even darker and more silent. No one was permitted on the streets after seven o'clock at night or before six o'clock in the morning. Lille was being disciplined. She was paying the penalty for a breach of the etiquette of war. A few days before a body of French soldier prisoners had been marched through the streets on their way to the train.

Lille didn't cheer. But Lille waved handkerchiefs and threw flowers. Cheering was "verboten." Waving of flags is forbidden, but no orders had been issued against the waving of dainty bits of lace. So Lille was punished by a week of nights indoors. One thought of the bad little girls who are sometimes sent to bed in the darkness. One believes that in the darkness Lille smiles.

The Germans let that go through untouched. I do not believe the Allied censors would have ok'd it, if the circumstances had been reversed. Here is another story from Germany, written in the early months of the war. Surely those who read it could see what war is like.

There is a river and a battlefield and a boy. The boy's name is on the list of the Iron Cross of the First Class. It is not possible to be more precise. Military reason.

He had just turned sixteen when the war began. He was one of those slender, erect, elegant little cadet officers one sees—children who are being trained for war—their boyish faces eager and candid, their straight little backs, their slim little legs fitted into tight breeches. Eventually he came to this battlefield and this river. He had become hardened, as cadet-officers will. His muscles were no longer pulpy. His lips were tight and firm and his eyes were not so widely open as they had been. He was a child who had been made a companion of death.

A long dip in the French half of this battlefield ran down to the river. It happened that this low-lying ground could not be seen from the German half. It was so long and wide that many troops could be assembled in it. German flyers bucketed over it now and then, of course, but the French knew its value. It was protected by the fringe of guns. The flyers were driven so high in air that they could not see. It was needful that an observer be stationed where he could watch the French.

"Let me go," said the boy. "I can swim the river."

This was in January. There was no ice in the river—or not much ice—though a hem of it formed at night along the banks. Those in command considered. If they hesitated it was not because of any compassion for this boy, with the little downy line of hair just forming on his lip. Boys are very numerous in any army, and no one thinks of life. Otherwise there would be no war.

"It is worth trying," said those in command.

So that night the boy strapped a reel of telephone cable to his shoulders and hung the telephone instrument to his body and slipped into that January water, dressed in full uniform. It was very dark and the river was swift. Perhaps he swam two hundred yards, paying out the cable as he swam, before he was able to make a landing. By and by the little buzzer sounded in the German trenches. The boy's trembling voice was heard:

"I have found a place," said he. "I do not think they will find me for a day or two."

It was not through fear that his voice trembled. Boys who do things like that do not fear. It was not that he was giving thought to what might happen when they found him, although no army is considerate of the observer who lies hidden in its midst with telephone and glass. It was only that he was very cold. He could not light a fire by which to warm himself and dry out that soaked uniform. Through the night the murmur of French voices came to him. It was January weather.

He has been there ever since. January—February—March—it is April when this is being written. Somewhere he managed to find himself a hole in which he burrowed like a beast of the field. No fire, no light, for three long winter months. All day long he watched through the peephole in his earth and telephoned to the German army the movements of the French troops. Then a gun began to play on this road or that fold in the earth. Many Frenchmen died. Horses galloped screaming and fell upon the earth and screamed. It is a frightful sound, the screaming of a horse. Once he telephoned:

"The Frenchmen are within yards of me now. I think they may find me. Listen! You can hear the tramp of their feet."

The man at the other end of the wire heard the scuffle of the steel shod boots of the French, but they did not find the boy. They knew he was there, somewhere, of course. The obliteration of companies just as they began to form, the destruction of wagon trains when they reached a crossroad, these things do not come by chances. They have swept that field in which he is hidden by shell fire. They have riddled it with shrapnel. But they did not find the boy.

At night he crept down to a hole in the bank and waited by the telephone cable. He had buried it as it runs from that hole to his earth. By and by the men on the other side of the river lift it, silently, on a pole, and a package of food slips down it. He got his blankets that way and eventually the heat of his young body dried them. Once he could not get to the bank for three days, because the Frenchmen were so near. Then came a snow and he waited, starving, in his burrow until it melted. He dared not leave a track. Each day he telephoned.

"You are over shooting," his soft, tense young voice would murmur. "Lower and to the left—ah—that shrapnel burst among them then."

They wanted to relieve him after a while. The men in command are not heartless. They thought this boy of sixteen had done a pretty tough tour of duty, and that someone should take his place. Perhaps they wanted to save that sort of a boy against another need. But he would not have it. He said that he knew his territory now. He knew every little mound and ditch and swale in it. If a new man came it would be days before he could be instructed in these things. Between times he telephoned the details of a map to headquarters.

"So that the man who takes my place will know all that I do," he said, "if they get me..."

One day headquarters telephoned. The General Commanding was himself upon the wire.

"I wish you to report at once," said the general. "Another man will take your place. You have been granted the Iron Cross of the First Class, and under the regulations your commander must pin this himself upon your breast. So you must come in."

The boy cried a little. He was only sixteen. They could hear his voice break over the wire. But he would not come in.

"The Frenchmen are doing something" said he. "I do not know what, but a new man here could not find out, and I can. So I will not come in."

Last night another observer took his place.

* * *

When that story was printed in the United States, both the French and the British protested, more or less officially. I never knew a more charming and generous and chivalrous man than Ambassador Jusserand, who represented France in Washington. He spoke almost as though he sorrowed personally for that brave boy who died on the bank of that French river.

"I wish that I knew the names of his parents," he said. "I would like to write to them a little note—after the war."

But he made it plain that the Allies resented the printing of such tales. They might help the German cause in the United States, he said. It seemed to him that almost the greatest task before the Allies at the time was the winning of the whole-souled and free-handed sympathy of the Americans. He was unquestionably right.

15

The members of the French and English military missions in Washington in 1917 were all wrong. Or so it seemed to me. We were not nearly as warty a little lot as we seemed to them. But it was easily possible to understand the amusement and contempt with which they viewed the early American enthusiasm for war and the intellectual whirlygig on which the nation—if it is a nation—was riding.

"I admire the manner in which you spend money," said one of the French mission. "It is—ah—a superb gesture. Like a somewhat drunken boy. But"—cautiously—"do you not think it might be well to conserve your resources?"

The English and the French had been compelled to count pennies and francs since the war began. At no time did they have our American idea that the war could be won by throwing dollars in the air. As representatives of the two most practical nations on earth, they knew that it would not be possible for them to take over the direction of the spending and leave to us only the job of providing the money, but they did the next best thing. They borrowed all they could and as rapidly as they could and they are not to be blamed. To reverse the Spanish proverb, God gives nuts to those who have strong teeth. They cracked the American nut as fast as possible, for it was evident to them that we were not capable of spending the money wisely. They misunderstood us completely except on two points. They could use for themselves the fact that our generosity had no limits.

"The one practical way to make use of your abundant manpower," they urged on President Wilson, "is to use your men as replacements in"—the English armies if an Englishman were talking and the French army if the speaker were French. From their wholly nationalistic and therefore selfish point of view they were right. It merely happened that they did not understand. We seemed absolutely insane.

"You have a Home Guard in Washington?" asked a Frenchman.

"This is true," I said. "A Home Guard, complete with uniforms and spurs and sabers and horses. It is a mounted Home Guard. If the Germans crush France and England and invade the United States and make a drive toward Washington after having ruined the American army, a mounted home guard will be able to retreat farther than an infantry home guard could possibly do. No doubt you know that the function of a home guard is to lead the retreat."

The Frenchman looked at me sadly. He did not laugh at all. He said: "Quelle folie!"

But it was not madness. The Home Guard of the District of Columbia may have been in part a dug-out in which bright young men could shelter who did not want to go to war, but it was also evidence of our national exuberance. Just froth on the beer. My first impression when I reached Washington was that everyone had gone completely cuckoo. They behaved precisely as did my Airedale pup when he first met a badger. He worked off his excitement in loud barking and prancing around. The badger bit him, and he was terribly disappointed and sheltered himself behind me and wondered why this strange animal should act that way and generally behaved like a canine moron. The next time he met a badger he went forward quietly, treading on his toenails. He went to bite and not to bark. Experience teaches.

In part I shared the feelings of the French and English about the world war that had been going on for two and one half years. New weapons and new methods had been used. The science of warfare had been somewhat changed. Fighting was now being conducted in the cellars and clouds. Guns were firing at longer ranges than ever before, and captains of submarines seemed to feel that they were doing their duty and were not "murderers" at all. Grant's campaign before Vicksburg and Sherman's march to the sea were still interesting items in our military curriculum but not precisely up to date. Yet, so far as I could see, neither our General Staff nor our people had the least comprehension of what had been going on or what was to go on. I may have misjudged the Staff completely. But the impression produced on me in 1917 was of pompous and light-minded ignorance. The French and English missions saw these things, too. What they did not see was the wide country, filled with lusty young men who could be rapidly heated up to go to war. It seemed to me at the time that the American attitude was:

"Well, we're in this damned thing. So let's make a good job of it. Now it's our war."

No one will ever be able to make me believe that we, as a people, cared one nickel-plated hoot for the Allies or their cause. It is true that along the Eastern Seaboard, where the influence of the internationalists and the bankers who had over-loaned themselves was strongest, real feeling was exhibited. Also, in the hinterland many had suddenly ceased to be pacifists and had gone blood-hungry, and there were ministers who saw the Finger of God pointing and professors engaged in a frantic chase after scraps of paper. But the West and the Middle West did not want this war, unless I was completely deceived in my soundings of opinion during a brief tour in 1917. Since we were in the war, though, the West and the Middle determined to make it a good one.

In 1919 Jay Williams, farmer and lawyer, and in the Big Business Class, was a sergeant in the occupied territory in Germany. One day he sat over a campfire with a German sergeant who talked very good English. The Germans asked: "Why did you Americans go to war?"

"Well..." Williams thought for a moment. "I don't know, exactly. I never heard any talk about the reasons in my outfit. It was a war and we were in it. That's all I guess."

But the German kept prodding.

"Idealistic reasons, I guess," said Williams in desperation. "To protect the sanctity of treaties—and then we did not like the way you invaded Belgium—and sank the *Lusitania*."

The German said those reasons sounded nonsensical to him. Heaven knows, he said, that France and England have torn up as many treaties as Germany ever has. He could not understand why, if we felt so badly about Belgium, we had not gone to war three years earlier, when the outrage was still fresh. And as for the *Lusitania,* everyone knows now, he said, that she did carry arms and that the Germans were within their rights in sinking her. And anyhow, that was three years ago.

"I'll tell you what we think," said the German. "We think that your American bankers were over-extended in their loans to the Allies and you had to go to war to protect their commitments."

Perhaps there is a certain amount of truth in that charge. Certainly, the bankers were ferociously patriotic in 1917. But it seems to me that the actual reasons we went to war—why we were tossed into war, head over appetite—were not understood then and may not be fully understood now. I am not certain they have ever been candidly discussed, for until lately we have been restrained by a curious loyalty to the Allies. A loyalty, I might say, that has never been reciprocated. We have been bludgeoned over the eyes with every verbal weapon in their armory and have not talked back. Here are reasons, then, why we went to war, as I saw them.

In 1916 President Wilson was re-elected because he had "kept us out of war." There is not now and never has been any doubt in my mind that he went to desperate lengths in his effort to hold us back from the cesspool. He was being abused by the Allies, who saw by this time that they would be defeated if we did not give unstinted help, and by the featherheaded Americans to whom the Allies had sold their war-pup and the businessmen and bankers who foresaw profits and safety only in an Allied victory. A reference to the newspapers of the day will satisfy the reader as to the truth of these assertions, I believe. American voters by a considerable margin approved of his course. They could not see why we should go to war to pull French and English chestnuts out of a very hot fire. Proof is in the difficulty with which the Draft Bill was passed later. On April 6, 1917, Congress declared war, in response to President Wilson's action. What had happened between the election in November 1916 and April 1917 to compel this?

In 1916 President Wilson became convinced that the Allies would certainly be defeated by Germany. In his more optimistic moments he may only have contemplated a stalemate, but at no time did he envisage Allied victory. Russia was cracking, France was showing evidence of that Gallic common sense which invariably enables France to identify the buttered side of the bread, and Great Britain could not carry the load much longer without aid. His sources of information were the best. His political diplomats in Europe were not worth—even allowing for a few exceptions—more than $10 a ton, perhaps, but Colonel Edward M. House was getting about on both sides of the line, unobtrusively gathering absolutely reliable information. There were other informants of lesser quality than House, but reliable and alert. The career men of the State Department were excellent.

President Wilson realized that a German victory would mean that a hungry, desperate, tremendously resourceful Germany would be at once turned loose on the world, avid to make up the losses sustained during the war. He paid no attention to the silly talk that Germany would demand a ransom of the United States. He did realize that Germany's best new markets would be in South American countries, if she could dominate them, and that the German war machine would have little difficulty in securing that domination. Germany would walk through the Monroe Doctrine like a bull through wheat. It has never been loyally subscribed to by all of the nations which we assume it protects. Some of them would certainly welcome Germany. Before he acted President Wilson asked for a departmental study of this question.

"What are our enduring national politics?"

The reply was:

"First, the Monroe Doctrine.

"Second, the avoidance of entangling alliances."

It was in order that the United States might be fit and ready to resist the German assault upon the Monroe Doctrine, which he was certain would follow a German victory without having recourse to the forbidden policy of alliances, that President Wilson obtained in 1916 the passage of the National Defense Act. To his intimates in Congress he also revealed that in the event of a German victory we would be threatened by aggression in South America from Japan. A few months previously the national association of Japanese bankers, meeting in Tokyo, had reached a conclusion as to the part Japan must play in the future of the world. The minutes of the meeting were kept secret, but a copy of them was secured through the means usual in diplomacy and the detective business. The conclusion ran something like this.

"Japan is hampered by its lack of money and of natural resources. The one thing of value we can export is manpower, thanks to the fertility of our people. This manpower must be exported or over population will threaten our security at home."

That was the gist of the resolution. President Wilson knew that—in the event of German victory—Japan's hands would be comparatively free. She had not sacrificed herself in the war, but had on the contrary a strong position. It was likely that Germany would offer her a good bargain to get back her eastern possessions. South America offered a paradise to the loyal, hardworking, frugal Japanese. They could out-work the native population readily.

The National Defense Act of 1916 was not at any time considered by President Wilson as an instrument to be used in the World War, although that was the popular assumption. It was designed only for our own protection after what he believed to be the inevitable defeat of the Allies. He proposed to uphold the Monroe Doctrine, even at the cost of war, against both Germany and Japan if need be. But events and the Germans and Allied propaganda forced his hand. The Allies had filled our young national head with the clamor that the German soldiery indulged in rape, child-killing, and murder in its off-duty hours. Americans who held these beliefs naturally loathed the Germans. But many Americans did not like the French and English, either, for perfectly good reasons.

In 1916 the submarine campaign was gradually reducing England to starvation. In desperation—and before the English course is too heartily criticized, get into a fight sometime with a man who has your head on the cobbles and see then what *you* will do—the English began seizing American ships bound for neutral European ports. This would be sheer piracy, of course, if sea law still existed. But in wartime the only law is that of might. The English needed the cargoes and were determined to keep those cargoes out of German hands. We protested bitterly, frequently, and vainly. The English replies were couched in a cynical and defiant vain. In order to checkmate, the Germans returned to unrestricted submarine warfare. They thumbed their nose at the United States, just as the British had done. We were the world's fattest push-over.

President Wilson's long series of protests, directed at both sides, against the outrages both sides had inflicted on us, had the effect of putting him on a spot prepared and located by himself. Something had to be done to save the national face. If he had been a free agent, I think it is quite probable that he would have declared against both sides a strongly supported and armed neutrality. There can be no doubt that his anger was almost as intense because of the British aggressions as over the German submarining. But that was not possible. He was compelled to choose one side or the other.

Of course, he could only choose the side of the Allies, having in mind a possible German-Japanese coalition against the Monroe Doctrine, and the Allied propaganda which had so drenched American newspapers and pulpits with yarns about German child-killing and the like. Then the British propagandists put an instrument in his hand without which it is more than probable he would have failed in winning the effective support of Congress. The British Secret Service turned over to him the Zimmerman letter, in which that incredibly inept diplomat planned a surprise attack upon us by Mexico. That letter unquestionably established the high point for silliness during a war which was not broadly daubed with intelligence at any angle. Our own Secret Service had never heard of it—or of many other things. The intelligence work in the United States up to this time had been almost wholly done by the British. And well done. The State Department gave out the Zimmerman letter for publication, without, of course, revealing the source.[1]

If the American people had realized at that time that they were being moved about like chessmen by the British propagandists they might have dug in their toes. But they did not know. The Zimmerman letter started patriot blood a-boiling in every saloon on 42nd Street. We were in the war—not precisely understanding why we were in the war—but determined to make an honest war out of it. Because we were by no means satisfied by the reasons assigned for getting into someone else's war, we steamed up our enthusiasm to a greater height. As soon as I could I got back to France, where war was being conducted in a mean and modest fashion. The Washington hysteria annoyed me.

In France the same bland disbelief that we were anything but a nation of hay-footed, thumb-handed farmers persisted. It was conceded that many individual Americans had rendered services to France, but to think that an American army could be constituted was plain idiocy to the French command. The one obvious thing to do was to send over as many men as possible for inclusion in the French ranks. There, under the training of officers who possessed the national flair for warfare, they might by dying save many good and more valuable French lives. This was quite openly urged upon us. The British were, as always, better diplomats. They wanted our recruits for the English regiments instead of the French, but they did not talk about sacrificing us to save more valuable English lives. They had a hunch that we might not respond to this reasoning.

Neither then, nor at any time since, did either France or England admit that we were fighting a war of our own, for as nationalistic reasons as they were fighting their war, and that our war merely happened to coincide in time and place with their war. It is that persistent misunderstanding that has been the groundwork for their clamor for release from debts they own us. That and a distaste for paying for dead horses.

---

1. In the telegram, German State Secretary for Foreign Affairs Arthur Zimmermann proposed an alliance with Mexico in the event the United States entered the war. The Zimmermann Telegram, as the proposal came to be known, called on Mexico and Germany to "conduct war together. Conclude peace jointly. Substantial financial support and consent on our part for Mexico to reconquer the lost territory in Texas, New Mexico, Arizona." The proposal suggested that Mexico invite Japan, which was then on the side of the Allies, to join the alliance.

16

"You can see for yourself," said the general, "that stories like that won't do, now that we have declared war."

We were talking in Washington in 1917. The armed forces of the United States, plus George Creel, many kind-faced old ladies, and almost all the professors and clergymen, were hard at work drumming up hate. It was a job that must be done, now that we had thrown our caps in the ring, and they were doing it well. Creel, poor devil, had his moments of anguish. He had been called on to transform the Washington correspondents almost overnight from a body of reporters to a body of propagandists and he found the going slow. He spoke of them only in words of one syllable. They used the same formula in speaking of Creel. The advantage was on their side, naturally, because there were more of them and they could say what they had to say in more different places.[1]

"It was a true story," I said to the general.

"Of course," he said. "I quite understand that. But your work—the work of all correspondents—from now on will be to teach our people to hate the enemy. If they do not hate we will not get the united support we need."

"I will tell tales of death and outrage," I said. It is perhaps possible that I knew more about my job than the general did. In times of war, newspaper-

---

1. Creel was the fiery head of the Committee on Public Information, which Wilson created one week after the United States entered the war. The CPI was the nation's first and only ministry of propaganda. The press came to depend on it for news, but many resented Creel, a former muckraker who was powerful and intemperate in pushing Wilson's messages. In the CPI's first days, Corey gave Creel the benefit of the doubt. "Very few editors seemed to realize that what Creel is really trying to do is broad and constructive work, and in no sense repressive" (Herbert Corey, *Cincinnati Times-Star*, June 25, 1917). As time went on, however, the CPI was often tendentious and played heavily on emotions, including hate.

men are the bellows that keep up the draft in the national furnace. They supply the wind. But the general cautioned me.

"Pipe down about death," said he. "That doesn't go so well in the South and West. Most folks out there think this isn't our war, you know. They don't see why we have had to get in."

It was a funny proposition, come to think of it. Creel and his aides were being called on to sell someone else's war to us at par or better. We were asked to "give until it hurts"—not realizing that the hurt was to become chronic—and to push our young men to go overseas and kill Germans. On our side, however, the war was to be bloodless and profitable. The Liberty bonds were the world's best investment, which they have proven to be, and the fact that some of our young men might be killed was discreetly oblique. The plan of campaign was a good one. It is, in fact, the only plan possible at such times. But poor Creel certainly had his troubles. We walked together one day.

"Dumb," he said of the Washington correspondents, "cheap, thick-heads, saps..."

It was a conflict between an irresistible force and a not so immovable post. It did not take long for Creel, the army and navy, the foreign diplomats and army officers, to convince the correspondents that the time had passed in which they could safely be reporters. Under a form of voluntary censorship American newspapers played their part well. Yet it has always seemed to me that most of the censoring was as silly as a sage hen. We went about in a tremendous state of secrecy.

Shucks! We had no secrets.

The battleship fleet was "hidden" down near Yorktown. No one knew where it was except everyone on the Atlantic seaboard and points west. It was hidden in obedience to that same instinct that makes little girls play house and little boys beat drums. The navy officers got a tremendous kick out of going about with their fingers on their lips and being portentous. Army officers went on "secret missions" to New York and Chicago. We persisted that German spies were desperately trying to find out the location of the steel plants of the Bethlehem company. The only secrets we really had to worry about were the times and ports of sailings. All the rest of the hush-hush was part of the machinery of working us up for war. It was a very necessary part, of course. But it was also very funny. The general said:

"I clipped out that story about Hans and have it in my scrapbook. I think it was damned good. But you can see for yourself that stories like that do not encourage the state of the popular mind we desire. We must have hate."

He was right, too. When a rookie is being given his bayonet exercise he is made to grunt when he sticks his bayonet through the hay-filled bag which is supposed to be an enemy soldier. The grunting, by some queer twist, helps him to work up the furious hate needed in bayonet fighting. A man may kill with a rifle at a distance in the best of humor, but bayoneting calls for blood lust and growls. No wonder the general objected to the tale of Hans. It seems worth reprinting now, just as it appeared under a Berlin dateline.

BERLIN. Hans's captain told us this story last night in the Traube Diele—which is a place where there are many pretty women and a good orchestra and bright lights and wine. We had taken the last table. The captain has just come home from Neuf Chapelle with a kneecap smashed because the bombproof was not bomb proof. Such places looked very pleasant to him, after six straight months in the trenches.

"I'll tell you the story," said the captain, "because you may be able to understand why Hans got the Iron Cross. Hans never will."

The day before it happened they had marched fifty kilometers, his captain said. That is something more than thirty miles. The man who does that stunt, carrying fifty pounds or more of baggage on his back, will need rest the following day. But one does not rest when on active campaigning. The next day his captain took Hans and five others out on a patrol afoot.

"We wanted to find out whether the enemy were in certain villages," he said.

The way one finds out, it appears, is by entering the villages. If one is shot—very well, the enemy is there. If one is not shot, then the enemy is not there. It seems quite simple. Here and there they were shot at, and here and there they were not shot at. They managed to keep in touch with those who wanted that information by sending the news through other passing patrols. Night fell. They had still other villages to investigate. They had walked many miles.

"We were sitting by the road eating our supper," said the captain, "It was quite dark. We were not talking, for we were very tired."

Time came when they must go on. The captain took out his map case in the darkness. Then he flashed his little electric torch upon it, carefully, that no passing enemy might see. The beam of light fell upon Hans's face. The big fellow was lying on his back. The tears were streaming down his face.

"Were you wounded, Hans?" asked his captain. It would be like Hans—a stupid, silent fellow—not to speak of a wound. But Hans shook his head.

"Only tired," said he, simply.

It vexed his captain. Here was this great lout, the largest man in the party, crying like a baby in the darkness, merely because a few muscles kinked and his bones ached. He spoke sharply to the big weakling. He could hear Hans sniffing by his side. One of the others spoke.

"He carried half of his brother's load all yesterday," said he, "because his brother had a fever."

That put a different face on it. His captain remembered how tired he had himself been the night before, after that tramp of fifty kilometers. And he had not carried half—a quarter—of the load that Hans had shouldered. They marched on through the darkness to the next village. It was empty. Even the peasants had fled. They went through house after house, flashing their torches in the empty rooms. There seemed a possible significance in this, that headquarters should know. He wrote a brief note.

"Report to the colonel quickly, Hans," said he. "The rest of us will go on."

"Jawohl," said Hans.

They heard his hobnailed shoes clatter over the cobbles of the village street as he started on his ten-kilometer tramp. One foot came down heavily. The other could hardly be heard. Hans was lame, then, as well as tired. But it could not be helped. After all, Hans could get back, and the others were strong enough to go on. In the next village they were grouped in the darkness while the captain considered the course. They heard military boots clattering over the stones. It was another German patrol. The front line, then, had been surveyed. They might return to their regiment. The captain and his men began to limp doggedly down the road.

"I was walking in a half stupor," said the captain, "for I was very tired. The morning was beginning to be gray. I looked up, to see figures approaching me along the road."

The Germans hid themselves behind a wall. Five limping men came toward them. One had taken off his boots and bound his bleeding feet in strips cut from his uniform jacket. Another was using his gun, muzzle down, as a staff. He swore steadily in Yorkshire as he walked. A third was pale and lurched from side to side as he walked, out of sheer fatigue. He was ten yards behind the others. A fourth seemed fairly fresh. The four were English. The fifth was Hans. The least wearied man of the four kept his rifle ready for use. Now and then he pricked Hans lightly, with the bayonet, as a hint that haste was needed.

"They surrendered when I called to them," said the captain. "It seems that Hans had walked right into them as they were sitting by the road. An English patrol had passed over the ground we had traversed—but after we did—and the four had been left behind. One was so tired he could not travel, a second was lame, and the third man's feet were so sore he was almost helpless. The fourth man—he who seemed fresh—had gone to sleep during a halt and had overslept."

So they took the four prisoners and the redeemed Hans back toward camp. They tramped wearily on, stumbling over the rough stones of the road. The sun popped up suddenly. Prisoners and escort labored on, their heads bent, silent in complete exhaustion. Only the Yorkshire man still swore. When they came to the outpost the captain snapped an order to his men. They stiffened up suddenly.

"Then," said the captain, "I saw this fool Hans return his heavy knapsack to the tired Englishman. He had been helping the man into camp."

His captain recommended Hans for the Iron Cross of the Second Class because he had been captured and recaptured in the course of the night patrol. But the reason that Hans got the cross was because the captain told those higher up of the knapsack and the tired Englishman. He told Hans about it, too, but Hans doesn't understand. He is rather apologetic.

"He is not strong like me—this Englishman," said Hans.

I feel no resentment toward the general for trying to teach me my business. He was quite right, just as the censors and propagandists on both sides had been quite right in insisting that only the wrong side of the enemy be turned to the front. But I did not agree with him when he insisted that the possibility that some of their sons might suffer death and mutilation be hidden from the mothers of the United States. In the first place, it could not be hidden, and it is always folly to waste time on things that cannot be done. In the second place, I had a better opinion of my people than he had. I did not think they would scare. I held that point of view throughout the months to come, when our men were holding Belleau Wood and working their way through the Argonne, a foxhole at a time, through complications of barbed wire and nasty corpses. If the correspondents in the field had been permitted to state our losses each day, in as much detail as possible, I think our people would have flamed hotter in support of the war. I am sure they would not have turned yellow. But the military belief is that the civilian supporters should only be shown the showier part of the war.

"That story about the dead Russian," said the general. "That was a good story. I clipped it out, too, and pasted it in my scrapbook. But don't write stories of that sort about the American troops when you get back to France. The women wouldn't like it."

There again I disagree with him. My experience is that no one so thoroughly enjoys a good, bloody murder in real life as the housewife who is sheltered behind a husband and a cook. Instead of dampening the popular zest for the war, I think stories like that about the dead Russian help to rouse it. If I seem to be referring too frequently to the files of stories sent from Germany, the explanation is that unpleasant forms of death still had a fascination for me at the time. Later on death became merely a trade risk. In any case, here is the story, as written in Berlin:

> BERLIN—The man who wrote the letter was a young Russian. They found him on top of a hill in the eastern theater of war. His strong young hands were clasped about the throat of an Austrian soldier. The fingers were almost buried in the flesh. It was as though in the heat of battle he had thrown away his weapon and sought to kill his enemy by strength alone. The Austrian had used his bayonet as a dagger. From the waist down he was drenched with the thick blood that had spurted from the other's wounds. Both men were dead.
>
> "He has been writing a letter, this Russian," said one of the burial squad that had been cleaning up the field. "Perhaps we shall learn his name—this murderer that kills men with his hands."
>
> So the man of the burial squad took the letter from the pocket of the long Russian coat and then forgot about it. His squad mate laid down the two long poles he had been bearing over his shoulder. A strip of canvas had been made fast between them. They tore apart the Russian and his enemy, so that they fell back stiffly on the wet sod. The Russian's hands

were lifted before his face, in the position they had taken during the long night on the hill. It was as though he were asking for pity. The big Russian was rolled upon the strip of canvas, between the poles. The two men took up the burden, one at either end. They trudged away to the trench in which he was to await judgement.

It had been a bitter fight on top of this hill. A mere pinpoint on the line of one of the great battles whose very name is unknown to us in America, three hundred men were found dead there when the Austrians finally took the height. Time after time they had assailed it. At last they won their way to the top, and there the Russians met them with steel. They fought together, grunting, like animals. The Russians used short entrenching spades as they would axes. They chopped downward upon their enemies, so that men were found there afterward with the flesh of their faces stripped by a slashing blow. Only the green bone was left behind—with eyeballs peering horribly. At night the men of the burial squad told each other of the sights upon that hill.

"I slipped—twice—to my knees on the greasy blood," said one.

They were quartered in a little roadside inn—a dingy, evil-smelling, noisy place. From time to time sullen villagers—their faces swollen and dark—slipped into the common room and took seats in the farther corners. They rarely spoke, even to each other. They watched the soldiers fixedly. Now and then a soldier's eye would catch that of a scowling peasant. Usually the peasant would smile ingratiatingly. The women of the inn hurried back and forward, calling to each other, shrilling. Flickering candles of tallow cast long, trembling shadows across the floor. The greater part of the room was in darkness.

"This Russian—this murderer—killed the man with his hands, although his very heart had been cut out with the bayonet," said the man of the burial squad. "What animals."

The squad was sitting about a table in the corner. A single tall candle threw shadows downward, so that their eyes gleamed in the light but the lower part of their faces seemed dark and uncertain. Bottles of the cheap country wine were on the rough table. Across the wood ran little gleaming channels of wine drippings, with here and there a ring made by the bottom of a wet glass. In one corner of the room a half drunken gypsy orchestra was playing. Sometimes the leader carried his men through familiar country airs, so that the tapping of boot-soles on the unswept floor furnished a deadened background for the melody. Sometimes he was swept away into improvisation, and overlaid a brilliant thread of fancy upon the humming undertones of the violins. At such times the gypsies' eyes roamed curiously over the room.

"There was a letter in the pocket of this Russian murderer," said the man of the burial squad.

He searched slowly and incuriously through his many pockets, puffing in leisurely fashion at his pipe as he did so. He brought out a multitude of unrelated objects—cartridges and a bit of sausage in a stained covering and a stub of pencil and what-not—and finally the letter. It was in Russian, in a huge boyish, unformed writing that straggled joyously across the paper. As he spread the letter upon the wine-soaked table it could be seen that each line strayed farther below the horizontal. A soft, greasy pencil had been used and the writer had brought all his strength to bear. The writing was smeared and smudged, and the lead came off upon the hands.

"Call Sacha," said the man of the burial squad. "I cannot read what this beast has written."

Sacha came—the educated man of the squad—proficient in half a dozen languages. He laughed as he picked up the Russian's letter.

"He has been writing to his mother," said Sacha. "Look. He calls her his 'little apple fair mother.'"

A roar of laughter went up from the burial squad. They settled themselves to listen. The gypsy musician gave his men a glance of command, and the waves of music sank to mere ripples, that the reader might not be disturbed. Sacha said that the Russian had not written down his mother's name and address. Nor had he time to finish it. Battle had intervened.

"Let's hear what the murderer has to say," demanded the man of the burial squad. Sacha translated, slowly. It was hard for him to puzzle out the difficult writing of a very ignorant man.

"It is now four months, my little apple fair mother," Sacha read, haltingly, "since this war began. How happy we should be that we are still upon this beautiful earth, and that each morning we are greeted by the golden sun. Last night the stars sparkled like little candles. I send my love to you, and to my four brothers, and to my sister. How happy we shall be when this war is at an end, and we shall no longer kill each other upon this tender earth. I kiss you, my mother, upon your honey sweet lips."

The men of the burial squad laughed, and beat with their fists upon the table so that the bottles leaped up. They slapped each other upon the back in exquisite mirth.

"Upon your honey sweet lips," they repeated, choking with mirth. "Ho, ho! Is not this a joke upon that Russian murderer!"

17

It runs in my mind that they were both sergeants. Certainly one of them was a non-com of some sort. They looked pretty lonely that afternoon, but that was because of the light, romantic haze that covered everything. I suffered the same defect of vision when I used to watch Susie Kirwin's light operas from the top gallery of the opera house in Delaware, Ohio. The music was rapturous, the colors lively, and the girls incredibly pretty. For the sake of their happiness in the future state, I trust that Gilbert and Sullivan never watched and listened to Miss Kirwin's presentation of *Pinafore*, but I can recall even now the ecstasies with which it filled me. That is why I thought the two sergeants—I'll call them sergeants—were lonely and tragic figures. The fact is they were two tough guys from the regular army. A tough regular is immune to the gentler emotions.

"How'ya feeling?" I asked.

They turned their eyes on me briefly. I was wearing the uniform of an officer and was therefore to be accorded outward respect. But I was a correspondent and the old regulars did not think much of correspondents en masse. Now and then an individual correspondent could make good with the old-timers, but as a class we were civilians who had been dressed up in khaki and were therefore to be mildly despised. This was quite understandable, but it took the wind out of the journalistic bladder. I had not cared whether other armies liked me or not, if they let me go along and gave me my beef and beans. The other peoples could go and get their heads blown off and I did not care a hoot. But when my own people went to war I was ashamed of myself for not being a fighter instead of a messenger. The show was better than ever, but I did not enjoy it as much.

"You comin'?" asked one of the two sergeants.

"No. I wish to God that I could come with you. But correspondents are not allowed."

The two sergeants glanced at each other. Not a flicker on their leather faces. Not an atom of expression on their hard eyes. They merely exchanged a telepathic report to the effect that I was a damned liar and had no desire at all to be going into the trenches. The sergeants were the first Americans to enter French trenches on a fighting mission. They were the forerunners of the hundreds of thousands of other Americans who were to go into the same filthy, ratty, stinking troughs and fight for some reason they did not understand and for peoples they did not even like. The silliness of the thing hit me like a brick, and for the first time. The hell of it was that it was not merely asinine. It was irrevocable. I could have bawled. What I did was to go to Chaumont later with Wythe Williams and Reginald Wright Kauffman and get laboriously drunk.[1] Brandy had no bite that afternoon.

Four or five officers dodged about behind the four- or five-hundred-year-old stone sties that made up the little French village. A group of correspondents stood with their feet in the rich French mud and swore. A couple of straggly trees made a Japanese effect against the sky. The two sergeants and their men waited until the sun declined a bit farther so they would be invisible to the German watchers as they walked the forty yards to the trench mouth. One sergeant said to his men:

"Pick up your feet when you get on them goddam duckboards. Don't make no noise."

The other sergeant added: "And don't get into no fuss with these goddam French."

Nothing about King and Country or Marianne or the Stars and Stripes. Nothing fussy. Just folks.

The lonely sergeant set loose the bile that had been slowly gathering in my system. I had returned from a fleeting visit to the United States with the conviction that Americans did not know why they were going to war, nor

---

1. Williams, as noted in the introduction, was a correspondent for the *New York Times*, and Kauffman was a correspondent for the *North American Review*. Both were outspoken critics of censorship.

how they were going to war. I had landed at New York on the day Congress made the formal declaration and soon went on to Washington to find the elected and appointed representatives of the people in bubble bath. As soon as possible I returned happily to the peace and order of France. It is true that a war was going on in France, but by comparison the country was sane. Supplies were getting to the front on time, men were being killed, the wounded were being shipped to hospitals in long trains of straw filled freight cars, officers on leave sat in front of the Café de la Paix and sipped mild drinks, Paris was being bombed from the air, girls wore black, and the telephone system was no worse than it had been during peace time. A routine procedure had been established.

In the United States . . .

What a mess that was. Old ladies in khaki breeches as noisy as magpies. Orators blasting away everywhere. A Home Guard organized to defend Washington, and to make it perfect the Home Guard was to be mounted on horses. Everyone getting up everywhere when any martial tune was played and standing at bugling attention until the tune was over. A General Staff that seemingly did not know its way about; the French and English military missions apparently running things. Grandiose plans filling the air. We were to have a million airplanes and thousands of concrete ships. Idealistic froth, talk of saving civilization, of the danger of a German invasion of the United States, confidence that we could win the war by spending money, graft in plain sight. Washington sounded and smelled like a madhouse.

I did not get the idea then, but the fact is that I had been a practically perfect representative in Europe for my own people. I had not known anything about Europe or Europeans. Neither did they. Long after the war U.S. Senator William B. McKinley of Illinois—now dead—was a guest at a royal dinner in Belgrade given in honor of a delegation from the Inter-Parliamentary Union. During one conversational pause an associate was horrified to hear McKinley ask the foreign minister of Jugo-Slavia: "By the way, how do you elect your president in this country?"

Yet McKinley was an extremely intelligent man and well informed on all matters that interested him. I had not cared about the rights and wrongs of the reasons for the war, or for the perils to small nations or the assault upon civilization or any of the other succulent shibboleths which had been fed to us. Neither did my people. The war had been a swell show, and I had liked it at first hand, and my people liked the fancy stories and the color and blood and pathos the correspondents sent them, and which were printed on every page back to the one that carries the ultimate statistics on bull beef. I had been getting a good salary—well, pretty good; McClure was no spendthrift—and a reasonable expense allowance. My people back home had been selling wheat and copper and gunpowder, and with the money paying off mortgages, and getting into trouble with widows. I had been just a little spot compared to 125,000,000 people, but I carried the same color.

Then they went to war, pants over applecart, knowing in a general way that they were in for it but too much excited to figure out precisely what they were in for. I had an edge on them there, because I had been seeing it, and I was angry enough to kick a door. Therefore I did not fully understand what I saw. To put it differently, I suffered from a gnawing grumble all the time I was in Washington and believed things I should not have believed. Once I said to an officer of the General Staff that it seemed to me the Staff did not know much about what had been going on in Europe.

"Didn't you get any reports? You had military attachés over there?"

"We got reports alright," he said angrily. "All about what a good time the young pups were having drinking tea."

Now, I knew better than that. I had seen the attachés at work, and knew what difficulties they encountered, and how conscientiously most of them did their duty. But I rolled that under my tongue for months. Charley Sweeney had resigned his commission in the French Foreign Legion, after a fight with the War Office that almost became international and had come home to help his own people. As I wrote earlier, the French considered him, with good reason, one of their finest officers. He is the only man not of French blood, so far as I know, ever to reach the rank of colonel in the Legion. I found him in Washington. I asked what he was doing.

"Digging trenches," he said, "out at Fort Myer."

Whether it was jealousy or ignorance that put him on a day laborer's job I never knew. It didn't matter, for the French soon got him back. But things of that sort were evidence to me that as a people we did not know what we were up against. The first soldiers to reach France were volunteers spread on a thin backbone of the old regulars. A good many of them were drunk when they volunteered. They were carried away by the tide of hooray and bravo, and a couple of noggins had sent them to the pen and ink. They made grand soldiers. Back home they were being cheered as heroes—and they were—but they were in fact an outfit of reckless hellions who would have fought King George and his Dragon as cheerfully as they fought the Germans. What did they care?

One consequence was that I was unable to put two and two together and get anything like the right answer. I came to three principal conclusions, of which only two were right.

One was that the rank and file, the bone and sinew, all the other nice things that the tax-paying and gun-toting millions can be called, did not know what it was all about. They did not care much, for that matter. The folks back home only knew that we had declared ourselves in and that was all they wanted to know. Later I was to talk with hundreds of doughboys, and if one hundredth of one percent of them knew anything about the reasons for the war they fooled me. They had no feeling for France or Great Britain, and they had never heard of Mittel Europa and it was all right with them if a grand duke had been bumped off in Sarajevo. They were tough babies, mind you. No tougher in the war. But they fought because they were in a fight and for that reason only.

The second conclusion was that if any European power had gone to war as we did, it would have blown up like a toy balloon. We had no army organization to speak of. The navy was good enough, but then battleships did not play any part in the war. No other country could have afforded to waste time and money as we did while we were getting ready. The explanation, of course, is that we were protected by the sea, and that war is a part of European business and plans are made accordingly.

The third conclusion was that we would never have an effective force on the continent, and there I was as wrong as any man could be. Black Jack Pershing,[2] tough, hard, savage, ruthless, should have the credit for this. He demanded what he wanted, and the folks back home gave it to him. This had not seemed possible in the early days of 1917. He straight-armed the politicians and made an American army when Washington was meekly willing to have our men used as replacements by the French and British. He whacked 2 million independent, sassy, bull-headed, free-speaking Americans into what was to become the best army in Europe. They never did like it, but they took it. No one loved Pershing, but the AEF stood for him because he got results. He hazed the buckos like a top sergeant, and they cursed him and obeyed him because the men knew he was doing what must be done. They had a phrase for it:

"He's a son of a bitch. But he's OUR son of a bitch."

2. General John J. Pershing was the commander of the American Expeditionary Force.

18

My pro-French American acquaintances in Paris were more than usually distasteful in the months following our declaration. It seemed to me that they were completely cock-eyed in their insistence that the United States had gone to war to save France and civilization, and it is probable that my rebuttals were marked by noise and vulgarity. They were sincere in maintaining the French position that our delay had been occasioned by greed and that we had only acted when we did because we were fearful of what might happen if France went down.

"A nation of contemptible dollar-grubbers and cowards," one born American said of their own people. The French loved that.

Because of this misunderstanding the American forces in France were in hot financial water from the moment of landing. The bills of costs presented were likewise misunderstood. The Americans maintained that if, as the French said, we were in France to save France, then we should not be asked to pay rent for the ground occupied by our trenches. If we were on our own business and only in France as a convenient field of operations then it was perfectly proper to pay the trench rents. But the pretense that we were trying to save France must then be abandoned. In the end Charles Gates Dawes was named as principal buyer for the American army, charged with the duty of haggling until he got a fair price for what we needed, and possessed of the nerve to take first and settle afterward if too much interference was offered. General Dawes has written his own story of his experiences. He could write a better one if he cared to be more candid.[1]

This French misunderstanding of the American attitude was responsi-

---

1. Dawes was, as Corey indicates, a general in the AEF, as well as banker, diplomat, composer, and vice president of the United States under Calvin Coolidge.

ble in large part, too, for the frantic effort of the French government to take over our men as replacements, and to oppose the creation of an independent American army. War is a business in Europe, and conducted for profit if possible. Not for one moment did any French statesman believe that we had no selfish aims and would not demand a share of the loot when victory came.

"If you have an army in being," was their stance, "and can point out after the war that you took this territory and that territory, you would be in a position to get a greater share than if you functioned merely as a reservoir of men and money."

Great Britain and France began their jockeying on the prospective division as soon as it became certain that Germany could not stand up under the American hammering, but their united opposition to the presence of our battle flags in France had been evident almost as soon as our men had learned how to live in dugouts. In 1917 my friend François Monod, a French civil servant attached to the French press service, put this point of view before me clearly.

"Washington," he said, "has accepted the French position. If you have no army here, but merely send your men into our cadres, then it will be easier for your government to explain to your people why you will not accept compensation for your efforts."

He paused a moment.

"You see," he said, "I am accepting at full value the American protestations that you will not ask for any territory or other indemnities."

I said that I did not believe that Washington had agreed to put American soldiers into either the French or the British armies.

"In the first place, we are entirely sincere when we say that we will not ask for any loot. Therefore there will be no need for any explanation. In the second place, I do not believe that the United States Congress would permit any such action to be taken. You do not understand at all why we are in this war. Maybe we do not either. But if President Wilson were to agree to any such thing, anything might happen at home. Anything. Impeachment, even,"

"But that is folly," said Monod. "I tell you, it has been agreed to."

American headquarters said that no such agreement had been entered into. But there was a certain hardness about the jaws of the men interrogated which led me to believe that there might be a rat in the cellar, and so I wrote a story, in which Monod's statements were accepted, and sent it on to the censor at Chaumont. It was stopped, as I knew it would be, but as a result an explanation was given me. It is offered under full reserve at this time. I do not know whether the statements made were true. I do know the officer who made them is a fanatically truthful man.

Here is what he told me:

> The French insisted that no American army should be constituted. They gave as their reason that Americans are of doubtful military value. They have never been tested in continental warfare. They say that our officers are untrained and that our men will not follow them. They say that the only practical way of making use of such questionable material is to impose the strict French—and English—discipline on them, and to bury them in bodies of trained and war-hardened troops. This demand was refused by General Pershing. Then it was made again in Washington.
>
> I am not in position to say what was the reply made by President Wilson.
>
> General Pershing again declined to yield.
>
> Then a meeting was called of a war council, at which General Foch presided. He had ceased to ask General Pershing to assent to the Allied wishes. He commanded. The two men sat at either end of the table and glared at each other.
>
> "No," said Pershing.
>
> "Here are my orders," said Foch.
>
> He pushed a typewritten paper across the table to Pershing, on which had been tabulated his requirements. The American army was not to take part in combat. As fast as its men were trained, they were to report to the French—and British—authorities and would be dissolved in the Allied armies. Foch was backed by at least two other generals and by a member of the cabinet. On the other side of the table sat two British generals. They assented.
>
> "This must be done," they said.
>
> General Pershing picked up the paper and read it. Then he very deliberately tore it in two. Then he tore the two pieces crosswise. Then he threw them on the floor. He rose.
>
> "You can go to hell," said he.

That story may not be true in detail. I do not know. That it was true in spirit is certain. I hunted up Monod and told it to him. He had nothing to say.

Then I went to AEF press headquarters, and found Colonel Sweeney, second in command to General Dennis Nolan in G2, and told the tale to him.

"Why were the French so anxious to have that story printed?"

Sweeney's theory was that when Monod told it, the French had not yet given up hope that the American army could be suffocated in its swaddling clothes and were still working hard at their propaganda to that end.

"They will go on trying," he said. "But they don't know Pershing."

19

Toward the end of the war I became reconciled to the Good Time Girls. Bless their dear hearts, they had added color and introduced a few funny lines into a plot that would otherwise have been black as a crow. It was easy to see, too, that they were as truly representative of our people as I had been as a correspondent, wandering about Europe and having one good time and writing home about it. We are a different people from the European breeds. Lighter-minded, maybe, and more casual, and with more of the gambler in us. Our forefathers had been in the habit of hitching the horses to the wagon and tossing a plough and a barrel of flour and the wife and a few kids in behind and setting out for California or Oregon or somewhere. It did not seem to make much difference to them. The year 1929 was a long way ahead of us, but it seems to me the slogan of Americans when they bust was "zip goes a nickel."

Our Good Time Girls were offset by our Good Time Men. Congressmen, preachers, lecturers, writers on all the high-toned subjects, businessmen who were able to think up some excuse for going to France for a good time, landed right in the middle of our war. Barring most of the preachers they all came thirsty.

It is true that as a nation we got drunk, hollered, shot out lights, kicked one another in the stomach, fell off docks and swam ashore, sang the funniest bawdy songs ever written, and made something of an alcoholic mess of ourselves. This had been going on for generations. Over in Europe whisky was swallowed with plenty of water and moderation, but we shot ours hand-over-hand. The firmly held opinion from Land's End to Budapest was and is that we are not a nation of gentlemen, and I had been infected for a time with this snobbery and complained because our officers swore like mule-drivers in restaurants and took to liquor like calves to milk. Harry Leon Wilson caught the national spirit when he had his immortal Ma Pettengill invite a friend to "Come up and split a bottle of Scotch with me."[1]

Before the end of the war I had recovered from this temporary Europeanization, for I had re-discovered something I had known all the time. Our men do their drinking more along cowpunching lines than the Europeans do, but you can trust them with women where you cannot—taken as a mass—the men of other races. Our women know it. The Good Time Girls ran a little wild because they knew that somewhere in the neighborhood a well-soused American, not perfectly shaven, somewhat open at the neck and with his leggings dripping down toward his heels, would show up and take care of them. He would also undertake to lick the armies of all the Allies if they interfered with him. He didn't like the Allies very well anyhow. There is the classic story of the American soldier who met a Tommy. The American asked:

"What was that you called me?"

"Nothing."

"You called me something?"

"A bloody bastard."

"You dirty sonofabitch."

So the fight started. I am getting away from the subject. I had to take an American congressman away from the table of the general commanding at British GHQ one evening, and that was distressing. Congressmen, writers, humanitarians, businessmen, all of the American persuasion, got unpleasantly drunk all over the safer parts of France and either sang or yelled. But they could be relied on in other activities. I am sure it came as a shock to us as a people when our allies welched on their debts to us. With very few exceptions we believed the promises we made to enemies and friends alike. We did not want to make a profit out of war. It was a surprise to us, and an infuriating surprise, when we found the allies were trying to break up the American army in France so that we would be hampered in claiming our part of the spoils.

I dislike saying this because it will hurt the feelings of our late allies. But before the war was over it seemed certain to me that we were the cleanest and most honorable outfit in the whole round-up. What if we did drink a little and make uncouth noises as we rambled home at night? I got so proud

---

1. Wilson, an American novelist, wrote *Ruggles of Red Gap* and made the term "flapper" famous.

of Americans toward the end of the outbreak that I was offensive. Especially after dead Americans were to be seen in the field. That does something to you inside. For one thing, you begin to hate.

Another result of this shift in sentiment is that nothing seemed very much worthwhile. Most of the men who underwent that tap-tap-tap on the nerve ends that one gets in war began to feel about the same way, I think. Damned good scouts today were just bags of rags on the mud tomorrow. If their friends grieved about them they could not do the job, and that job was to hold the trench or bomb the Germans or bang a truck down a road in spite of the shells. When they got home that deadness persisted in the nerve ends. So it seems to me. It was handed on to the others. There were some years when it was of mighty little difference to those of the AEF who got home whether the young folks made dancing and drinking fools of themselves. The AEF had seen their dead. They had seen the Good Time Girls in France singing in barrooms and sneaking along hotel corridors after midnight, and the Good Time Men being pushed head-foremost into taxicabs. What of it?

Just this of it, I think. There is in the hearts of the men who fought in France something of a fury against those who trapped us into a war that was none of our making and who tore up their notes after the war was over. Never think we will not fight again. We are as little pacifistic as a nation as were the old-times bargemen on the Mississippi, but the next time we fight it will be for our own hand.

I revere tough old Jack Pershing as I could not the Pope even if I had been a Catholic for forty generations. I remember Colonel Hamilton Smith and the way he died, and Ben Hough and his regiment, and Father Duffy and his New York Irish unit, and Lieutenant Colonel Frederick Wise and his Marines at the Battle of Belleau Wood, and another hundred whose names spring to the memory. And the women who slaved for our men so devotedly. What difference does it make if a few Good Time Girls raced through the streets and that some of our men drank like wild horses at a desert well? These little men and women and mistakes need not worry us.[2]

---

2. Smith, with the 1st Division of the AEF, died heroically of wounds on the battlefield. Father Francis Duffy, a chaplain to the 69th Infantry Regiment, a unit of the New York Army National Guard, was frequently with the troops in combat. He is considered the mostly highly decorated cleric in U.S. Army history.

20

I was assigned to the 26th Regiment, 1st Division, when I returned to France. I believe the 26th lost more men in action than any other regiment in the AEF, and the 1st Division lost more men than any American division. At any rate, the regiment and the division lost more men in sharp sequence than any other. It had been Pershing's own division at one time, he knew it and relied on it, and he was forced to use it mercilessly while the arriving divisions were being hammered into shape. The 1st would be popped into battle, be fairly well torn to pieces, pulled out, deloused, fed, shaved, refilled with men, and popped back again. Of course, the division was sore about it. It said so with all its profane voices. But it never failed to do the job sent it. It had been made tough early in the game.

My billet was with Major (now general) Edward Croft's battalion in some little Lorraine village which had for generations taken a just pride in the size of the dung heaps under the front windows of its homes. No doubt the Lorrainers are good farmers. They appreciated fertilizer as no other farmers on earth do and keep it where it can be guarded against thieves. Croft polished up that village until there wasn't a smell of cow manure within a mile of it. If I lighted a cigar on the village street, I put the burned match in my pocket, for if I threw it on the ground a police squad would double down the road to pick it up. The incensed villagers carried their injuries to the government in Paris and representations were made to Croft.

That did no good, either. Croft was an old-style regular, and he knew his job. Years later I listened to an American officer tell Croft at a party precisely how much he hated him for his tyranny. Yet it was not tyranny. No other methods could have broken in the Americans in time to do the job they were in France to handle. My sympathies were with the army, for in a rash moment earlier in life I had almost joined the National Guard. Fortunately, the proper blanks were not at hand, and before they had been sent on from Columbus I had discovered that I could not lick the sergeant. This conclusion came to me slowly but in the end was irresistible, and so in the end I refused to sign. In France I sorrowed with the men who were being worked over by the old regulars, but my reason told me that only in this way could they be made into an army.

The explanation is that Americans are responsive to leadership as are no other men in the world. Or so it seemed to me. Perhaps the French tie them in this, for the French and American relations as between officers and men seemed to have been cut from the same cloth. The English and German troops were forced into rigid molds by an iron discipline. The Russians were ox-like peasants who were handled by their officers as though they were cattle. Americans accepted all the discipline necessary, saluted when they should, stood at attention according to the book of words, but they followed leaders and not brass tabs. They got the idea quickly. It was up to them to get tough. And they were tough.

Let me take time for a few illustrative anecdotes. Not many. Only enough to make the point.

I found a doughboy once sitting on a hill near Mills Feuilles. All alone. Smoking a cigarette. His pants as wrinkled and coming-down-behind as a doughboy's pants usually were. His leggings mere rugged lumps of cloths. The Americans never did learn to tie their legs up handsomely.

He said, "I come out here to see how come I got away with it yesterday."

There was a limestone cavern under the hill, and by luck the doughboy had sat down to get a smoke in the one place which commanded the entrance. There were 165 Germans inside, with machine guns and food and blankets and everything they needed. He knocked over the first two or three to appear, and they thought he was a regiment. So he went on knocking them over as they came out until he had bagged twenty or thirty.

"I had to kill 'em dead," he explained, "because if they had known I was all alone they could have ganged me."

Help came along and the Germans who were still alive surrendered and were glad to do it. I suspected the doughboy was lying, but I checked up on him and he wasn't.

Another doughboy was taken prisoner and searched somewhere near Belleau Wood. The Germans forgot his knife. That night he knifed four of his guards and came home triumphant.

I played a small and deeply regretted part in the hardening process. Just before the fight at Cantigny what was left of the 26th was stationed in the very dirty little town of Broye. Headquarters was in a lovely limestone cavern, thirty feet deep, which we penetrated by means of a stair that might as well have been a ladder. Every inch of the village was under direct observation, and when the Germans saw a nice chance to bag some game they used to shoot at us with a field piece. Therefore the intelligent doughboys stayed under cover.

Colonel Hamilton Smith had been put in command of the 26th Regiment. A fine, scholarly, kind gentlemen, but he knew his job.

One morning Colonel Smith said to me, "Suppose we take a walk, Mr. Corey."

That was the equivalent of a royal command. We climbed the ladder and got out into the sun and saw bright doughboy eyes peering at us from cracks in the piled-up masonry and from behind remnants of wall and the remains of the old church that had once fronted the goose pond.

Like squirrels, we walked down the middle of the main street. Colonel Smith had a little switch, and I had a fine Malacca cane with which I swished at things. Now and then Colonel Smith would address a doughboy, and that sorrowful gentleman would crawl out of his hole and come to attention and tell Colonel Smith where he came from and how he liked his food.

We did that four mornings. The Germans shot at us, of course, but missed us. As we strolled down main street on the fifth morning, swishing our sticks, jaunty and debonair as a couple of dudes in Manhattan, Kansas, and at least one of us scared until my mouth tasted like a ball of chalk, it seemed to me that these exercises boded no good for someone, probably me. I could not say to Colonel Smith that I did not like them, and so my protest was placed on a high moral ground.

"Your life is a very valuable one, sir. Do you think that you have the right to risk it in this fashion?"

"It is the only way I can teach the boys to disregard shells," said the colonel. "Shells are a part of their business, and they are dodging them. If I were to lecture them I could do no good. If I walked out here alone they would merely think that I was on an errand. But when they see a civilian walking with me they say to themselves, '"If a civilian can do that then I can, too."'

So we went on walking.

The system worked. The Americans took Cantigny with a force that a few months before had been law-abiding, peaceful, kindly clerks and farmers and schoolteachers, except for the thin skeleton of old regulars that made the backbone of the attacking regiment. But the youngsters were as tough as any regulars ever dared be. They dug the Germans out of their shelters with bayonet and hand grenade. I have always thought that Jimmy Hopper's experience at Cantigny is an evidence of what can be done by training. A year before Jimmy had probably been as case-hardened as nine out of ten men in the 18th Regiment. He had had worldly experience. But in the intervening year they had been steam-hammered. He hadn't.

He is a nice, rough, jolly, bushy-headed little guy who once was a star football player. Then he became a writer of fiction. He represented *Collier's* during the war. One would think the corners had been rubbed off Jimmy, but the night after Cantigny he appeared as excited as a boarding schoolgirl at her first marriage. He had gone into Cantigny with the attack force.

"I did not intend to," he said. "I was sitting in the trench, waiting for the whistle to blow. Then I planned to go back to camp and write my story. But when I saw those guys disappear into the fog I got so lonely I couldn't stand it, and so I got up and ran after them."

He did that all the way into Cantigny. When he caught up with the men he would sit down and bless God that he had recovered his sanity. The moment he lost sight of them his loneliness descended on him like a blanket and against all the judgement he had he would rise and run after them. The story as he told it was one of the funniest ever told during the war, what with Jimmy's bushy hair and his wild blue eyes and his waving hands. But when he wrote the tale it was a flop. The point is that the well-toughened doughboys would not have gone emotionally up in the air as he did. The basic material was the same, but the doughboys were no longer soft.

At Soissons the 26th was held up by a nest of machine guns. At the division council that night a superior officer said to Colonel Smith, "If you can't take those guns I'll send someone to take over your regiment who can take them."

Colonel Smith would not order his men to go against the guns again. He loved them too well. But he went along his line, saying goodbye to those who were left. Elliott and Mood and Roosevelt and a score of others were already gone. Then he walked into the open and started for the guns. Seven men followed him.

"Go back," he said, turning to them. "I'm going alone."

"Like hell you are," said the seven men.

The 26th took those guns. The next day I saw the brown lines of dead. Among them were Colonel Smith and the seven men.

21

There is no punch in this story. There is no kicker at the end. It is merely the relating of what happened in the Restaurant Weber, down around the bend on the boulevard. If you have an architectural soul you sit in the Restaurant Weber and look at the Madeleine. If you have not you look at the girls passing by. Part of it I saw. Part was overheard by a shameless waiter. He had no ideals, that waiter. It was not yet noon, and he had been drinking. Merely for the hope of a tip he repeated to me, breathing warmly in my ear, things he had heard in his professional capacity. If I were to give the story a name I would call it "The Three Who Won the Cross."

We were in that middle room of Weber's. An officer had been sitting at one of the bare brown tables writing a note. As fast as he completed the note, he tore it up. Finally, he gave the chasseur whispered orders about that note. Almost before the chasseur reached the street the officer had overtaken him and taken the note back. He began patiently to draft it over again. A lone woman sat at another table with a glass of coffee before her. She sipped from time to time, but it did not seem to grow less. She had friendly eyes. The confidential waiter hobbled about, putting cloths upon the little brown tables. In this room the tables resist the linen until the very hour of dejeuner strikes.

Two of the party I was afterward to watch sat down at a table that had been reserved for them. The father was a slender, fragile, white-haired man who might have been a professor. His eyes shone. From time to time he put his hand upon the unwounded arm of his son. Their relationship was evident at a glance. Sometimes the hand went up to the boy's shoulder, and once he patted the Cross of the Legion that hung on the young man's breast, with a half shy, half laughing glance about the room. They were immensely happy.

They were joined by another pair. This father was a grossly fat man, with an air of arrogance and stupidity. In spite of his clumsy bulk there was something suggestive of the soldier about him, as though he might have fought in 1870. There was the ribbon of a decoration in his lapel. His eyes were those of a boar grunting himself into a rage, and he took his seat with almost a growl of recognition at the others. One noticed, however, that he helped his son very carefully into his chair. He was almost angry about it, it seemed. He glanced at the boy's bandaged leg with a frown. It seemed as though he deliberately refused to look at the cross upon the boy's breast. The boy was a handsome, well-set-up, thick-eyebrowed chap. The two young men beamed upon each other. They sat with their hands clasped as they exchanged questions and answers. The fathers talked perfunctorily, watching their sons.

Others joined them. These others became merely a bit of the background. The confidential waiter muttered something indistinct to me about "friends—three crosses—Armand." I could hardly get him to stay with me long enough to violate the rules of his profession. A chair was vacant at the table, and the party apparently waited for someone. The servitor had not yet learned the identity of the missing one. He made a guess.

"Is it not thin Armand, then?" he asked.

A rather pretty young woman took the chair. She had that air of wifehood that some women acquire the moment the padre pronounces the benediction over them, and that some women never acquire. In a paper cornucopia such as the flower sellers on the Place de la Madelaine serve their wares she had some small clusters of blossoms which she handed to the men in the chairs. Her dress was modest, but becoming. It was the sort of dress a young wife might wear in an hour of happiness at a café. It was a little celebration we were looking at. These were more than acquaintances. They were friends.

"They are telling her how they won their crosses," said the waiter, drifting alcoholically across to me.

The youngsters were being prompted by the young wife and by each other and by the fathers and their friends. Hospital walls had taken the tan from their cheeks, so that at times their blushes might be seen. They frankly enjoyed telling their stories, just as happy, clean-hearted boys like to repeat their adventures. It had seemed when the young wife joined the party that a shadow of constraint had settled down upon it, but this had passed away. Two or three times there were roars of laughter. Once the boy who had been wounded in the leg stood up, balancing himself upon the chairback and on the shoulder of that silent, hard-faced father and rehearsed his tale dramatically. There was an interval of silence—a rather embarrassed silence it seemed—and then the young women began to speak.

"Devil," said the waiter as he plied across the room, "she is telling them about Armand."

Animation made her face almost beautiful. One can imagine there are times when her face is unforgettable. Her hands were marvelous. As she made play with them I noticed that she wore the wedding ring only. I recall now that there was no color in her face. It was almost as though a film of ashes had spread over her cheeks. Her eyes were noticeably brilliant. But I do not think I consciously saw this at the time. For as I watched her I became suddenly aware of the emotion her story was producing in her audience. The two boys were crying with the naked candor of honest youth. They wiped away their tears with great white handkerchiefs and their shoulders heaved. The father whom I had imagined a professor was looking at the ceiling, as though he were not interested. But his lips twitched continually. The gross fat man was staring at the girl. The tears were running down his heavy cheeks and his rather small, thick-lipped mouth was half open. Now and then he put up a short-fingered, round, fleshy hand to clear the tears from his eyes.

"I cannot get it all," the waiter said, "but this Armand was wounded between the lines, and his comrades could not bring him in. He rolled into the hole made by a shell, and for three days he stayed there, where the Germans could not see him, calling directions to his comrades. At night he warned them of the German attacks. He was the farthest outpost, Madam says. He saved his friends."

The girl's manner changed. It seemed as though she addressed herself to one after another of the party. The big man wiped his eyes savagely and crashed his heavy little fist down on the table. Then he rose and kissed the girl's hand and said something in a rough, guttural voice to his son. The agitation of the others passed, and they put in their buttonholes the little bouquets the girl had brought with her when she entered and bowed to her very formally. The waiter hovered about their table. Then, as I watched, she pulled at a little chain that was around her neck. She laid her hand, palm upward, on the table. It held the Cross of the Legion. The waiter came back to me.

"Name of the devil," he said. "This Armand is dead."

The peculiar merit of my particular job was that it called for much sitting around in cafes on an expense account. Other reporters had to deal with the sordid details of battles and diplomatic maneuvers. They sent their news by wire, and news editors three thousand miles away asked them why they did not get signed statements from Foch and Clemenceau.[1] I was held responsible for little human stories that peopled the dark background with men and women, and these were most easily found in the cities, where we sat late drinking wine in curtained restaurants and walked home through darkened streets. Not until the AEF came to France was any American correspondent permitted to stay in the field. There were too many unpleasant things happening at the front, and there was always the possibility that a correspondent might be indiscreet and a censor sleepy.

Two more stories, if I may.
Late one night at L'Ane Rouge I heard the story told of Alexander Cowden, who learned how to pilot a fighting plane by reading books and without ever taking off.

"What would you do," asked the French examiners, "if you were piloting an aeroplane, and a German plane attacked you?"

Mr. Cowden didn't hesitate a moment. That problem had been contained in his fourth lesson.

"I would get on top," said he, "and then I would shoot him down."

Which is precisely what he did when the test came. It is one of the reasons why Mr. Cowden now wears the Croix de la Guerre. It is not the principal reason why this story was written. There are many aviators who have won the cross, and there are many others who have shot Germans out of the air without getting it. But no one ever did precisely what Mr. Cowden did. Even when I wrote it, with evidence of its truth before us, I found it somewhat hard to believe.

Cowden is a polo player when he is at home in New York. He may be other things. No one in Paris seemed to know. Inquiries at the few places where he was known suggested that Mr. Cowden was slender—the Americans called him "skinny"—and wore a stingy mustache. No one knew whether he was rich or not, though it was presumed that he was because he played polo, and his father and brother were in San Francisco.

---

1. Georges Clemenceau was a French journalist and politician who served as prime minister from 1906 to 1909 and from 1917 until 1920.

Cowden decided to come over to France and fight for the Allies and more specifically for France. If he had convictions about this war he did not air them widely. General opinion in the American colony here was that he wanted to have some fun. Polo playing had paled on him. It seems hardly worthwhile merely to get a bruise on the ankle from some other player's club when the glorious prospect of having your head shot off was being offered. After he reached Paris, he looked about a bit. He found that as a foreigner he must enlist in the Foreign Legion.

"That," said Mr. Cowden to himself, "is not good enough."

No reflection on the Legion is here contained. Some units of it did wonderful fighting. Mr. Cowden seems to be a sure thing player. He wanted to make sure of excitement. He spent two months as an ambulance driver. That proved to be not good enough. The men who are doing the fighting were ridiculously careful of ambulance drivers. The moment one saw a chance to get himself nicely shot he was sent off to the rear and out of danger. Mr. Cowden grieved about this unsportsmanlike attitude of the soldiers.

"I will join the flying corps," he decided. "Other Americans have done that. Billy Thaw is a flyer and got a cross the other day. I can do whatever Billy Thaw does."

According to the unanimous testimony of the American colony, Mr. Cowden had never been in an airplane in his life. Allowing for the colonists' anxiety to make a good story, it is still certain that he had never piloted a plane. He had never touched the levers. I range myself flatly on the side of those who say he had never been in one. I prefer it that way. Anyhow, there was not a dissenting vote. All who knew him hung together in this statement. He was a good motorist, of course, and knew all about engines.

So he read up on piloting airplanes. He absorbed all the knowledge that can be found in books. Two or three of the French military fliers were his particular friends, and they told him things. He used to go out to the flying fields near Paris and hang around. He didn't ask any questions, of course, because someone might find out that he was a greenhorn. But by and by he volunteered for the flying work and came up before the examiners.

"What do you know about flying?" he was asked.

"I am a pilot." said Mr. Cowden, simply.

Pilots are aristocrats. One doesn't tell a pilot to show that he can fly any more than one insists upon a jockey proving that he can ride. He was given an oral examination which he passed with flying colors. Every now and then some question came up which had not been covered by his source of cramming. Then his French promptly became lamentable. His stock answer to unanswerable inquiries was "Fifty horsepower."

It is inconceivable, of course, that anyone should insist that he is a pilot when as a matter of fact he has never been in a machine. The examiners had no suspicion. Cowden was taken on and sent to the field to fly. If he had any early adventures in getting up and down without breaking his neck he did not tell of them. So by easy stages we came to the fight in which he won the Croix de la Guerre. Cowden's only comment on it was that it beat polo playing.

He was on a reconnaissance with his observer when he was attacked by two German machines. One of them was an Aviatik and the other one of the new double-motored battle planes. It was his business to get away if he could, and he tried to do so. When he found that he could not he turned to fight. His machine was a "pusher" type, with the propeller set behind the wings. The Aviatik had the propeller in front. In this type, at that time, no shots could be fired directly from the front, because the bullets would strike the propeller. Cowden mounted steeply, turned, and charged the Aviatik. "He couldn't get away," was his one comment.

His observer was in charge of the machine gun, the barrel of which ran out over Cowden's head. They dashed down upon the Aviatik like a thrown knife. A stream of bullets poured out over Cowden's head. The Aviatik dodged and twisted and tried to escape, but it was no use. Suddenly the pilot stood up in his car and then plunged stiffly out. The Aviatik began to turn over and over. Then it fell, in queer, sidelong dashes as a shingle might if dropped from a height. Cowden whirled his car up again, to guard against the battle plane.

"Then I found my machine was dead," Cowden told his friends. "At first I thought my controls had been cut."

Later he found that the main "strut"—whatever that is—had been cut almost off. The battle plane kept up an incessant fire on him. He could not manipulate his plane at all. He found that his engine and the radiator and the connecting pipes and almost everything else had been perforated. Hot water sprayed from the gashed radiator. The engine kept on turning for a time and then it died. There was nothing to do but to volplane to earth, and they were fifteen kilometers from the French lines, and in German territory.

"We'll try it," he said, grimly.

So he started to volplane. Fortunately, he was very high. Far below him he could see little dots running. He knew they were German soldiers.

"Drop the bombs," he cried to the observer.

That lightened the machine. As they descended, they came in easy rifle range of the German lines and bullets whistled about them. They began to rush through the air at an uncanny angle because of the dead controls, but he kept on his course. Finally, he landed behind the French lines and in safety. His machine was a wreck.

"But I got a new machine," Cowden said, very happily. "A faster one this time."

That is how he got the Croix de la Guerre.

The little American woman who told the story of the three cooks cried quite openly during the telling. Not that her nerve was broken. She had gone through what everyone else had gone through in Paris and had been as brave as everyone else had been. No braver. Night after night she had hurried down to the cellar when the bombs began to drop. She had seen women killed in the streets. She had met the long trains of boxcars filled with wounded, lying frozen on straw wet with their blood. She had helped men die.

"I think," she said apologetically, "this is the only time I have cried."

This is the story:

The three cooks have returned to the trenches. The fat cook wept when he said goodbye. The middle-aged cook kissed her hand. There is something of the distant aristocrat in the middle-aged cook. One remembers reading of certain seigneurial rights and of certain seigneurs who exercised them very long ago. The little young cook stood up very straight. He had that way with him that so many Frenchmen have of saying theatrical things in an untheatrical way.

"It is for France," said he.

She was an American woman. When French soldiers came home for leave it occurred to her that many of them have no homes to which they may go. Their homes—the places where their homes were—are behind the German lines in northern France. She began to worry at nights about these men. At last she went to the War Office.

"Will these men be given leave?" she asked.

"No," said the officials. "It is regrettable, Madame, but what would you? They have no place to go."

She canvassed her friends for money. One day she returned to the War Office.

"Send three of these homeless men to me each week," said she. "I will give them good meals and a bed to sleep in, and they shall see this brave Paris. As for the money, my American friends will help me out."

For a time there was silence. Then, one morning, there came a little tinkle at her bell. A timid tinkle. It was as though a good child had touched it. Madame the American went to her door, and there stood three men looking at her wistfully. They were clothed in the French uniforms of blue mist, which had been stained from heel to shoulder with trench clay. They did not speak. One of them—the middle-aged cook—bowed with something of grace and offered her a paper. The others took off their caps and stood at attention. It was the order from the War Office, quartering the three homeless soldiers with Madame the American for a week.

"But come in," said she. "Come in. I am so glad to see you."

They entered in single file. The middle-aged cook and the fat cook and the little young cook. Once inside the door, they stood at attention. Their faces were precisely the color of those bronzes one sees in shop windows upon the Rue de la Paix, but Madame would have sworn they were blushing. She asked them to sit down, and they sat upon the extreme frontier of the chairs and held their caps firmly in their strong fingers and looked unhappily before them. It is of a certainty, says Madame the American, that they were missing the trenches.

Madame is very certain that she prayed that night that these three men might have a good time in Paris. They were such very dear, helpless, simple souls, for all their uniforms and mustaches and the trench clay.

The three cooks had worked in the same town in northern France. One was a pastry cook and one a meat cook, and the little young cook had a marvelous way with legumes. It was but natural that they were members of the same company when the mobilization orders came. Unfortunately, they were not assigned to the kitchen. They handled rifle and spade, just as less talented soldiers do. For one entire year they had done their full share of the fighting. No doubt they had killed many Germans, but they never spoke of such things. Madame took them to music halls and theaters and rode them about Paris. They enjoyed it all immensely, but they were painfully unvocal. They were good children—big, silent, wistful children—but they were frightfully hard to entertain.

"And the food in the trenches?" Madame asked one day. "No doubt it is disgusting?"

Their eyes snapped. They began to speak all at once, each apologizing to the other for continuing to speak but nevertheless continuing to speak. It appeared that the food was very good indeed. Somewhat monotonous, one comprehends. What would you expect in time of war? But of an excellence beyond doubt. There was one dish especially. Madame did not recognize it by its technical descriptions, but she believes it was stew. It lacked but a very little—that touch of the artist—to become a creation.

"Perhaps," said Madame by an inspiration, "you would like to see my kitchen?"

It was only then that Madame noted that whenever they sat down, they sat down facing the door which led into the kitchen in Madame's modest flat. Sometimes that door opened. Then one secured entrancing glimpses of polished coppers hanging on the wall, and adorable utensils of clay, and the wide top of a tiled stove on which pots simmered. The three faces brightened. They had been immobile, these faces, and perhaps rather sad, as becomes the faces of three children who are consciously upon their good behavior. Immediately they became broad rather than long. Crinkles appeared at the corners of the eyes. They seemed to be setting white caps straight upon their heads.

"If Madame pleases?" they responded insinuatingly.

There were but four days more of that delightful leave, but for that four days three cooks were happy. They begged permission to make little dishes. They pampered Madame's husband until that gentleman panted unpleasantly at the top of the second flight of stairs. They flattered Madame with dainties. They so praised Madame's cook—and so opened her eyes to the culinary possibilities inherent in meat and flour and vegetables—that the good woman glowed upon them. She had not glowed before in Madame's recollection. Madame used to watch her. That glowing woman would go from cook to cook, patting them unconsciously on arm or shoulder, as one does very loveable little children.

"And the petite saucepan?" said the fat cook. "Tres jolie."

Perhaps it isn't a saucepan. Madame doesn't know its name. She only knows that it is a quaint little trinket of copper which she found in an old shop one day, and which has been hanging on her kitchen wall ever since because of its decorative effect. The fat cook fell in love with the petite saucepan. He cooked delights that would tempt an anchorite away from his refuge. They still went to the music halls at night, but in the pauses Madame could hear them talking.

"A pinch more of the moutarde, comprenez vous?"

Until the day came when their leave was over, and these three cooks must go back to the trenches. They bade farewell to the cook, and Madame's husband, and to Madame, with much decorum. They shook hands again at the door, and again when Madame announced that she would go with them to the railway station. They gazed at the door of the little apartment house mournfully, as though they never again expected to see this place where they had found happiness. At the gates of the train station the middle-aged cook kissed Madame's hand with much of the grand manner, and the little young cook said, "It is for France." Then came the surprise. Madame's cook appeared from where she had been hiding, with the petite saucepan in her hand. It was tied up in paper, but no one could mistake that saucepan. So she gave it to the fat cook.

And the fat cook went away crying, and very ridiculously wiping his eyes with a hand in which was clutched that saucepan which was "tres jolie."

22

The rapidity with which Pershing and his old regular army officers and non-coms made over a mob of fine young men dressed in khaki into a force governed by steel discipline was marvelous. It was hard going, of course. I remember that Heywood Broun's generous anger was stirred once by Pershing's rebuke to a soldier who had not properly saluted during kitchen inspection. Pershing took the hide off the poor kid. One of the first companies to get into action was unlucky enough to draw a visit from Pershing the day it got back from the wire.

"Where are your buttons?" Pershing roared at the two or three officers whose clothing had suffered. "Fall out!"

He probably grinned—a grim grin—when he got away. But that was the stuff to give the troops. The AEF called Pershing everything but "Black Jack" in those days. The men hated him far more than they did the Germans. But he made them into an army. Back of him was a line of stiff old soldiers who had been corporals and sergeants and lieutenants and very infrequently captains in our old regular army. I suspect that the old regular army staff was a pretty sad lot, but the old regular soldiers were grand old men.

Major Edward Croft, with whom I billeted in some dirty little town in the manure belt, was as tender as a mother when one of his men got into real trouble. He always went to the front, just as did all of the old hardshells from the regulars. The youngsters soon caught the idea. It was not necessary for the old regular sergeants to lick very many of them into discipline, but where it was necessary, they were licked. A sergeant starts with a tactical advantage over a recruit. He does not bandy words, as is apt to be the habit of the young man who has been raised by a loving mother in a good Christian home. He just socks the young man in the front teeth. Incidents of this sort are most unpleasant, but there is no question that they aid in the manufacture of soldiers. The men meant well. They wanted to be disciplined. But at first they did not know what discipline is.

There was, for instance, the story of Captain Barney Legge and Company E. I do not know that this story is true. I can only say that I was in the little French town when it is reputed to have happened and have never heard it denied. Before Colonel Hamilton Smith took over command of the body of green men, slightly leavened by old regulars, which was called the 26th Regiment but had not yet become in fact the 26th Regiment, Company E was in a sad state. It had several very headstrong hell-raisers in it, and several captains had failed with it. The captain commanding when Colonel Smith took over had established a sort of a soviet. It was the understanding that if Company E did not make too much trouble, he would close his eyes to its delinquencies. Company E was as sloppy and no-account a company as could be found in the AEF, but it loved its captain.

"Take over E Company," said Colonel Hamilton Smith to Acting Captain Bernard W. Legge. "The company seems to be getting out of hand."

E Company revolted. It demanded that its dearly loved captain be returned to it. It became drunken in a large way and walked up and down the streets cheering for the former captain and denigrating Acting Captain Legge unpleasantly. He was just a youngster, new to command, but with the guts of a grizzly. At Company E's quarters he found an old regular sergeant, and a Christian soldier who had volunteered to make the world better and had been annoyed by the brandy drinking customs in Company E, and a young man who could not drink because he had stomach ulcers.

"Fall in," shouted Acting Captain Legge.

At the head of the sergeant, the Christian, and the ulcer man he marched down into the village. Presently he caught a man from Company E. The old regular sergeant put a bayonet on the man's stomach.

"By the right flank—March!"

The canal was frozen over. Thinly but competently. While the sergeant held his rifle on the rebel from Company E, the Christian soldier and the man with stomach trouble got him by the head and heels.

"One—two—three"—splash.

Through the ice he went. Acting Captain Legge indicated to the Christian soldier that he go into action with a pole that by a fortunate chance had not been burned for firewood. The Christian placed the end of the pole on the back of the rebel in the ice water.

"Hold him under until he bubbles," ordered Acting Captain Legge.

When the bubbles were satisfactory, the rebel was let out and chased up and down the towpath until he was in a pleasant glow. Then:

"Fall in," ordered Acting Captain Legge.

The erstwhile recruit wore a grin wider than the hole in the Arc de Triomphe when the detachment returned to the village. One by one the rebels were picked up and bubbled and warmed. Company E followed Captain Legge thereafter with fanatic devotion. There is a sequel to this story. In time to come Legge became a major, and one day I met him in the shell-torn ruins of what had been a village. He looked like a military tramp, he was so grimy and ragged and pale beneath the dirt. Barney Legge is a sentimentalist at heart. He loved his men as they loved him, and he stopped just long enough, regardless of the gas that tainted the air and the shells that were continuing to drop, although with a decreasing rhythm, to tell a story.

"For a day," he said, "I have been trying to take some machine guns."

His battalion flopped on its bellies just behind the comb of a little hill. A shallow valley intervened between it and the next little hill. Behind the peak of the next little hill the German machine gunners lay. They had trained their pieces on the topline of Legge's hill so that if a scrap of khaki showed it was cut into ribbons.

"There we lay, helpless, for twenty-four hours."

Then a fog began to rise in the shallow intervening valley. Foot by foot it crept up the two slopes. Presently it would mask the top of Legge's hill and he could order his battalion forward.

"I had my whistle at my lips. Ready to order the advance. But I didn't blow it. I heard the men on either side of me say, 'Come on. Let's go.'"

The American wave inched over Legge's hilltop and trotted through the narrow valley and up the slopes of the other hill, from whose top long streaks of fire told that the Germans were keeping their watch.

"We had more than 500 causalities out of our 700 men," said Barney Legge. "But we speared every bastard at his gun."

Company E—what was left of Company E—was squatting in the mud by the roadside as we talked. Company E's eyes were on Major Barney Legge. At such times men forget the formalities with which life has taught us to protect ourselves. They do not present a more or less blank surface to the world but display their emotions candidly. Company E's eyes made me think of the eyes of good dogs. The men had been through purgatory and wore that peculiar, tallowy pallor which is the unfailing evidence of that ecstasy of terror and rage. But their grim mouths seemed to wear a half smile as they watched their major. If Major Bernard W. Legge ever wants to charge hell, I know one company that will be at his heels.

23

The first detachments of the American army to reach France consisted entirely of tough babies. Tough. This was before the Draft Act had caught the 4 million, more or less, who are now calling for another pull at the pap bottle of compensation graft. The first arrivals were real fighting men. Enough hard old officers had been withdrawn from the regulars to give the new army a steel backbone. On it had been plastered a layer of young and middle-aged men who wanted to get into a fight. Any fight. They cared no more for La Belle France than I do for horse liniment, but if there was a fight going they wanted to get into it. They had volunteered from docks, farms, churches, bar rooms, colleges, and bawdy houses and still carried civilian fat and peered at the new country through soft civilian eyes. They were as unimpressive a layout on their first marches through cheering villages as ever had been seen, with their wide campaign hats and their drooping shoulders and their uncertainties about "fours right."

We were a graceless outfit in those first days. No doubt about it. We were inclined to play, like young bull terriers, and it took a knowledge of the breed to give confidence that one of these days the pup would bite deep and hang on. Every day the Americans were exercised and trained in bayonet work and charging and bombing and the other pretty little methods of bumping the other fellow very much off. The men took the work as a joke which wore thin after a few days, but was nevertheless funny. The officers were keen as mustard. I can still see that look of intent youth in their eyes. The hell of it is that some of the passionate youngsters I remember most clearly died in Champagne and in the Argonne and on the Somme in someone else's war. I wish I could forget their clear and lively eyes.

The training period was playtime for me. Back home the great international brains which have always plagued us were still worrying about Dear

France and Good Old England, of course, but the men and women who buy papers wanted to know about the Americans in France. A clearer American point of view is to be found in a cornfield than in a lecture hall at any time. I had been saddled and ridden so long by the Allies that I had more of a grouch against them than against the enemy. I did not want to see either the French or the English armies for one damned long time, and the privilege of mixing with my own blood again was simply grand. There was, also, the satisfaction of knowing that I was safe. I would not be bounced out of the country if I happened to offend some English admiral or French general, so long as I put a reasonable limit on my offending. I had only to please my own people. There were, of course, exceptions to this rule. Westbrook Pegler furnished one.[1]

"Why doesn't Peg come back?" I asked one day at Neufchateau, where American press HQ had been established. Pegler had been representing the United Press most efficiently. He did not regard a general with the reverence which had been hammered into me for three years, but he was a good reporter.

"Peg has been given the gate," I was told. "He went to England on a visit and wrote something funny about an admiral."

He should have known better, of course. One does not write funny things in England about the admirals, or generals, or princes, or God. I have always wanted to read that piece. It was probably good. The difference between the American and the Allied point of view toward the press was disclosed about this time by Floyd Gibbons.[2] One of the adventures available to reporters toward the end of the summer was to spend a night in the fire trenches. These nights were messy, muddy, damnably uncomfortable, and toilsome, and as the training area was about as active as prayer meeting night in Marysville, Ohio, most of us laid off that particular amusement after the

---

1. What actually happened is more complicated and revealing. Pegler, the youngest reporter accredited to the AEF, shared a sense of frustration with the old-timers over the restrictions placed on the press. When he expressed these in a letter to UP management, British censors intercepted the letter and returned it to AEF headquarters. General Pershing asked Roy Howard, the president of UP, to replace Pegler, and he did.

2. Gibbons was one of the most colorful correspondents of the war. The *Chicago Tribune* reporter made a point of traveling to Europe on a ship likely to be torpedoed by the Germans, as indeed it was. His resulting story was a frontpage sensation. When Gibbons covered the Battle of Belleau Wood, he violated censorship rules by reporting that he was with the Marines. He was wounded and lost his left eye while attending to a Marine. He wore a signature eye patch from then on. For his heroism he was awarded France's greatest honor, the *Croix de Guerre* with Palm.

first experience. But Floyd wrote a piece that fretted an American general. The general said that Floyd's story of a night in the trenches revealed a lot of important facts to the enemy.

That was all bosh, of course. The enemy knew more about us than we knew ourselves during the training period. They did not think much of us at this time, either. The enemy could see our soldiers wandering around over the face of the earth, as careless of possible shrapnel and snipers as though they were back home in Missouri and playing with the village maidens—this was a favorite sport—and sitting on stoops talking to the village kids. These things took place back of the line, of course, but were calculated to make the enemy believe that our hearts were not in this war. Our advanced trenches were, of course, known in every inch to the enemy observers. The probability is that Floyd said something about the general instead of about the position. At any rate, there was a hell of a hullaballoo and the general wanted Floyd sent home. He was not sent home.

There was not an army in the war, on either side, which handled the press with the intelligence and comprehension shown by the Americans. For this General Dennis Nolan may be thanked.[3] Part of the thanks go to two of his assistants, too. Colonel W. C. Sweeney directed us like a wise and lenient managing editor until his love of a fight overcame him and he managed a transfer into one of the active divisions. Major A. L. "Jimmy" James was the second. James was one of the finest men and best soldiers I have ever known.[4] But the tale of the censorship will come later. One story of the doughboys and the correspondents might be told here, however.

We—the correspondents—ran heavily to fur collars on our overcoats. There was good reason for this. The air in the Lorraine country was raw and

---

3. Army intelligence was ill-quipped for the war. Nolan created a modern G-2 (intelligence) unit in France that included four divisions: Information, Secret Service, Topographical, and Censorship and Press. In those days press relations were often located in intelligence units, which worked as secretly as possible. Eventually Nolan included propaganda as an element of the G-2's work.

4. Frederick Palmer, who was for a time in charge of press relations, is conspicuously absent here. Corey admired him as a reporter, but not in his AEF role. In a letter home in April 1917, Corey mentioned that censorship had improved. "The only yowls I have heard from the correspondents—the only fervid ones, at least—are when Fred Palmer gets on the job of censoring. It is odd that a man who had been in the business all his life should display lack of insight and bradth [sic]." Around this time Palmer was given other duties. Corey to mother, April 15, 1917, box 3, HC.

cold. Most of the time it rained. The roads were hard enough underneath but were covered with a soup of mud. The army cars in which we rode by day and night were open Cadillacs. They stood up magnificently, but they were not warm. If we—the correspondents—had sense enough to bring blankets we wrapped our legs in them. It is the reportorial habit to believe that Elijah is still in the raven-feeding business. Few reporters ever lugged blankets to a car. If any reporter ever borrowed a blanket on a cold night he never returned it. In some respects we are a lousy lot. The fur collars helped keep us warm and made us look like generals. When our cars flashed through the French villages in which American soldiers were stationed, the soldiers loafing on the street would leap to their feet and salute respectfully. We—the correspondents—always returned the salute. But the American soldiers were having the minutiae of discipline hammered into them at this time. They had learned to know the real thing in saluting. A reporter saluting does not look military. He looks like an angry hen. The next time our car flashed through that village we got another kind of a salute. It had its origin in the Bronx. The soldiers always said in tones that were quite audible, no matter how fast our car was flashing, "Dirty sons of bitches."

That was all right. It is good American language. Later on some German prisoners were captured at Soissons, where Americans had burst through resistance using butt and bayonet indiscriminately. The prisoners were pale and shaken when they shuffled into camp. At the height of that furious charge every one of them had faced a sloppy death at the hands of some panther-muscled, leaping, yelling American. When they got safely in the bullpens as prisoners and on terms with their guards, they asked in German to be told the meaning of the American war cry.

"The Americans haven't no war cry," said the interpreter, who came from Milwaukee and talked good German in consequence.

"Oh yes they have," said the prisoners.

"That's damn funny," said the interpreter. "I never heard of one. What does it sound like?"

The earnest, inquiring Germans repeated it as best they could. Every one of them had heard it. It had been yelled in their teeth by the men who galloped through their strong points. When the interpreter heard it he laughed himself into a cough. This is it: "Kill the God Damned Sons of Bitches!"

This seems to be a good place in which to make a public apology to Irvin S. Cobb. I have not made it to his face because for one thing I lack the courage and for another Cobb has probably forgotten all about the incident—he is that sort of a man—and I would have to preface my apology by a laborious explanation of why it is offered. But I was ornery to him one night. Just plain ornery. That goes for Martin Green of the *New York World*, too, who got the same treatment from me and did not resent it any more than Cobb did. Sixteen years after I am bowing low before both of them.

Neither side took the war seriously in the Lorraine country. The Germans used it as a rest ground and a place in which to use the divisions of old men who thereby relieved younger men to die where real fighting was going on. The French never dreamed of starting anything in Lorraine, being well content to leave it alone. The Americans were sent there for training because it was a quiet sector, and they could get used to a little lazy shrapnel bursting and machine gun firing without suffering any loss. But as soon as our outfit began to get its legs we honed for action. One day it was announced that the Iowa regiment and the Ohio regiment in the Rainbow Division would put on their first shows.

I had been living at the regimental HQ of the Ohio regiment of the Rainbows at Domjevin, with Colonel Ben W. Hough. We had a large, old-style French farmhouse, half-barn and half-home, which was in clear view of the German outposts. They could have shelled it off the face of the earth any day, but in that case, we would have blown out the nice chateau in which Hough's opposite number was living, and so an informal armistice had been declared. My room was in the second story, with windows facing the enemy. Consequently, they had been well blinded with blankets. The only light permitted in the room was a candle set in a box which had contained canned peaches. Cobb came out to see the two shows along with Martin Green, the *World*'s best reporter.

"You can take your pick," said Hough. "Stay with me and we'll take a trench this afternoon, or go with Corey up the road thirty miles and see what the Iowa outfit can do."

After some debate Cobb and Green decided to see both shows. Hough planned his racket for the afternoon. It was not intended to be more than a warming up gallop. The Iowa outfit would put their entertainment on after dark. I worked out a schedule by which Lincoln Eyre of the *Morning World* and I would go up to the Iowas, where a real fight might be expected, and in which we were interested, and would send the car back for Cobb and Green.

"If you make it snappy you can see both," I told them. "The connections will be close, so be ready to hop into the car when it comes back."

Eyre and I went into the fire trench to see the Iowa outfit go over. At this distance I can only remember two incidents, except for the charge itself. Two corn-fed brothers were stringing a wire into the trench. The sergeant brother was bossing the job, but the private brother seemed to think he knew more about wire. There was more or less German shelling going on, for they had gotten wind of the fact that something was brewing. Finally, the sergeant ordered his brother to report himself under arrest.

"You must be a damn fool," said the private peevishly, "to think I'm going to stand for arrest just when there's a chance for some fun."

That was good American. It was that kind of an army that Pershing bridled and saddled. The Americans wanted to see the fun but at first they had only rudimentary ideas of discipline. The other incident had to do with a tall, serious sergeant, who was nursing his platoon in the forward trench, waiting for the whistle to go over and kill themselves a mess of Boches. The boy's teeth clicked in the darkness like typewriter keys.

"What's the matter, Sergeant?" asked his lieutenant.

"I don't know, sir," said the sergeant. "It's damn funny. I think I must be scared."

Cobb and Green did not reach us in time to see the show, and Eyre and I hoofed it along the railroad track to the ruined mill behind which the car returning for us had been ordered to take shelter and wait. We had had no supper, for Iowa was concerned with other things. The Germans had been stirred up by this unprovoked attack upon their trenches and were spilling shells over the American layout with a total disregard of cost. A sad, mean, penetrating rain was falling. We hid behind the ruined mill and no car came. And no car came. Five hours after it was due the chauffeur wearily wheeled it in, and we asked why he was so late.

"It was," he said, with complete indifference to military etiquette, "the fault of the big guy. The one who is always telling funny stories." He did not call Cobb "that big guy."

The Ohio show had been just a little one, as anticipated, and Colonel Hough had taken Cobb and Green back to HQ for something to eat and drink. The officers at HQ simply would not let him go, assuring him with some truth that the fight in Iowa would not amount to very much, either. The chauffeur stood around patiently where Cobb could see him. At last he ventured to approach Cobb, and Cobb asked him to wait a little while. When he dared not wait any longer, for he knew that Eyre had a deadline to make, he told Cobb his predicament and the Kentuckian told him to go. Eyre and I seethed through the thirty miles. We were so hot that the rain which entered the necks of our slickers came out in stream. Back at Domjevin, Eyre drove on to Nancy to file his story and I went into Hough's quarters for a bedtime drink. Then:

"I guess I'll go upstairs and go to bed."

"Bed?" said Hough quizzically. "You have no more bed than a chicken. Cobb took it."

That was the straw that broke the camel's back of patience. I stamped upstairs, to find large Cobb and little Green sleeping in my bed. They were sound asleep under the influence of clear consciences, a proper fatigue, and several tots of French brandy. When they seemed not to hear me, I stripped down the blanket and approached the burning end of a cigar to Cobb's white and exposed rump.

"Get up," I said, "or I'll burn you."

This statement was somewhat embroidered, as I recall it. Cobb and Green rose sleepily, and I gave them a blanket or two and they laid down without a word on the floor where the dimmed light of the candle half hidden in the canned peach box shone upon them. They looked precisely like a cow elephant with its calf tucked in its flank. I laughed myself almost into hysterics. Just when sleep almost overtook me the ridiculous picture would start me going again. Neither said a word. In the morning they were on their way before I woke up. They might have been sore about it. In their places I would have been as angry as an English colonel always is at sight of an American, and that is pretty angry. But if either held it against me, neither has ever said a word. Again, I bow to them. The fault was mine.

During this preliminary period General Pershing did his best to whack discipline into his army, as I have said before. The men simply did not understand it. They were willing to obey orders sharply and implicitly and they realized the importance of doing a job well in which failure might be paid off by death. But they could not and would not aspire to the West Point perfection of snappiness Pershing demanded. Then the tone was relaxed, almost overnight. It was long after the war when I discovered what had happened. Colonel Hjalmar Erickson of the old regulars took his courage in his hand one day and approached Black Jack.

"Don't do it," he said, using, of course, the proper military formation for his protest. "You can make the best army God ever knew out of these men. They will learn to obey their officers absolutely and do anything that any soldiers anywhere can do. But they simply do not understand the West Point discipline you demand of them, and they never can understand it. Ground them in the fundamentals and do not worry so much about how they salute."

Pershing listened in silence. That was one thing about Black Jack. I have always looked on him as the best commanding general on either side in the war. He was a stiff, stern man, but when someone had something to say he listened. He made no reply.

"I thought," said Erickson later, "that I had cooked my goose."

But the discipline was relaxed. Long afterward Pershing wrote Erickson a letter of thanks for his protest against unnecessary discipline. That letter is in Erickson's files today. And the discussion of discipline recalls an incident in which Erickson figured somewhat later. He had become a general and his division was on its hurried way to the front one night. Sharp fighting was going on and Erick the Red, as the army called him, was needed at the front line. He earned the reputation of being one of the finest combat officers in our army. The roads were filled with marching men.

"Turn on the lights," said Erickson to his driver. "I must make time."

That was against regulations, for the German airmen would spot the lights and know that an important officer was on his way and earnestly bomb the roads in the effort to get him. Incidentally, it was to be expected that they would knock off a good many soldiers. As Erickson's car sloshed through the mud and the weary soldiers stumbled right and left to get out of the way a cry arose and carried along the line. "Turn off that light."

Other words rose naturally to American lips. When Erickson finally reached the head of the line and halted his car, he turned to his aide. "Get out of the car," he said, "and go back along the line and take the name of the last man who called me a son of a bitch."

Erick the Red was one grand fighting man, and that kind of man always leads grand fighting men. In one of the three-day fights that came later, Erickson was lying in a doghole with Captain Rice H. Youell, now at the head of the Prison Department of Virginia. He had been attacking one of the first line German divisions, and make no mistake about it, the first line Germans could put up a fight worthy of any man's army. The Americans had been pretty well shot to pieces, but were holding on with their teeth, waiting for the order to go forward again. The lieutenant colonel and three majors of the regiment were out. Erickson noticed a black blotch on the back of Youell's shirt, on the third day.

"You've been hit," he said.

"I know it," said Youell. "That was day before yesterday."

Erickson stripped off the shirt and found that Youell had been shot through the body alongside the spine. A quarter of an inch nearer, the surgeons said later, would have finished him.

"Go on back and get fixed up," said Erickson.

"I'll do no such damn thing," said Youell. "Think I'll leave my outfit in the middle of a fight?"

Erickson barked, "Runner."

The runner squirmed up to him. Lying on his side, because the doghole was shallow, Erickson wrote a recommendation to headquarters.

"I've just asked that you be promoted major," said he, "taking effect at this minute, for gallantry on the field."

24

There was a real party at the auberge the night the 26th heard the "light heavies" were to go to the fight. Everyone sang. After the white wine began to lie cold on the stomach, Lieutenant "Bill" Jones brought out his famous cocktail recipe and mixed it in the black pot Madame ordinarily reserved for soup.

"Tell her this is a very auspicious occasion, Pop," urged Jonesie, "Eli is goin' up there and irritate the Dutchmen with those li'l guns of his. We just got to have a cocktail."

"For the brave Americans" Madame consented graciously. The drink is constructed on the basis of Benedictine or kirsch or brandy or anything else handy, mixed with whatever it is possible to get. Toward the end of the evening the mixture varied widely. Friends who heard of the drink-making operation came in with offerings. Jones served it in the aluminum cups of the mess kits to a sort of a chant. Madame herself passed the pot.

Madame was a billowy person, as one should be who had kept the leading inn of the village for more than forty years. She floated on her own waves. The auberge was better than it looked. One entered it by what appeared to be a back door after skirting a pond which ducks and geese and cows and horses and sheep used at will, and the water of which was of an appalling nastiness. The rafters were covered with a black mold of soot, and chickens picked crumbs from the uneven stones of the floor and dogs dreamed miserably in the corners. A fire alternately sparkled and smoked when the wind puffed down the stone chimney. But the white wine was good and the soup delicious.

"Where is the little devil with the long hair?" Madame asked frequently. She did not want Eli to get out of her sight. "The one who mixed that last potful—the one who made me dance for the first time in forty years of inn-keeping in Picardy. If the Germans do not kill that little devil, he will become very great."

Everyone loved Eli Lyman, but all hated his little guns. They were the 37 millimeters. Nasty little things that one man can carry and which fired shells that weighed about a pound, and which had the meanest, naggingest whine any gun ever had. They got everyone into trouble except Eli. It was his habit to stir up the Germans and then dismount his guns and withdraw his battery by the process of legging it to shelter. Each man carried some part. The men whose job it was to sit in the trenches could not follow him. Hence, they hated his little guns.

"There's goin' to be a real time tonight," said Eli. "Like we used to have down on the Rio Grande."

Mademoiselle surprised us. We had not been paying much attention to Mademoiselle, except by being polite to her and by trying to pay her compliments in bad French, as is the American way. But we had been more interested in the wine she served than in the girl. She was large and frankly rounded, with big blue eyes set far apart and fine teeth and the dead white complexion that often goes with an abundance of red hair. When she pulled a cork she held the bottle firmly between her knees. Once a cork stuck, and Highpockets Dye took the bottle and twisted out the cork by some trick of his own. Mademoiselle was impressed. From that moment she stood behind us listening to the singing. Sometimes she smiled at the Nebraska boy.

"How does the 'Marseillaise' go?" asked Highpockets. "March-ong, march-ong..."

Mademoiselle stepped forward, one hand in the air.

"Ecoutez," she said. "Listen."

And she began to sing. There was a story in Mademoiselle, if one could but have learned it. Her voice was a fine contralto, almost masculine in some of its tones. That girl had not learned what she knew of singing by serving petit verres to thirsty travelers in a smoky inn. She put her hands on her hips and threw back her head and her deep breast swelled and the little room fairly rang to the great song. A French soldier who had been sitting quietly in a corner bowed to her.

"If Mademoiselle will permit," he said, "I will bring my violin."

Perhaps Mademoiselle was only having fun with us, but while he was absent she told us his name. He was well known in the orchestra of the opera at Paris, she said. It is certain that he was a fine musician. Mademoiselle did not look again at the tall boy from Nebraska. Her eyes were on the violinist's face, and once I am sure they were wet. It was after she had sung to the accompaniment of his bow a little simple song. An old chanson, perhaps—a thing of repeated phrases and odd little strains that ran in and out through the melody—something no American there had ever heard before. It was after that song that Mademoiselle disappeared.

"And I who am old must serve these strangers," Madame grunted.

She was not old enough to resist Eli Lyman's magic. He talked to her in Mexican Spanish and made her understand, while the rest of us told of his light heavies, and how he had stalked German batteries in the Toul sector— "the doggoned little guns sound like pug dogs yapping," said "Bill" Jones— and then run like the dickens, laughing. Day after day he used to set ten miles of battle front chattering, just because he liked to shoot. He told the most amazing stories.

"Those little guns can out-shoot a rifle," he said, "and you can run 'em like a six-pistol. Come out with me some day, Pop, and watch me get some of these German working parties. It's the funniest thing."

But I never did, for nature planned me for holding a position, and not for legging it through tall grass with strangers shooting at me. If he had coaxed, I might have fallen, at that, for he had very pleasant phrases. He charmed Madame until she danced again for him, and the dance of a lady whose waves overlap is a remarkable thing to see. Then the Canadian visitor gave the "Face on the Bar-room Floor" and the musician from the grand opera in Paris picked his violin like a guitar while Old Cebu sang some little mournful thing he had learned in the Philippines, and we drank some more and were intensely sad.

Long before we were up in the morning Eli and his light heavies were plodding through the early mist, on the way to a position before the early shelling began. Mademoiselle was very quiet when we saw her next, and not at all like the buxom barmaid of a dirty little inn. Madame was again grumbling.

"Gone, has he?" she asked. "They always go. If the Germans do not get him, he will become very great—that little devil with the long hair—he who made me dance for the first time in forty years in keeping an inn in Picardy."

A monument should be erected on the place where "Bill" Jones and Madame passed that cocktail together. Monuments have been erected on many places less historic. That night marked, in a way, the emergence of the AEF from its pinfeathers. For months the first arrivals had been wallowing in trench mud and complaining about the lack of proper uniforms and boots and blankets and jabbing at bayonet bags and learning that a charge is conducted at a slow walk by separated groups. There is little to be said or, for that matter, remembered of that period. I sympathized with the Ohio lad who told once of the high enthusiasm with which he had volunteered, "I oughta knowed better," he said. "Once before a strange lady left me holding a baby."

My last memory of the training area has to do with Colonel B. W. Hough, who is now a judge, and his orderly. "Red" furnished the humor for the Ohio regiment of the Rainbows. He was tall and stoop shouldered and red-headed and had a mighty appetite for drink, which his C.O. could not always control. On the day that Hough turned over his position at Domjevin to the tired French regiment which was to rest there I drove over to say good-bye. None of us knew what would happen next or where it would happen. The Germans had noted unusual activity on the roads, and as I approached the old farmhouse in which Hough had his headquarters they began to throw shells at it like corn to chickens.

"Step on it."

The driver did not need encouragement. We tore down the straight road like Barney Oldfield on a dirt track and slewed around a right turn with gravel flying to drive through the double doors of the barn and ran into the farmhouse. The soft brick walls would not have afforded us the least protection, of course, but we wanted to get under cover. Inside Red was hovering about like a nervous hen. His freckles stood but like copper pennies on vanilla ice cream.

"Mr. Corey," he asked, anxiously, "have you any whisky?"

"Not a drop, Red."

"Or any brandy?"

"Not a drop."

"My God, Mr. Corey. Haven't you even any vin rouge?"

"Not a bit."

Red turned away disconsolate.

"Not that it's for myself," said he. "I was just thinking of the colonel."

25

It seemed to me that a little visit to Paris was prescribed after my close encounter with German shells. A few dinners at the Restaurant Griffon were a part of the prescription. Not only was the cooking at the Griffon of an excellence only to be approached in a small number of other restaurants in Paris, but the headwaiter of the day was the only Frenchman I can remember who carried his gratitude toward Americans far enough to be really practiced. On several occasions he had insisted that the next bottle should be on the house, which is an honored American custom. One night my wife and I were sitting at table in the Griffon, discussing one of her emphatic needs. "I have no cigarettes," she said, "and I must have cigarettes."

She was at that period rising at dawn each morning and getting on the telephone to Truck Headquarters and getting the promise of a truck on which she loaded as many wounded Americans from Hospital Number One as the truck would hold, and taking them on a sight-seeing trip around Paris. The trip would not have been wholly successful if she could not provide cigarettes.

"Excuse me," said an American at the next table. "I think you have forgotten me. I used to see you in the *Globe* office in New York."

The speaker was Harry Reichenbach, the most noted press agent of his day.[1] His exploits are a part of New York tradition. He had been appointed on one of the travelling committees of the Committee on Public Information

---

1. This encomium of Reichenbach is no exaggeration. He was famous for his publicity stunts and self-promotion. While with the CPI in the United States, he dreamed up the idea of an American July 4th Loyalty Day celebration in 1918 that promoted a patriotic outpouring abroad as well as at home. When Reichenbach was sent to Europe, he became difficult, however. He misrepresented himself as the agent for the National Film Corporation and said, according to a military intelligence report, "The present staff of the Bureau of Public Information were a bunch of 'boobs.'" Reichenbach was "a genius in some ways," George Creel said after firing him.

for which George Creel was unjustly blamed. Those committees were gallivanting carnivals, equipped with the most expensive cigars and cigarettes and silk stockings at the cost of the taxpaying suckers of America, and if they ever did anything except get in the way I never heard of it. Except that Harry Reichenbach made good.

"I have heard your talk," he said, after we split another bottle. "I want to give lunch to Mrs. Corey's soldiers."

He called the headwaiter, and then ordered a luncheon that will always live in my memory. When the guests came the next day, they were in the pajamas of Hospital Number One. Their legs were in splints and bandages, and their arms in casts, and through the rents in the pajamas one could see the hospital gauze that bound their bodies. They smelled of iodoform. And the Griffon is a fastidious restaurant. Harry Reichenbach's lunch was the best that the chef knew how to cook.

"You will permit me that I honor myself," said the headwaiter. "I shall provide the wine."

It was the understanding among our better classes at home that the doughboys did not drink, and if the authorities of Number One had discovered that wine had been served to them—or, to be more precise, if the authorities feared that someone might blab to the old ladies back home—I do not know what might have happened. But no one interfered, and these cheerful, humorous Americans who had gotten shot to pieces in someone else's war had a grand time and were finally loaded into taxicabs under Mrs. Corey's direction and carted off to the Casino de Paris, and Harry Reichenbach and I stood on the pavement and waved them goodbye. And then went back in the Griffon to finish the day.

The war was full of stories like this. Here's another.

The American Ambulance had long been submerged in France under the flood of Americans in uniform, but in the earlier days of the war it had played a lively and interesting part. These reminiscences of hospitals and bandages bring it to mind, and by a natural train of thought the story of the Petite Yvonne is recalled. Most of the men of the American Ambulance knew the Petite Yvonne. That's what they all called her. She was petite, and Yvonne was her name. Also, that title seemed subtly descriptive of the lady.

"It gets her number," as Bill Ahlstrom said.

The Petite Yvonne was a product of one of those quarters of Paris through which tourists sometimes shudder under competent escort. Haggard, black toothed women sit at open windows and smile horribly at the passersby. For 10 cents one who can resist the promptings of curiosity can achieve a table d'hote which is at least excellently filling. Coffee may be had for a penny, and coffee with a liqueur for 3 cents in many corner shops. The alleys are rather more animated at midnight than at noon. The men shoulder against greasy storefronts and eye the stranger in a sort of tranquil hostility.

Still, the Petite Yvonne was really very pretty. She dressed well by an instinct. A girl of Whitechapel accentuates her bunchiness by tangles of ribbon, and wears carrots in her hat. Yvonne knew the value of line.

Her particular Duval had been taken to the American Hospital at Neuilly. It was during this time that the men of the American Ambulance met the Petite Yvonne socially. She didn't miss a visiting day. On other days she was almost certain to stroll down the Avenue d'Inkermann, past the front of the hospital. If a khaki clad American hailed her she would respond in her scraps of English.

"Find out about my little Duval—he with the knife cut across his cheek."

Whereupon the obliging American would penetrate Duval's ward, and come to Yvonne with the information she desired. Never the same American two days in succession. The Petite Yvonne doubted all men. She would check the report of one by the report of the next. Eventually Duval was transferred to one of the French military hospitals. The men of the Ambulance followed his fortunes through the gossip of the French drivers.

"He is convalescent now, that Duval," it was reported, "and is keeping drunk by buying wine at a franc the bottle and smuggling it into the hospital for sale to the other patients at a franc and a half."

Duval was quite as characteristic a product of his environment as was his Yvonne. He had been swept up in the first days of mobilization and put in a uniform. Many of these criminal parasites made good soldiers. They had a rat-like intelligence that was of use in the fire trenches and a rat-like desperation in the fight. Duval had been twice wounded and once praised by his captain. If he had not been Duval, he might have been given the Cross. He looked crookedly at the world. He rasped his words from an absinthe-bitten throat.

"You are to have a week's furlough," said the chief physician of his hospital. "Then you are to go back to the front."

Duval growled his thanks and started for his quartier on the arm of Yvonne. He was quite strong again. But he did not want to return to the front.

He was of the opinion that he had done enough for his country. He let his old friends know this. By and by one of them came to Yvonne mysteriously.

"Pierre knows how to save Duval from the front," he reported. "But he will not tell."

Pierre is the keeper of a wine shop on one of the little back streets that are hidden behind Boulevard Montparnesse. He had long appraised Yvonne's good looks at their full value. But she clung to Duval as a permanency. She coquetted with Pierre.

"If Duval were out of the way I should be better pleased," said the keeper of the wine shop. "But I bear him no grudge because you love him and do not love me. Let him know that a soldier who has been twice wounded need not return to the front if he prefers to stay at home. Let him refuse to go. Tell him not to gossip this about. It is not desirable that many know."

Duval faced the chief physician of the hospital the next day. He need not go back to those infernal trenches, he insisted. Full of bad wine, he defied the chief physician. He promised that official a knife between his ribs if he attempted to force him back to the firing line. If the physician succeeded in getting him off to the front, he pledged himself to find revenge at the first opportunity. Duval was quite sincere. He really believed that having been twice wounded, he had the right to remain at home. He thought the chief physician was persecuting him. Next day a file of soldiers sought him at his hold in the quartier.

"You're off for Pont-a-Mousson," they told him. "It has been asked for you especially. You made threats against persons in high authority."

"I was wrong," the wine shop keeper told the girl. "I had been misinformed. He has been sent to Pont-a-Mousson for punishment."

Firing was continuous at Pont-a-Mousson at this period. Those who went into the fire trenches expected to be killed. Duval was petulant. He said there was a man he wished to knife before he died.

"The chief physician," said one who had heard why he had been ordered forward to Pont-a-Mousson.

"Not the chef physician," said Duval, in that queer, wine-bitten growl. "Another."

His desire did not lead him to spare himself. There was an assault one night upon the German trenches, on that angle overlooked by the statue of Joan of Arc. Duval had made himself quite drunk before the word came to leap over the entrenchment. He staggered as he tore his way through the wire entanglements. He had forgotten his gun, and when he stumbled into the German trench he was snarling, well down in his throat, like an animal, and thrusting upward with his knife. There was a push of the close-packed enemy away from him—not in fear so much as to get room in which to use the bayonet or the butt of a gun. But Duval crouched and pressed upon them.

"Four at least he killed," his mates told the ambulance driver. "We found his mark upon them—an upward slash, with a twist, so that they died. No one else handles his knife quite like our little Duval."

It seemed at first that Duval was not seriously hurt. Duval was known to be a man of enormous strength. His heavy arms, covered with black hair, were the boast of his company. So that he was passed on through dressing station to field hospital, and thence to the clearing station, and then ordered back to a hospital near Paris. Duval made no complaint. His dull black eyes watched those who passed, but he rarely spoke, and then only to demand wine. But in the hospital near Paris he died. A constitution based on bad wine and little meat could not stand the shock of the third wound. His surgeon said there was no reason why he should die. Nevertheless, he died.

"So that day," the orderly at the hospital near Paris told the American Ambulance man who inquired, "the Petite Yvonne came for his body, and with her was a man named Pierre who keeps a wine shop in the Quartier Latin. I went to the front hall to call them. I found them sitting on the bench. Yvonne was kissing Pierre.

"It is true," I said to them, "grief cannot be eternal."

Yvonne put her hand in Pierre's as they followed the orderly down the hall toward the mortuary.

"Ah, Monsieur," said she, "when one is young, it is such strength as that of our dear Duval that attracts one." Then she stopped there in the hallway, on the way to the mortuary, and again kissed this wine shop keeper Pierre. "But when one matures, you comprehend, one admires the treasure of the mind."

26

It is not in the French nature, one comprehends, to laugh at the suffering of a comrade. But whenever the laughing sniper gave out that weird whinny through his megaphone the whole trench would laugh with him.

"Hysteria, perhaps," my companion said thoughtfully. "Some of the men caught their breath in sobs. There was something in his voice."

He had been sitting at the next table on the café terrace. A most attractive boy. One had to look closely to find the inch of ribbon that told his rank as lieutenant. After a time he joined frankly in the conversation.

"I am lonesome, you see," said he candidly. "Today my four days' leave in Paris comes to an end and I have seen no friends. My home is in the north."

He seemed to enjoy talking of his life in the trenches, but he needed prompting. A question would start him on a story, but at the end he would relapse into silence to watch with smiling appreciation the pretty women as they passed and repassed in front of the tables. Slender, blue eyed, blond, he seemed modest as a girl, and yet one could feel the fire and spirit underneath. A distinctly French type but a most unusual one.

It is the sniper who is particularly dreaded by the man in the trench, said he. A shell storm is a very shocking thing, of course. Under it, the moral fiber of the human targets disintegrates in harmony with the destruction of their trenches. But ordinary shell fire was hardly regarded. It was always going on, and one could usually hear the missile on its way in time to dodge. It was quite different with snipers. A moment's forgetfulness—a second's pause in an exposed section of the line—and you were dead.

"Here," said he, taking a match from the box on the table, "just like that." He broke the match sharply in two.

The laughing sniper had been at work in one of those canyons in the Vosges where the enemy trenches approach each other closely among the tall, slender pine trees. He was a man of infinite daring, this German, and infinite skill. At night he would hide himself where he could get a clear view through the multitude of tapering boles. Then he waited with a deadly patience for his victims. He rarely fired more than twice from the same hiding place. When night came he would move to another blind. He did not often miss a shot. He was known all along the lines because he laughed when he killed his man.

"That was devilish," said the other man with us.

"No," said the boy, thoughtfully. "It was not the laughter of a wicked man. It was as though he were very greatly amused. One laughed with him."

The laughing sniper must have carried a megaphone to his daily post, the boy thought. Perhaps, he explained, it was merely a roll of bark or a bootleg, although there are collapsible megaphones that take up little space. At first the French soldiers cursed this laughing killer. Then the laughter got on their nerves. They jeered back at him in futile defiance. Now and then he missed his shot but laughed because he thought he had been successful. Then a perfect storm of laughter rocked up and down the trench, the boy said. Men held their sides and gasped weakly when they could laugh no more.

"I do not understand now," said he. "But it was very funny."

He was an irritation, this laughing man. Usually one fights, the boy said, without feeling the unpleasantness of personal hate. As a Frenchman one hates the Boche, of course. But after a time the feeling becomes impersonal, especially if the Germans had been fairly quiet for a time. It seems rather silly to hate men one has never seen. He had known men to spend a month in the trenches without having once caught sight of the enemy. The men were too apt to fraternize across the lines. The officers were forever forbidding these amenities.

The boy himself was a sniper. But he did not go out to kill in any spirit of hate. That would seem—the boy blushed as he tried to make plain the way he felt—rather petty. He was trying to kill for his country's sake. No doubt the man he was trying to kill felt the same. It was that large charity that gave a dignity to war. It was this dignity that the laughter of the sniper disturbed. The animosity it seemed to suggest disturbed him. The uneven laughter of his own men in reply seemed spiteful to him. He tried to repress it. It was indicative of a nervous weakness.

"Yet I laughed with them," he said. "There was something in his voice."

Everyone had tried for the laughing sniper, the boy said. The best shots had been deployed against him. When his exultant cackle was heard of a morning, sharpshooters came from all along the line. Sometimes days would go by in which he was not heard, for he was very careful and very methodical. He never took up an unsafe position and never fired unless he were sure. But every night, after he had abandoned his covert for the day and was crawling back to his own lines through the company of the dead that the growing grass was trying hard to shroud, he would laugh once.

"It was hideous," the boy murmured. "It was like nothing human, that laughter from the darkness, amid the decaying dead. There was something in his voice."

As time went on the men became used to the laughter. Perhaps they became sullen, or perhaps their nerves were under better control. The boy had conquered that desire he once felt to join in the laughter that came from the green forest. Nor he was irritated by it. It seemed to him that he was a better and stronger man for having resisted this bodiless attack upon him. He said as much one day to the lieutenant of the next trench section, who was paying him a visit. The other lieutenant had that day received a letter from home, in which a loving message had been sent to the boy. The young officers had been friends at school.

"We should not direct our rage against the man," the other assented. "It is his country we must hate."

He rose to say goodbye. A ray of the setting sun shone in through the porthole and illuminated the blue-gray of his cap. Somewhere out in the obscurity of that wire entangled wood a rifle cracked, and the young officer fell forward into the arms of his friend. Laughter echoed through the tree trunks. It was so inspired by an impish mirth that the men in the French trenches forgot their new decorum and laughed savagely with the sniper. Then all became silent again.

"That night," said the boy, "we opened fire with rifle and mitrailleuse upon the sector of the line within which we knew the sniper had taken cover. It kept him in his burrow. From time to time there were pauses by prearrangement. At such times I crept noiselessly through the openings in the wires and around the gnarled roots of trees in the darkness. Sometimes my outstretched hand fell upon a bit of cloth. Then I drew myself in another direction. Then the firing stopped, and I laid there silent, my rifle thrust out before me. I heard a noise—but a little noise—and at my gun's end a heavy body seemed to take form in the night. And so I fired.

"Then I too laughed out loudly in the darkness."

27

Who now remembers the case of Mary Davies? I'll lay a bet that she did not get a decoration.

Davies was an English woman, a nurse by profession, healthy, pretty, and young. Her father held a high official position in India. For some years Miss Davies had been studying bacteria at the Pasteur Institute. When the war broke out she attached herself to the American Hospital at Neuilly. There she came in contact with Dr. Kenneth Taylor.

Dr. Taylor had been the bacteriologist of the Imperial Cancer Institute. Before that he occupied the chair of bacteriology at Minnesota University. Although a young man he was a distinguished scientist. Incidentally he was a modest man. He tried to keep this story out of the papers. Not all scientists—even in wartime—shrink from a little earned praise.

"Watch the gas gangrene," said his superiors in the hospital to Dr. Taylor.

Gas gangrene had never been heard of until the Germans began using asphyxiating gas. Unpleasant details may be skipped as far as possible, but this much of a hint at the quality of gas gangrene may be given. Gas forms in the muscular tissues of the sufferer. His entire body swells. The only practicable treatment has been to slash open the flesh of the man's arms and legs in order that the rapidly forming gas may escape. By and by he dies. In that way his agony is eased.

Surgeons experimented furiously in the effort to conquer the disease. Perhaps the surgery was sometimes rough and ready, but no matter. The men would have died anyhow. They could not suffer more than they were suffering. Human endurance has its limits. Dr. Taylor had recourse to the faithful guinea pig, like any other bacteriologist. After the one hundredth—or one thousandth—had been used up he was able to make an announcement in *The Lancet*.

"The quinine treatment seems promising."

That, to the lay mind, was about all that Dr. Taylor said. He had injected a preparation of quinine into the inoculated guinea pigs and some of them lived. Some of them, mark you. The experiment had not been completed. But it seemed promising. Here ensues a gap in the narrative. It has not been stated whether Dr. Taylor has used his preparation on a soldier victim. In any case that treatment might not have been successful.

"You see," said another physician, "there are so few pure cases of gas gangrene. A man may have a dozen different dangerous organisms preying on him in the trenches but he doesn't know it. Then something happens, and he goes down. His case may be labelled this or it may be called that. In fact it may be a combination of many things. The principal ailment may have many collateral relations at work upon the patient."

One day Mary Davies said goodbye to Dr. Taylor. She was going away, she said, for a rest. She might be gone several days. She did not know. What she really did was to take a room across the way from the American Hospital and for four days put herself through a course of dieting. She really trained for what she was about to do. When she thought that her top note of health had been reached she deliberately injected the virus of gas gangrene into her thigh. Then she waited. Two hours after she walked across the street and into the American Hospital.

"Send for Dr. Taylor," she said. "I have inoculated myself with gas gangrene. I can feel the first symptoms."

It was that undoubted case of uncomplicated gas gangrene for which Dr. Taylor had perhaps been hoping in his soul of a scientist. No trench maladies were present here. Nothing in the world was wrong with the young woman except the dread disease of the war. It has not been possible to fully explain gas gangrene to the reader. There are some things which must be taken for granted.

"Good Lord," said Dr. Taylor. "Hurry."

For twenty-four hours he fought for her life. All the familiar symptoms appeared, but one by one they were conquered. For three days she was a very—very—sick young woman. The issue remained in doubt. Then she recovered sufficiently so that, very pale and shaken, but on the road to health, she was put on board a boat for England.

"And don't come back until you are strong again" were her sailing orders.

Not many deeds in this war topped that for pure heroism. Science is rightfully proud of the devotees who have given their lives in her service. Malaria was checked by one sacrifice. Yellow fever has been harnessed because a young American gave up his life. That "spotted fever" in Idaho which puzzled the medical world has been conquered because a young surgeon of our Public Health Service bought knowledge by his death. The list might be extended indefinitely. The courage of these men is the greater because the death they faced came in loathsome form. They were not cheered on by comrades frenzied with the battle lust. They hoped to evade death but they knew they could not escape suffering. Mary Davies was as heroic as any one of these.

Only—it was a useless heroism. It did not prove anything. No one knows today—knows—whether gas gangrene can be cured by this quinine injection or not. Never another patient will come to the surgical ward as Mary Davies did—healthy, robust, glowing with perfect health. Instead they will reach the surgeon after long hours of agony in the mud of the trenches or the sand of the open field on which the sun beats down or chilled by a cold that bites through to the bone. Their strength has been sapped by the most cruel test of endurance ever put to man. Their very flesh may be alive with hostile organisms.

It is men like these that the scientists hope to cure. Not clean, well-kept, hearty fellows who have but to walk across the street into a surgical ward, within two hours after the infection has begun its work. Nine-tenths of the men for whom the surgeons hopelessly battle against this putrid enemy have been suffering for hours before a friend can reach them. It is the aid that will help these men that Taylor and his confreres want.

Mary Davies did not stop to think of that. She only knew that men were dying, and she wanted to help. She counted her life as nothing. She took the risk of the most hideous suffering that even prolific war has devised for man. No one knows today whether her courage was productive of the very least good. The quinine treatment will be administered to soldiers, and it is by the effect upon the soldiers that it will stand or fall. It is true that her life was saved, but her's was not a typical case. It doesn't prove anything. No real knowledge has been gained.

Only . . . heroism is not to be measured by an inch rule. There has been no greater bravery than that of Mary Davies in all this war.

28

During a slow week on the American front in the summer of 1918 I obtained permission to visit British press headquarters. It was as though I had dropped into another world. I might have gone to sleep in a backroom filled with cigar smoke, typewriter clatter, male and female voices, and the clink of glassware and wakened in a hushed gentleman's club. The pace was different. So were the men, rules, and manners. The American correspondents were no more dignified than American reporters usually are. An evening at Meaux, where our press HQ was then established, might include "The Rolling River" by Floyd Gibbons, a ballad by Fred Ferguson, a loud debate between Jimmy Hopper and Bill McNutt, beginning at a fixed point and moving in all directions, reports on the flora of Kansas City by Otto Higgins, comments on our low morale and mental ratings by Bill Forrest, and violent wrangles with the censor by Edwin L. James. It was a full cast.[1] Other things might happen and almost certainly would happen, but this outline affords a general idea of the operations. We were noisy, profane, addicted to drink and anecdotage, and incredibly argumentative during our off hours. Each day each man rode scores of miles in army cars driven over roads crowded with guns, trucks, tanks, and marching men by a young man wrapped in thoughts of the girls back home in Kansas. The reverse journey was made at night over the same roads, still crowded, on which no lights were permitted because of the flyers overhead, and at a higher speed because the drivers were now thinking of chow. Each reporter wrote a few thousand words on the day's doings before he could settle down to drink and acrimonious camaraderie.

1. Ferguson was the replacement for Westbrook Pegler of the UP. McNutt and Hopper were correspondents for *Collier's Weekly*; Higgins represented the *Kansas City Star*. Wilbur Forrest was a correspondent for UP until 1918, when he switched to the *New York Tribune*. James, with the *New York Times*, later became that paper's managing editor.

The system lacked dignity, gave each reporter almost complete liberty of action, a short-cut right through to quick results, and produced a daily crop of top-notch news stories.

On my first night at British press HQ, I was reminded of the sextet in *Floradora*.[2] I am still reminded of it. The correspondents are remembered as moving with that slow grace characteristic of the sextet's girls. They were very courteous and hated each other bitterly. No one raised his voice, and it seemed likely to me that each correspondent prayed nightly that all the other correspondents would drop dead. Each had a batman who polished his brown leather and brushed his uniform and served him tea and whisky and spoke in low tones. It seemed to be the rule that each was accompanied by an officer when he went to the lines daily. Nightly lectures were given by a staff officer and army operations and plans were pointed out on a wall map. The British system was highly efficient and resulted in the production of quantities of high-class literature. It was as different from ours as the Seaforth Highlanders are different from the 101 Ranch.[3]

The task of the British correspondents was to present a picture to England and through the English press services to the world which would enlist and retain sympathy, confidence, and support. This was superbly done. The broad outlines of the picture were brushed in by the press officers in collaboration with the press chiefs in London, but there was no interference with the detail work by the correspondents. Early in the war—about as soon as Lord Kitchener's hands could be tied—it had been recognized that the manner in which fact was presented to the world was of more importance than a park full of heavy guns. Propaganda had become a weapon. In order that it should be thoroughly efficient, direction by a central authority was essential. Some months later on I said to General Pershing:

"It is my belief that because of the Allied propaganda and of their control of all news channels, there has not been a moment from the beginning of the war that the United States has had a true understanding of what was going on."

He banged his big fist down on the table.

"By God, Mr. Corey," he said, "you're right!"

2. *Florodora*, an Edwardian musical comedy, became a highly successful Broadway show in 1900 after it left London.
3. The Seaforth Highlanders infantry regiment was known for their bagpiping. The Miller Brothers 101 Ranch in Oklahoma was the site of the 101 Ranch Wild West Show.

The Allied propagandists succeeded in selling us a $40 billion pup. If they had not so thoroughly enlisted American sympathy for the Allies' cause we would either not have entered the war at all or would have entered it on other terms. Other terms might have meant the defeat of the Allies. If I continue to emphasize the importance of the part that propaganda played in the world war, it is in the hope that when the next war comes we will profit by the lesson. It will not only be possible for us to slather the right pigmentation on the canvas in order to keep the other fellow from putting on his colors. It was not necessary for our press officers to do anything of the sort in 1918. The picture was on the line. All they needed to do was to keep over enthusiastic Americans reporters from slapping in a sour tint here and there.

George Creel's pothunters were all over the place by the end of the summer, of course. This is not to be taken as a crack by ricochet at Creel. He not only did the best he could, in my belief, but I think his best was useful at the outset. Then the joyriding began, and the Committee on Public Information got away from Creel. Show an American—any American—and that goes for British, Italian, Greeks or Chinese—a chance to become an envoy on an expense account and he will leap to it. Millions of dollars were spent by our own propaganda department in 1918, and it is doubtful if a nickel's worth of good was done. By the time our propagandists got to work the picture had been painted. The world's opinion had been formed. The only thing left to do was to fight it out.[4]

That paragraph flew off at a tangent. What I am writing of now is the work of the American correspondents. General "Denny" Nolan—every one of us spoke of him as "Denny" and not one of us ever spoke to him that way—was the head of the press service. Nolan is a tall, lean, humorous, wise Irishman who knew reporters as though he had made them out of wire and beads. The American reporter is a cynic if he has been on the job any length of time. He does not believe in statesmen, diplomats, army officers, or handsome ladies. He knows they are all out to do him out of the truth about what-

---

4. Initially the Committee on Public Information confined itself to domestic propaganda in the United States. But once the "inner lines" were secure, as Creel put it, the CPI sent commissioners abroad. Corey's view of this overseas work was a common one: The undertaking was marred by poor management, clumsy propaganda, poor judgment, and discreditable deception. Some of it, however, was useful and well done. More significantly, it established the concept of what is today called "public diplomacy"—that is, the idea of seeking to shape the attitudes of citizens overseas.

ever it is if they can. Often they can see through the arts of silence, procrastination, or bluff, and occasionally have friendly relations with someone who knows the owner. He is unbribable—I have never known a reporter who sold out—sometimes scareable, and as reliable as possible. If "Denny" Nolan had said to his reporters, "You must do this and that," they would have ignored him to a man. Instead, he told them what they must not do. They must not anticipate events, put poison ivy down the necks of our allies, tell facts that might be of aid to the enemy, or identify units. These rules offered plenty of openings for fights with the censor. Otherwise, they could do as they pleased. Some of us preferred to stay with the forces in the line. Those who were responsible for daily cable stories lived at press headquarters and were kept informed on army plans and movements, within reason. When GHQ had prepared its plans for a battle we would be directed to assemble at press headquarters.

"Cars will leave at such-and-such an hour."

Sometimes Pershing himself read the map for us. When the Saint-Mihiel movement was ordered we were ridden halfway across France to Nancy, and Nolan gave us that night a lecture with the map on what was planned, which put the whole picture before our eyes. When the guns began the next morning most of us were out in the fog watching the men move forward as the barrage lifted. The American plan was to make it as easy as possible for the reporters to get the facts they wanted. Then it was up to the reporters and the editors back home. Now and then, of course, we ran crosswise.

When Chateau-Thierry was the hot spot a daily automobile trip of four or five hours was necessary to get to the line from Meaux and get back again at night, and so Lincoln Eyre of the *World* and Tom Johnson of the *Sun* and I commandeered a vacant house we found in the outskirts. It had been the home of the prefect of Chateau-Thierry and more recently had been used by a German general and his staff. It was equipped with brass beds, box mattresses, a fine cookstove, and three dead Germans in the garden. Someone got rid of the Germans after a day or two. We settled down there to do a little light housekeeping. An old French woman was found to do our cooking. One day she did not come back. I do not know what had happened.

The drawback was that the town was being bombed almost nightly. In the precise center of the ceiling of the ground floor hall was a black iron chandelier from which a round iron ball was suspended. When we heard the alarm, it was our custom to shiver in bed until the bombs seemed to us falling somewhere near. Then we would rise, and six-foot-something Eyre would take my hand and I would take Tom Johnson's hand, and we would feel our way through the pitch darkness down the stairs and into the hall. Johnson and I would listen breathlessly. Presently Eyre's forehead would strike the round iron ball. Eyre would swear painfully. The little column then executed a half right and found the door to the cellar and sat in the cellar on boxes until the bombing was over. This was an involved method but the only one feasible. Eyre never missed the ball. One day he shouted through the door: "Father Duffy's here."

Every New Yorker in the AEF, at least, knew Father Francis Duffy. He was on his painful way to the rear, shaking with fever, weak from starvation and fatigue, and angry enough to fight the whole army. His assistant chaplain, it appeared, had rejoiced unduly when he was sent back. Duffy had been holding him in reserve and had arrogated to himself the privilege of comforting the dying in the front lines. When Duffy's superiors ordered him to go back and get well, the assistant had openly rejoiced.

"I'll be having a chance to do a little something in this war," he said.

"I had a mind to crack the blaggard over the head," said Father Duffy.

We enlisted a doughboy and built a fire in the bathroom and boiled buckets of water, and he had his first bath in weeks. Then we set him down to a hot meal and in the evening tucked him between clean sheets—we had found some poor old Frenchwoman's store of fine linen in a wrecked home—and gave him a bottle of whisky and a novel.

"Whatever ye do in the days to come," said he with a huge sigh of content, "I'll give ye absolution for this."

Someone spoiled our little sideshow, and we were ordered back to Meaux. Now that it is all over, I am inclined to look at that as a proper paying out for a bit of needless meanness on our part. One day Arthur Ruhl of *Collier's Weekly* came through Chateau-Thierry, and I invited him to spend the night with us. He did not spend that night, being in fact engaged in sitting as deep down in a doghole as possible during a shell storm which knocked off some of his temporary comrades, but the next night he drifted in. Eyre and Johnson and I had had another quarrel. By this time everyone's nerves were jittering, and we barked at each other on the least provocation. Ruhl was frozen out. There was no reason why he should have been except that he was a good reporter, and we were running a closed game. I have been ashamed of that ever since and inclined to blame the others for it. But to be truthful about it I do not know who was at fault.

It was about this time that an invitation came through for Eyre and I to visit the French front. For more than two years we had been permitted to see the French front only at intervals, but now that we had our own people to write about the French authorities began to miss some of the love and kisses we had blown at them in our persistent efforts to get out where something was going on. It was suggested that we were writing too much about the Americans and not enough about La Belle France and her troubles. Perhaps the same invitation went to other correspondents. In any event, this being our first chance to be haughty, we were haughty as could be, and refused to go.

We did, however, make a tour of our own front and returned to report that the Germans were on top of us everywhere in the air. That did not get by the censor. The Germans knew it, of course, and our troops knew it, but knowledge of that sort might—in the opinion of HQ—have harmed the martial spirit at home. I could not believe that at the time and do not believe it now, but our eloquent pieces were stopped. It may be that we had not fully comprehended the reason behind the stoppage. By this time it was becoming more certain each day that sooner or later we would burst through the German lines and the war would draw near its end. The French and English, although not attempting to minimize the value of the American effort, might have been well pleased to let Americans know that we had our weaknesses. They were already making their plans for the political battles which were to follow the armistice. Our headquarters were not admitting anything.

The reference some paragraphs ago to the city of Nancy brings to mind the queer ways in which fear will operate. During the Saint-Mihiel drive, I kept rooms on the top floor of the Hotel d'Angleterre, and when possible got back to them for a wash and brush up. The Angleterre was within a stone's throw of the railroad station and yards, and the yards were presumably the target for the German flyers. As a matter of fact, their aim was either very poor or an arrangement had been made about the railroad station, for it was not hit nearly as often as the odds indicated. Almost every night the Germans flew overhead, bound for somewhere in the rear. The siren always notified us. Early in the morning they flew over again, homeward bound. The sirens told us. If they had any bombs left, they dropped them. Overwise they winged back silently.

Night after night I had been getting up at the first alarm and going to a damp and crowded cellar and listening to the serial stories. Each time I carried my typewriter, for not even the sanctifying influence of war, which was one of the things we wrote about in those days, would protect a portable from a thief. Each morning I repeated this at the second alarm. Eventually the performance staled, and I determined to stay gallantly in bed. It was very apparent to me—during the sunshine—that no attack need be feared. If one were made it was not probable that the first hit would be scored on the Angleterre. As it was not possible to sleep, I provided myself with a bottle of light wine and a novel for the twice nightly raid.

Night after night I turned on the light when I heard the siren, opened the bottle of wine, lighted a cigar, and began on the novel. The flesh is weak, and it shivered more or less, but I was so certain that I had worked out the logic of the case that I was able to remain fairly comfortable. Then—night after night—good Cal Lyon came panting up the stairs. We rode together most days and were partners after a fashion. At each alarm, each night, he would take a census of the refugees in the cellar.

After each census he would say, "Good God! Corey's still asleep." Whereupon he would risk the arteries of his heart by running up six flights of stairs to waken me and force me into safety. Each time that he burst open the door of my room, I was moderately comfortable and happy, and no more frightened than my reason told me I should be. One look at Cal Lyon's startling eyes and one note from his voice invariably reduced me to a state of jittering panic. I leaped like a gazelle on my way down the six flights. Once I forgot my typewriter but returned in time to meet it in the hands of a French soldier. We agreed that La Belle France was pretty swell and that nothing should be done about it.

The Saint-Mihiel drive wasn't much of an action, as actions went in the war. It was more of a battue than a battle. But it was a beautifully handled affair from the staff's point of view. My own idea of it was gathered from the men of the Ohio regiment of the Rainbow Division. I knew this outfit, rank and file. Most of them came from Columbus or thereabouts, and so did I, and when the chance came, I always looked them up to see what they had been doing. Here is the story I wrote of them after the drive:

> With the First American Army in the St. Mihiel Salient—
> It was a revel—a romp—a giddy steeplechase for the men of one

Ohio regiment. Captain Henry Grave of Columbus took thirty prisoners by his own hand. Lieutenant Walter Christensen captured a nest of machine guns with an empty pistol. Lieutenant Edwin Shoemaker of Lancaster got the drop on the crew of a pair of heavy guns and the crew threw up its several hands. Three companies waded a river, deep to their necks, and took the gun that swept the water surface. So it went on. The men from Ohio just galloped through.

"The hike up was worse than the fighting," they said. "The battle itself was a rest."

This regiment had had no rest since Feb. 15. I was with them when they held the line in the Nivelle sector. Then they helped smash the Boche offensive of July 15. After that they encountered the Germans' desperate rearguard resistance on the Ource—and then they were pulled out of the line. They were bathed and shaved and put in clean clothing and permitted to sleep at night. Then replacements came in. They were men from Indiana and Kentucky and good men, but for the most part they knew nothing about war. They were in the pinfeather stage. Some of them had only been in uniform for six weeks—not six weeks in France but six weeks in uniform. The veterans of six months fighting looked down upon them:

"You green guys want to watch us," they said. "Do what we do and you'll come through."

On Sept. 5 the greenhorns began to find what it means to do what veterans do. They marched all that night in the rain and slept all the next day in the rain in the woods. Four more nights this was repeated. The American army crept upon the German position like a cat on a mouse. As far as possible the villages were avoided, so that no unwise tongue might betray the secret. They felt rather than saw the artillery and the Stokes mortars and the machine guns and the tanks coming up alongside of them on other roads. On the night of Sept. 11 they did not start until midnight. Up to that time they sat disconsolately in the mud by the road in the rain. It was very dark.

"March," the order snapped down the line.

That was a joke. No man could see the man ahead. Each man seized the coattails of the man ahead, and so, clinging to each other like a herd of trained elephants, they slushed through the mud of the greasy road. Not a private soldier knew where he was going. Few knew even in what part of France he might be, for hiking under fifty-pound packs does not encourage map study in leisure moments. The barrage began behind them, so they knew they were near the take-off line. Its rose-colored flames ran and flickered ahead in the curtain of black fog. The non-coms began to herd their men.

"You greenhorns," they said, "watch us, and you'll be alright."

It was five o'clock of the morning of Sept. 11 in the neighborhood of Seicheprey. The old-timers sat grumpily silent in wet holes in the mud. They could not smoke, and this prohibition became an outrage and a travesty. The greenhorns shook ever so little in their shoes. They had gathered something of the nonchalance of the men with whom they had bunked, but the jump-off was a new experience to them. A whistle blew.

"Come on," said the second lieutenant, shlepping through the mud at the left end of their platoon fronts. "Come on," said the sergeants. "Get on there," said corporals. "What'n hell's the matter with you?" The greenhorns shivered but stepped out into the greasy mud, into the dark that was just beginning to gray, toward the clamoring conflagration on ahead. The old-timers put a wad of gum in their cheeks and started. If the field had been visible it would have been seen as severed with little strings of men. Each string walked parallel to another, head-on to the enemy. The steady old-timers grunted at them. Sometimes they kicked the greenhorns angrily.

"Can that stuff" they said. "That ain't no way to do it. Come on outta that."

The barrage lifted on ahead. Its red line ran quivering along a farther bank of cloud that was thinning under the rising sun. The crackle of machine guns began in the mist ahead. It seemed deadened by the fog and rain. The old-timers spread out on either side of them. "Come on, you," they said to the greenhorns. Some of them stolidly flopped in the mud and began to dig little wallows with their shovels. On ahead they would see a sudden flare of bursting bombs, or a petulant, wet snapping of rifle shots. Then a second lieutenant would call back to them.

"Come on, you."

At eleven o'clock of the morning of Sept. 12 they came to the little River Rupt-des-Main. Like most of the little French rivers it was hardly twenty yards in width. Its swift brown water ran neck deep. Captain Henry Grave of Columbus, Ohio, was in command of the company that first found the Rupt-des-Main on the half-mile front the regiment covered. On the other side machine guns screened by the willows of the bank were popping. They were set almost at a level with the water, so that the bullet sometimes glanced against its surface, dull under the sunless sky.

"Come on, you," said Henry Grave.

That could not do it. The water hissed under the bullets and the men pulled back and dug in, stolidly, on the bank. Captain Grave sent for a tank. It came rattling and lurching up and searched the opposite bank for the machine guns. Their bullets ricocheted from its turret. The tank could not cross the river—but while the Boche had been fighting this devilish contraption Captain Henry Grave and some of his men had worked their way down the river and up the river.

"Come on, you," said Captain Grave.

Some of the Germans were brave and died at their guns. For the most part they ran. The little, comic, ugly figures in gray-green, running with hands flapping across the wet fields, dropped one after another in the mud. The old-timers hurried after them, pausing now and then to soothe a rifle butt against a wet cheek and fire. They came across an unexpected machine gun nest in the open field. Lieutenant Walter Christensen ran at it from the side, firing his pistol. The Germans surrendered and begged. Then Christensen re-loaded his pistol in their presence. Before the capture had been completed his gun was quite empty.

There was a line of bushes which might shelter a battery position on ahead, and Lieutenant Edwin Shoemaker of Lancaster rushed through it. The crew of two German guns—150 in caliber—were busy at their places. When he dropped his gun on them they surrendered and the guns were his. Corporal Sensabaugh of Crestline thought he saw a furtive figure crawling behind a rise of ground. He ran it down a hole, as one might run a rabbit. At the bottom of the hole he saw a white patch. It was the face of the German, on his way to a deeper compartment of the dugout:

"Come on, you," said Sensabaugh, and nine Germans meekly climbed out, hands high, and smiling at their captor. Lieutenant Bannden of Bowling Green had the Stokes mortars, which were dragged and carried through the mud by their impatient crews. At the second shot the machine guns fired in the air like mechanical fountains, and the Germans who were left alive came shrieking for their lives.

There was danger ahead at Pannes. The Germans always organize these little towns like fortresses. Machine guns guard every inch of the streets. A man from Ashland jumped out and drew fire and jumped back again, and so did men from Springfield and Akron and Chilicothe. The men from the Midwest have confidence—and pride—in tanks now, just as they have in our artillery and our air service. Cooperation had been established. Runners were sent back for the tanks, and soon the little fellows came up. They leaped and bounded over the rough ground with an odd suggestion of playfulness—as though these quaint beasts enjoyed their work.

They nosed into Pannes and the Germans fled—and as they fled the infantrymen who had worked around behind the town took their pay from the runners. So they went on until they reached the limit set for them by the army. They might have gone farther, but they obey orders now. The men of the army have been taught that trick. They always go where they are told, but they go no farther. It doesn't pay.

So the men of the regiment did sixteen kilometers in twenty-seven hours, across a country unknown to the fighting men, and in the face of an enemy who had machine guns well placed and the best of the ground—who had everything, in fact, but the will to fight. They have loot—German glasses and pistols and maps and boots and blankets and coats are on every side now, not to speak of wagons and guns—and they were credited with 700 of the 959 prisoners taken by the division in the fight. The old-timers say it wasn't a battle at all. They say the hike was the worst of it and fighting was just play. The greenhorns—but they are no more greenhorns now.

They became veterans in that twenty-seven hours.

29

One story of the war of mine has never been printed. It has to do with the grief of a man who for four years had been the greatest man in the world. I will not debate this classification. It did not get into print because the four correspondents who got it had broken the rules and were in punishment. They could not get a word through the censor. By the time this edict had been relaxed too many other pots were on the fire to go back into the past. The present was too engrossing.

Fighting had stopped. The Armistice had been signed. The Peace Conference was being assembled. Five of us—Lincoln Eyre of the *New York World,* Fred Smith of the *Chicago Tribune,* Cal Lyon of the Newspaper Enterprise Association, George Seldes of the Marshall Newspaper Syndicate, and me—determined to go into Germany to see what the conditions really were there.[1] We could not get permission. By that time American correspondents were thick as fleas. If all were permitted to go, the expedition would have resembled a regiment. If only a few were selected, the others would have raised a resounding hell. Colonel House, who was still President Wilson's advisor, gave us a note. "I have no authority to grant you permission. But I know you and approve of your plan."

---

1. In addition to his AEF assignment, Eyre was the Paris bureau chief for his paper. Frederick A. Smith had been a city editor for newspapers in New York, Chicago, and St. Louis. The Newspaper Enterprise Association was part of E. W. Scripps's empire; Lyon had edited Scripps newspapers in Ohio. Seldes, the youngest of the lot, had taken a break from working for the *Chicago Tribune* to write for the Marshall Newspaper Syndicate. Corey's original manuscript does not mention Seldes, whose name we have inserted. He considered Seldes a tagalong who had not been expressly invited. Seldes had to turn back before the others because he ran out of funds; he exited Germany via Luxembourg and was sent to AEF headquarters for questioning. As Corey points out later, he and the other three were arrested in Berlin and sent back.

House said that if we got into trouble that might help us out. He thought we would get into trouble. The English and the French would not like it. The plan was to let the English and French correspondents get into Germany first.

"We have returned to the prewar-power politics," he said. "The sooner Americans get out of Europe the better our recent allies will be pleased."

The first morning out of Metz we drove through the retreating German army. There never was a happier body of troops. If they had been defeated, they didn't show it. They trudged along, laughing and talking, delighted that the fighting was ended. Now and then we saw groups of officers on the Saar hillsides, mounted on the magnificent horses German officers always rode, looking down at the marching troops on the roads. It did not dawn on us that anything had gone wrong. The village streets were decorated with Arches of Triumph, flagged, and flowered. The villagers cheered and the girls kissed the soldiers. If this was not the march of a victorious army, it had all the marks of one. A non-com stopped our two cars and examined our papers. Then he tied little red flags to the hoods of our cars.

"That will pass you right into Berlin."

"You are a non-com," said Lincoln Eyre, who was the only one of us who spoke even a little German. "How come you have this authority?"

"There are no more officers," said the sergeant. "The army is on strike. This is revolution."

We rollicked along with the revolutionists. Everyone was friendly and cordial except the occasional groups of mounted officers on the hillside. We ate a bit more peas porridge than we wanted, but our hosts ate it, too. At Kassel we put up at a superb little hotel on a hilltop and began to eat roast goose. In the end we tired of roast goose. Our rooms were large, luxurious, sparkling clean, and the service could not have been better. As we sat at dinner that evening, enjoying a meal that was about as good as a meal could be, washed down with a pink German wine, a scrawny, under-sized German captain paused at a respectful distance from the table. He saluted. Eyre said in German, "What do you want?"

The other three said to each other: "Here it is. This is it. Our luck has been too good to last. Well—it's been a good story."

The little German captain—and I wish to stress his apparent insignificance and shabbiness and scrawniness and generally third-rate aspect—said, "You are the American correspondents?"

We agreed rather jovially. Our dream had blown up, but we had gotten farther than we had hoped. We said that, yes, we were, and would he sit down and have a glass of wine with us? He said that he would not. He wanted to know if there were anything he could do for us. He was in command of the rebellious army, he said, and our coming had been reported to him, and he was sorry that he had not been able to give us a proper reception. However, he wished us to know that he was completely at our service. Was there not something he could do for us in Kassel?

We said no. We were still jovial. It appeared that we were getting along all right. No one was peevish with us, except, maybe, back in the American army. We asked him again if he would not have some wine. Again he said no.

"There must be something I can do for you. Would you not like to have an interview with General Von Hindenburg."

We laughed a little at that. Hindenburg had been the greatest general in either army, from the day he drowned 100,000 Russians in the Mazurian marshes. He had been licked by sheer weight of muscle in the end, but we did not kid ourselves that anyone on our side had displayed finer generalship. We had heard our own generals admit this too often.

"Of course we would," we said with one voice. "But that's out. Hindenburg would not receive us."

"You will not leave before nine o'clock tomorrow morning?" the little captain asked. I am sorry I did not get his name. At the time he did not seem sufficiently important. None of us believed him. We thought he was some kind of a nut, probably.

"No. We will wait for you until nine o'clock," we said. "But not a moment longer, mind you."

"Until nine o'clock, then."

On the following morning our luggage was piled in a heap in the hotel lobby. We had just finished our breakfast—and a good breakfast it was, ham and eggs and hot bread and fruit and coffee—when the waiter clicked his heels and said the captain was waiting. He approached us, meek and lowly, and said the limousines were at the door. There were two of them, of the perfect style the German army affected, long and wide and black and polished, with two soldiers on the driver's seat. The footman leaped out and saluted and opened the doors and we got in. We rode over a series of good roads to the War College. The little captain followed us in his battered little car. At the door of the War College we were greeted by several soldiers. I do not remember whether they were of officer rank. The fact is I felt slightly stunned.

"General Von Hindenburg is waiting for us in his office."

We walked through several long corridors and climbed two flights of wide stairs. Two soldiers stood at attention at a door. The little captain said something and they opened the door, and we followed him in. As I remember it, the room was perhaps forty feet long and half as many wide. A dozen or more soldiers were at work on books and writing letters. In the most distant corner of the room, kitty-corner from the entrance, was a small wooden desk. In front of it was a wooden army chair. On the chair, his arms on the desk, staring at the wall, sat the immense figure of Von Hindenburg. He did not stir as we entered. I do not think he heard us. He was as motionless as though he were a monument of granite. The soldier who had preceded the little captain said something. The general did not respond. The soldier turned to the little captain. He said: "My general."

Von Hindenburg stirred heavily. Presently he rose, an enormous figure of a man. He asked, "Who are you?"

The little captain clicked his heels and saluted formally. A new tone came into his voice. For the first time I respected him. He said, "I am Captain So-and-so. I am in command of the German army. In absolute command. I have ordered that you see and talk to these American correspondents."

Von Hindenburg was silent for a moment, staring at the little captain. Then he said: "My kaiser has run away. My country has been crushed. My army has been defeated and is in revolt. And now you—you call yourself the leader of these rebels—attempt to order me to talk to these Americans. I will not. This is the bitterest moment of my life."

Von Hindenburg turned his back on us and sat down again in the little chair and replaced his massive arms on the desk. The little captain shrugged his shoulders and turned and led the way out of the room. The soldiers at the desks ceased all movement. The little captain led the way down to the two great black limousines and gave the drivers instructions and got into his battered car. We never saw him again.

I had no reason to like Von Hindenburg. I had been in Berlin during the early days of the war, when the Germans were trying their best to bluff us. He made the group of officers who constituted the American military mission stand in the sun, waiting for permission to see him, until it became apparent that they were being deliberately insulted. As soon as they could get their passports they went home. But that day I felt sorry for the man who had risen so high and fallen so far.

We were eventually arrested in Berlin and taken to Chaumont and court-martialed by General Dennis Nolan. Then we were sent to Paris to plead our case before General Pershing. When the others had said what they had to say, Pershing said, "And now, Mr. Corey."

Pershing sat at a huge polished desk in the drawing room of the huge chateau. The only articles on the desk were an ink stand and penholder of bronze. I said, "General, we have been correspondents ever since the United States got into the war. We have loyally supported the common cause. But when the armistice was signed, we recognized that the roads of France and Britain would diverge. We thought the American public should know the true conditions in Germany as seen through American eyes."

General Pershing brought his big fist down on his desk. The inkstand leaped. The ink spurted. He said, "By God, Mr. Corey, you were right."

Our characters were cleared. But we did not get permission to print our stories. In the end the Allies were too much for us.

"Runaway Correspondents"

Editors' Postscript

AEF headquarters treated the trip into Germany as gross insubordination. AEF files contain a bulky set of papers titled "Runaway Correspondents." These detail what the correspondents did and how the military brass responded.

The crux of the issue from the correspondents' point of view was a natural one for journalists. The war was over. The kaiser had fled Germany and the country was in turmoil with strikes, military mutinies, and a possible Bolshevik revolution. The reporters wanted to witness what was happening first-hand. They also wanted to understand what conditions were like for the German people as a result of the continuing blockade of food to the country. It was a chance to get an important story. As Lyon cabled his editors, "If I reach Berlin can deliver biggest bellringers of entire war."[1]

The military saw matters in a different light. The Armistice had brought about a cease-fire. Fighting could resume at any moment. An Inter-Allied agreement sought to limit travel to enemy territory, and the AEF did not want to violate that even if correspondents who were unaccredited found a way inside the country. The AEF's view that the war was not over was reflected in its refusal to end censorship for comments critical of the French and British. Accredited correspondents, each of whom wore an officer's uniform and were subject to AEF regulation, had signed a specific pledge "to be governed in his movements by the direction of a press officer."[2] By violating that, the military insisted, reporters disobeyed orders and had to be punished.

The AEF quickly tried to locate the reporters and, that accomplished, sent a senior press officer to Germany to ensure they were expelled. When the German military located the correspondents in Berlin, they were turned over to the AEF.

The judge advocate, General Walter A. Bethel, thought a six-month prison sentence appropriate.³ A subordinate believed that "any punishment other than death would be imposable."⁴ Fellow correspondents, angry at being beaten on a big story, pressed for a stiff penalty. The final decision was to prohibit the correspondents from filing stories about their sojourn in Germany.

Having one's stories killed as punishment was not unprecedented. Wythe Williams was detained early in the war when he went to the French lines without permission. He was brought back to Paris and put in the Chere Midi, the military prison that once held Alfred Dreyfus, the French officer of Jewish descent who was falsely accused of treason in one of the great French political scandals. When Williams was released, his punishment was to be "forbidden to write anything concerning my trip to the battlefield."⁵

Anything harsher than suppressing the stories of the "Runaway Correspondents," the AEF brass concluded, would make martyrs out of them in the eyes of the public and work to the disadvantage of the army. In addition, even if this were only a cease-fire, the war was nearly over.

Corey (and historian Emmet Crozier) said they were subject to a court-martial. AEF records indicate they had a "conference" with General Nolan.⁶ Early in the meeting, which was transcribed, he told the correspondents the punishment he was meting out. They gave him their side of the story. Lincoln Eyre, a tall, broad-shouldered presence who wrote for the *New York World*, did most of the talking. He stressed the importance of their stories. "The Entente Governments do not see peace propositions eye to eye with President Wilson. We believe that it is very likely that in interested quarters the truth about Germany may not be desired to be known and that very strenuous efforts may be made to prevent the truth about Germany being made known."⁷

Nolan was unmoved by their pleas to be allowed to file their stories. The punishment was mild, he pointed out, and, besides, other correspondents were getting into Germany and writing similar accounts, which made the runaway correspondents' stories less critical. He said they could do as they wished with their stories if they relinquished their credentials with the AEF. The correspondents said they were reluctant to surrender their accreditation. That would reflect poorly on their wartime service and prevent them from getting other stories from the AEF; and in any case they might be censored by the French.

Seldes, who went on to be one of the most significant press critics of the twentieth century, commented years later about the trip in a memoir. He said Hindenburg's statement that Germany had been defeated deserved "to be headlined in every country civilized enough to have newspapers.... I believe it would have destroyed the main planks of the platform on which Hitler rose to power," namely that Germany had not lost on the battlefield but because of betrayal by Jews, Communists, and other civilians.[8]

In 1919, when no longer with the AEF, Corey wrote an article based on the trip for *Everybody's Magazine*. It appeared in April while the treaty negotiations were underway—treaty negotiations among the winners, that is. The Germans had no place at the table. Corey reported how much the Germans had relied on Wilson to deliver a just peace when they agreed to the Armistice. The German politicians he had met, he wrote,

> blandly insisted that peace had been made as an item in an implied bargain. "We might have fought for another year," they insisted, "but we relied upon Wilson's fourteen points." Putting aside the kernel of future danger enclosed in the boast we often heard that "the German army had never been defeated in the field," it is probably true that the average German does not hate America as he does France or England. The average German—the barber and clerk and tram driver—has been taught by the German press since the armistice was signed that the one hope for Germany in the peace negotiations is in the disposition of America to be just.[9]

When the Germans received the treaty at the Petit Trianon in Versailles on May 7, they did consider it a great betrayal. The head of the German delegation, Count Brockdorff-Rantzau, denounced the Allies for allowing thousands of Germans to die because of the continued blockade of food after the Armistice was signed. The agreement carried impossibly heavy reparations as well as loss of territory. The harsh terms were "a godsend" for Adolf Hitler's propaganda, British historian Margaret MacMillan wrote.[10]

The squashed stories by Corey and the other runaway correspondents were, in fact, desperately needed.

Notes

1. Lyon to Cleveland Press, n.d., box 6133, entry 228, AEF. This is the location of all other AEF citations unless otherwise noted.

2. "Correspondent's Agreement," sample copy. An excellent discussion of this reasoning and the entire episode can be found in Caitlin Marie Thérése Jeffrey, "Journey through Unfamiliar Territory: American Reporters in the First World War," Ph.D. diss., University of California, Irvine, 2007.

3. W. A. Bethel to Commander in Chief, December 14, 1918.

4. Francis E. Neagle to Commander in Chief, December 14, 1918.

5. Wythe Williams, *Passed by the Censor: The Experience of an American Newspaper Man in France* (New York: E. P. Dutton, 1916), 120.

6. "Conference in the office of General D. K. Nolan," December 7, 1918, 1.

7. "Conference in the office of General D. K. Nolan," 14. On Eyre's personality, see *New York Times*, September 10 and 11, 1928. In the first of his suppressed stories on the trip, Corey wrote, "We had the mandate that every American reporter has to get the news. We believed we could get it. Events proved that we were right. Since we got back we have been assured that we had the nerve of the College of Burglars." Typescript, n.d., box 9, HC.

8. George Seldes, *Witness to a Century* (New York: Ballantine, 1987), 100.

9. Herbert Corey, "Germany—At the Beginning," *Everybody's Magazine*, April 1919, 97.

10. Margaret MacMillan, *Paris 1919* (New York: Random House, 2001), 2.

Index

Note: Page numbers in italics refer to illustrations.

Adlon, Louis, 42. *See also* Hotel Adlon, Berlin
AEF. *See* American Expeditionary Force (AEF)
Ahlstrom, Bill, 183
airplanes (flyers), 19, 80, 117–18, 140, 158–61, *193*, *198*
Albert, Heinrich, 39–40
Albert, King of Belgium, *75*
Aldershot (military prison), 17–18, 24
Alexander I, King of Serbia, 100
Allied Powers: Balkan politics and, 96–104; debts to U.S., 100, 128, 148; likelihood of victory, 38, 84, 86, 125. *See also* France; Great Britain; Japan; Russia
Allied propaganda, ix–x, 7; American diplomats and, 86–90; American support and, xiv, 3–4, 7, 61–62, 194–95; censorship of correspondent stories, 47, 51, 58–59, 83–88, 91, 95, 118, 121, 208 (*see also* American censors; British censors; French censors); criticism of war correspondents, 36–42; on German atrocities, 127 (*see also* atrocities, German); sinking of *Lusitania* and, 68; Wilson and, 115
ambassadors. *See* diplomats
ambulances, 64, 67; drivers of, 20, 79, 159, 183–86
American Ambulance, 183–86
American censors, 91, 95, 103n5; editors, xiv; military secrets and, 130; stories of death and, 129–37; War Department, 55n2. *See also* Allied propaganda; censorship; Committee on Public Information
American Expeditionary Force (AEF): 1st Battalion, 165th Infantry, 42nd Division, 77n2; 1st Division, 56, 149n1; 3rd Division, 55; 18th Regiment, 153; 26th Regiment, 2, 56, 150, 152–54, 166, 178; 42nd Division, 2, 4, 77n2; 166th Regiment, 95; accredited correspondents, ix, xvi, 5, 74, 107, 109, 113, 138, 209–11; casualties, 57; censorship of news, xiii–xvi, 2–6, 209–11 (*see also* censorship); Company E, 166–68; formation of, 128; leadership and discipline, 150–54, 165–68, 174–76; press headquarters, 146, *193*–96, *198*; Rainbow Division, 173–74, *181*, 199–203; training, 142, 165–81; uniforms, 22; volunteers, 169. *See also* battlefield reports
American Hospital at Neuilly, 183, 190–91
American Mercury, xi
American national character, 46; British perceptions of, 60–61, 100–101, 115; French perceptions of, 61, 115; as "Good Time Girls" and "Good Time Men," 147–49
AP. *See* Associated Press (AP)
Argonne, Battle of, 134
Armistice, 204–8
Associated Newspapers, vii–xi, x, 1–2, 7, 37
Associated Press (AP), viii, ix, x, xv, 12, 23n4, 41
atrocities, German, 15–17, 43n6, 54–55, 92n1, 127
Austria-Hungary, 96n1
Austrians, 7–8, 60

Austrian soldiers, 97, 134–35
Aviatik planes, 160

Balkans: Allied Powers and, 96–104; trouble in, 8. *See also* Ferdinand, Franz
bankers, 8, 124–26
Bannden, Lieutenant (of Bowling Green), 202
battlefield reports, xii–xiv; about American soldiers, 55–57, 151–54, 167, 197–203; about death, 131–37; about German soldiers, 36–39, 51, 56, 69–72, 91–95, 118–21; aerial fights, 160–61; in France, 78–82. *See also* casualties; front lines; shell fire; trench warfare
Battle of Argonne, 134
Battle of Belleau Wood, 134, 149, 151, 170n2
Battle of Cantigny, 153
Battle of the Marne, 55–56, 59, 92
bayonets, 131, 134–35
Belgium: front lines, 49, 73; German invasion of, viii, 23, 92n1, 124; king of, 75
Belleau Wood, Battle of, 134, 149, 151, 170n2
Berlin: correspondents in, 29–35; Hotel Adlon, xiv, 34–35, 41–43
Bernstorff, Johann Heinrich von, 48
Bethel, Walter A., 210
Bigart, Homer, xii
Blythe, Samuel G., 22–23
bombings, 116–17, 149, 167, 196–97, 198–99. *See also* airplanes (flyers); shell fire
Boston Globe, x
Boy-Ed, Karl, 48
bravery. *See* courage; heroism
British army: accredited correspondents, 4n8; American soldiers in, 122, 128, 142; casualties, 51–52; leadership and discipline, 151; officers, 21–22; strengths of, 59; uniforms, 22. *See also* British prisoners
British censors, 13–15, 24, 78–79, 91, 170n1. *See also* British propaganda; censorship
British correspondents, xiv, 4n8, 193–94, 205
British Navy, 8
British prisoners, 17, 133
British propaganda, xiv, 10–18, 28, 42n6, 62, 127–28, 194. *See also* Allied propaganda; British censors

British Secret Service, 23–24, 127
Brockdorff-Rantzau, Count, 211
Brooklyn Eagle, xiv, 49, 88
Broun, Heywood, 5–6, 30, 165
Brown, Cyril, 29–32, 34, 49
Brown, Edgar, 84
Broye, 152
Bryan, William Jennings, viii, 3–4
Bryce, Viscount, 15n8
Buckmaster, Stanley, 14–15, 24–25
Bulgaria, 99, 104
Bülow, Karl von, 92n1

Canadians, 21–22
Cantigny, Battle of, 153
Casement, Roger, 32
casualties: American, 103, 149, 150–54, 167, 182–83; French, 183–86; gas gangrene, 190–92; German, 64–67, 120–21, 131–33; jaw injuries, 81; medals and, 133, 156–57 (*see also* medals); Russian, 134–37; Serbian, 97–99. *See also* ambulances; hospitals
censorship, xiii–xvi, 55–56, 139n1; after Armistice, 209–11; "Corey Charges British Censor is Forging Dispatches," 13–15. *See also* Allied propaganda; American censors; British censors; Committee on Public Information; French censors; German censors
Central Intelligence Agency, 77n2
Chamber of Commerce, xi
Chateau-Thierry, 196–97
Chaumont, 139
Chemin des Dames, 86
Cheppy, 57
Chere Midi (military prison), 210
Chicago Daily News, ix, x, xvii, 26, 29, 31–32, 49, 55n2, 61, 82n3, 84
Chicago Tribune, xi, 48n4, 170n2, 204
Christensen, Walter, 200, 202
Cincinnati Enquirer, vii
Cincinnati Times-Star, vii, 7
civilians, 135–36, 152
Clemenceau, Georges, 158
Cobb, Irvin S., 5, 172–75

Cohan, George M., 36n1, 53
Collier's Weekly, ix, 22, 24, 49, 82n3, 153, 193n1, 197
Committee on Public Information, xiv, 3n4, 88n3, 129n1, 182–83, 195
Coolidge, Calvin, 143n1
Corey, Carolyn, 81, 104, 182–83
Corey, Herbert: as AEF accredited reporter, ix, 1–2 (*see also* battlefield reports; front lines); attitude toward U.S. involvement in World War I, xv, 1–9, 10–18, 19; books by, xi; death of, xvii; journalism career, vii–xi; lectures given by, xviiin13; magazine articles by, xv; memoir writing, x–xii; opinions on World War I, xv, 1–9, 10–18, 19, 40, 44–47, 123–28; personality and writing style, xii–xiii, xvi–xvii; photographs of, 105–7, 109, 112–13; suspected of pro-German sympathies, x, 18n11, 38–39, 68–74, 208–11
correspondents, viii–xii; AEF-accredited, ix, xvi, 5, 74, 107, 109, 113, 138, 209–11; American soldiers' attitudes toward, 138–39, 172; British, xiv, 4n8, 193–94, 205; British attitudes toward, 25; criticized by Allied propagandists, 36–42 (*see also* censorship); French, xiv, 205; German propaganda and, 32, 38, 50–51; loyalties of, 45; medals for, 75–78; salaries of, 41–42. *See also* British correspondents
courage: of American soldiers, 177, 199–203; of British soldiers, 51–52; of German soldiers, 118–21; of medical researchers, 191–192. *See also* heroism
Cowden, Alexander, 158–61
Crane, Frank, x
Creel, George, 129–30, 182n1, 183, 195
Crillon Hotel, 72–73
Croft, Edward, 150, 165
Croix de Guerre, 158–61, 170n2
Cross of the Legion of Honor, 76, 155–57
Crozier, Emmet, xviiin29, 210

Daily Chronicle, 4n8
Daily Telegraph, 4n8
Davies, Mary, 190–92

Davis, Richard Harding, viii, ix, x, 97
Dawes, Charles Gates, 143
death, stories of, 129–37. *See also* battlefield reports; casualties
decorations. *See* medals
Desmond, Robert W., xviiin9
Dickey Dippy's Diary (comic strip), x
Die Vaterland (The Fatherland), 18
diplomats: American, 11–12, 45–46, 49–50, 86–90; French, 47; German, 48, 62; loyalties of, 45–46
disarmament conferences, 63
Domjevin, 173–75, 181
Donovan, William, 77–78
Dougherty, George S., 12
Doyle, Robert, xii
draft legislation, 125, 169
Dreyfus, Alfred, 210
drinking and drunkenness, 1, 21, 43, 58–59, 139, 141, 147–49, 166, 178–81, 184–86
Duffy, Francis, 149, 197
Dunkirk, 79–80
Duval (soldier), 184–86

Eastern Front, 30, 35–39. *See also* front lines
Editor & Publisher, xi
Ed Kennedy's War, xv
Edwards, Daniel R., 1, 62
Elliott, Clark, 2
Erickson, Hjalmar, 175–76
espionage. *See* spies
Estep, Ralph, 101–3
Everybody's Magazine, ix, 211
Eyre, Lincoln, 6, 173–75, 196–98, 204, 210

Ferdinand, Franz, viii, 7, 26, 96n1
Ferguson, Fred, 193
flappers, 148n1
Foch, General, 145, 158
Ford, Henry, 49
Foreign Legion (France), 28–29, 141, 159
Forrest, Wilbur (Bill), 193
Fox, Edward, 36, 38, 40
France: American correspondents in, 85–86; American perceptions of, 61; Corey in,

France (continued) 25–26, 28–29, 68, 72–74, 77, 87, 105, 197–203; cuisine, 80–82, 161–64; England and, 21; loyalties of Americans in, 44–45; medals and decorations, 76–78. See also Allied Powers; Allied propaganda

François-Poncet, André, 73–74

French army: American soldiers in, 122, 128, 141–46; leadership and discipline, 151; soldiers on leave, 161–64; strengths of, 59

French censors, 91. See also censorship

French correspondents, xiv, 205

French prisoners, 118

French propaganda, 10, 28. See also Allied propaganda

French Secret Service, 45

"frightfulness," German strategy of, 15–17, 43n6, 54–55, 92n1, 116–18, 127

front lines: correspondents' attempts to get to, 25–26, 34–35, 49, 158; fraternization across, 188; reporting from, xii–xiv, 73, 78–82, 115–21, 131–37, 197–203. See also battlefield reports; Eastern Front; trench warfare; Western Front

G-2 (intelligence) units, 16, 146, 171n3

gas gangrene, 190–92

gas masks, 114

gas weapons, 63, 83

gender roles, xvi, 19–21. See also women

General Slocum (steamship), 7

Gerard, James W. (Jimmy), ix–x, 11, 49–50

German army: American correspondents and, 29–35, 53–59, 115–21, 131–37; atrocities and "frightfulness" against civilians, 15–17, 43n6, 54–55, 92n1, 116–18, 127; leadership and discipline, 91–95, 151; rebellion in, 205–7; snipers, 187–89; strengths of, 58–59, 88, 198. See also battlefield reports; German prisoners; German submarine warfare

German censors, 91, 95, 118. See also censorship

German Foreign Office, 49–50

German prisoners, 17–18, 55–56, 133, 172

German propaganda, 7, 10, 13n5, 18; American war correspondents and, 32, 38, 50–51; compared to British propaganda, 62; for naval expansion, 48n4

German Secret Service, 31, 53

German submarine warfare, 127, 170n2; sinking of *Lusitania*, 63, 68, 115n1, 124

German sympathizers: American, 47–50, 121; correspondents considered as, x, 18n11, 36–42, 39n3, 68–74

Germany: American military mission in, 33–34, 36, 141, 207–8; anti-Americanism, 53–59; Corey's stories from, x, xv–xvi, 23–25, 29–35, 47, 68–72, 115–21; diplomats, 48, 62; Kaiser of (see Wilhelm II, Kaiser); likelihood of victory, 24, 88, 125–26; loyalties of Americans in, 44–45; national character and manners, 23, 53–54, 57, 60–67; postwar reparations, xvi, 211; postwar reports from "runaway correspondents," xvi, xvii, xviiin29, 204–11, 212n7; proposed news bureau in New York, 39–40; U.S. ambassador to, 11; U.S. declaration of war against, 83, 129, 140; War Office, 32, 54; Zimmerman letter, 127–28

Gibbons, Floyd, 170–71, 193

Gibbs, Philip Armand Hamilton, 4

Gibson, Charles Dana, viii

Gifford, Walter, 31–32

Good Time Girls, 147–49

Gordon-Smith, Gordon, 96–97, 100, 104

Grant, Ulysses S., 123

Grave, Henry, 200–202

Great Britain: American correspondents in, 12; cuisine, 81; France and, 21; loyalties of Americans in, 44–45; U.S. ambassador to, 11–12; War Office, 38. See also Allied Powers; Allied propaganda; British army; British censors; British propaganda

Great War. See World War I

Greece, 100

Green, Martin, 173–75

Griffon Restaurant, 182–83

Grundy, Fred, 17

Harbord, James G., 108

Harden, Maximilian, 49

Harper's Monthly, ix, xiii

INDEX

hate, 21, 60, 129–31, 133, 149, 188–89, 211
Hearst papers, 42
Hecht, Ben, xviiin1
Henry, O., vii, xii
heroism, 13, 33, 35, 69, 82, 87, 97–98, 141, 149n2, 170n2, 191–92. *See also* courage
Herrick, Myron, 50
Higgins, Otto, 193
Hindenburg, Paul von, 33, 36, 206–8, 211
Historical Dictionary of War Journalism, The, ix
Hitchcock, Raymond, 36
Hitler, Adolf, 211
Hohenberg, John, xviiin9
Home Guard, District of Columbia, 123, 140
Hoover, Herbert, xi, 12–13
Hoover, J. Edgar, xi
Hopper, Jimmy, 153, 193
Hospital Number One, 182–83
hospitals, 182–86. *See also* ambulances; casualties; nurses
Hotel Adlon, Berlin, xiv, 34–35, 41–43
Hôtel des Arcades, 79–80
Hough, Ben W., 149, 173–75, 181
House, Edward M., 87, 204–5
Howard, Roy, 41–42, 170n1
human interest stories, x, xii–xiii, xv, 58, 158

intelligence (G-2) units, 16, 146, 171n3
Inter-Allied agreement, 209
international law, 90
International News Service, x
Iowa regiment, 173–74
Iron Cross, 76, 118, 120, 131, 133
Italy, 81, 87–90

James, A. L. "Jimmy," 171
James, Edwin L., 193
Japan, 64, 126–27, 128n1
Johnson, Jack, viii
Johnson, Tom, 55, 196–97
Jones, "Bill," 178, 180
Jones, Casey, 56
journalists. *See* correspondents
Jusserand, Jean, 47, 121

Kansas City Star, x, 193n1
Kassel, Germany, 205–6
Kauffman, Reginald Wright, 139
Kennedy, Edward, xv
Kitchener, Horatio Herbert, 22, 194
Kluck, Alexander von, 92–95
Kohl (American consul at Salonica), 99
Kuhn, Joseph E., 33, 36

Lansing, Robert, ix
Lardner, Ring, xi
Lawson, Victor, 31n2
League of Nations, 61
Legge, Bernard W., 166–68
Legion of Honor, 76–77
Liberty bonds, 130
Lille, German occupation of, 116–18
Little Black Piglet (restaurant), 61, 64–67, 91–93
Lloyd George, David, 4n8
London Daily Mail, ix, 42–43, 79, 102
London Times. See *Times* (London)
Lorraine region (France), 150, 171–73
Loyalty Day (U.S.), 182n1
Lusitania (ship), viii; sinking of, 63, 68, 115n1, 124
Lyman, Eli, 178–80
Lyon, Cal, 16–17, 199, 204, 209

MacArthur, Douglas, 2–3
Macedonia, 96–104
MacMillan, Margaret, 211
Madden, Martin, 8
Manchester Guardian, 96–97
Manchuria, 64
Marines, 149n1, 170n2
Marne, Battle of, 55–56, 59, 92
Marshall Newspaper Syndicate, 204
Martin, Frederick Roy, viii–ix, 12
Matthews, Joseph J., xviiin9
McAdoo, Williams Gibbs, 40n4
McClure, H. H., 18n11, 69, 141
McIntyre, O. O., xviiin1, 7
McKinley, William B., 140
McNutt, Bill, 193
Meaux, 196–97

Medal of Honor, 77n2
medals, 75–78, 155–61, 190. See also *Croix de Guerre*; Cross of the Legion of Honor; Iron Cross
Metz, 205
Mexico, 127–28
Meyer, Leo B., 103
military secrets, 130
Milwaukee Journal, xii
Monod, François, 144–46
Monroe Doctrine, 126–27
Moran, Frank, viii
Morning World, 173
Mowrer, Paul Scott, ix

Nancy (France), 196, 198
National Defense Act (1916), 126
National Film Corporation, 182n1
National Geographic, ix, xiii, xvi
National Guard, 150
Nation's Business, xi
Neuf Chapelle, 131
neutral states: correspondents from, 23, 29, 50–51, 68, 90; European, 127
Newspaper Enterprise Association, 16–17, 204
newspapers: censorship by editors, xiv (see also censorship); foreign journalists and, 31n2; human interest stories, x, xii–xiii, xv, 58, 158; war correspondents (see correspondents); wire services, viii, x, 37, 158. See also specific newspapers
"New York Day by Day" column, vii, 7
New York Evening Post, 13n6
New York Globe, x, 13–15, 37, 39, 83–85, 182
New York Herald, viii, 96n1
New York Herald-Tribune, xii
New York Sun, 17, 36, 41, 55, 196
New York Times, ix, 6n11, 29, 31n2, 139n1, 193n1
New York Tribune, 5, 193n1
New York World, 3n5, 6, 15, 39, 40n4, 42, 73, 173, 196, 204, 210
Nicholas II of Russia, 82n3
Nicolai, Colonel, 31
Noel, Percy, 26

Nolan, Dennis, 146, 171, 195–96, 208, 210
No Man's Land, 56
North American Review, 139n1
Northcliffe, Lord, ix, 42, 82n3
nurses, 98–99. See also hospitals

Office of Strategic Services, 77n2
Ohio Regiment, 173–74, 181, 199–203
O'Malley, Frank Ward, 5
Oscar II (ship), 49
Outlook, xi

pacifism, 48–49, 115, 124, 149
Page, Thomas Nelson, 50, 87–88
Page, Walter Hines, 11–12, 89
Palmer, Frederick, viii–ix, x, 22–24, 25, 26, 171n4; "The City of Unshed Tears," 24
Pannes (France), 203
Paris: Americans in, 161–64; German march on, 91–95; hospitals in, 182–86
Paris Herald, 96
Parker, Sir Gilbert, 13–14
Parr, Bob, 20
Paterson, Cissy, 48n4
Pearson's Magazine, xii
Pegler, Westbrook, 170, 193n1
Pension Herrenschmidt, Paris, 81
Pershing, John G., 55n2, 108, 142, 145–46, 149, 150, 165, 170n1, 174–76, 194, 196, 208
"Petite Yvonne," 183–86
Philadelphia Bulletin, x
pilots, 158–161. See also airplanes (flyers)
Pinkerton Detective Agency, 12n4
Place Jean Bart (France), 79–80
Pont-a-Mousson (France), 185
Powell, E. Alexander, 3–4, 72–73, 78–80
Prince of Wales, 23–24, 78–79
Princip, Gavrilo, viii
professors, university, 3, 7, 46, 83, 129
propaganda. See Allied propaganda; British propaganda; French propaganda; German propaganda
"The Prush" (Prussian captain), 34–35, 49
public diplomacy, 195n4
Pyle, Ernie, xii

INDEX

Radio Corporation, 31
radio manufacturers, 31–32
Red Cross, 2, 65, 98–99
Reichenbach, Harry, 182–83
reporters. *See* correspondents
ribbons. *See* medals
Rimini, Italy, 90
Ripley's Believe It or Not!, x
Rogers, Jason, x, 85n1
Rogers, W. L., 85
Rohe, Alice, 104
Romanians, 50
Roosevelt, Franklin Delano, 30
Roosevelt, Theodore, viii, 18n10
Ruhl, Arthur, 49, 197
rules of war, 63
"runaway correspondents," xvi, xvii, xviiin29, 204–11, 212n7; discipline of, 208, 210
Rupt-des-Main River, 201–2
Russia: correspondents in, 82. *See also* Allied Powers
Russian army, 31, 35, 37–39, 134–37, 151
Russian prisoners, 37

Saint-Martin d'Esquermes church, 117
Saint-Mihiel (France), 196, 198–203
Salonica (Macedonia), 99–100
Salvation Army, 2
Sandes, Flora, 98n3
San Marino, Republic of, 90
Saturday Evening Post, xi, 18n10
Schuette, Oswald, 29, 31–32, 49
scientists, 190–92
Scripps, E. W., 16n9, 204n1
Scripps Howard, xii
secrecy, 130
Seldes, George, 204, 210–11
Sensabaugh, Corporal (of Crestline), 202
Serbia, 96–104
Serbian army, xii–xiii, 97–98
Sharp, William Graves, 4, 50, 50n8, 86–87
shell fire, xii, 1, 30, 37, 70, 80, 82, 91, 104, 120, 152, 174, 179–82, 187, 197. *See also* bombings
Sherman, William Tecumseh, 123

Shoemaker, Edwin, 200, 202
Signal Corps (France), 102
Simmonds, Emily, 98–99
Smith, Frederick A., 204
Smith, Hamilton, 2, 149, 152–54, 166
Smith, Roland, 81
snipers, 187–89
soldiers: Corey's stories about, xii; photographs of, 110–11, 114. *See also* American Expeditionary Force (AEF); battlefield reports; British army; casualties; courage; French army; German army; heroism; Russian army; Serbian army; trench warfare
spies, 26; German, 39–40, 45, 130; in Italy, 89; in Switzerland, 86–87
Spurgeon, Jack, 15
St. Omer, 78–79
Suydam, Henry, xiv, 49, 88–90
Sweeney, Charley, 28–29, 141
Sweeney, W. C., 146, 171
Swing, Raymond, 29, 32, 38
Switzerland, 86–87

Taylor, Kenneth, 190–92
Thaw, Billy, 159
Times (London), 14n6, 40, 52, 82
Titanic (ship), 7
trench warfare: American soldiers and, 56, 139, 173–74; beginning of, 92n1, 93; fire trenches, 174, 185; German soldiers and, 64, 185–86; photographs of, 106; reporting from, xii, 170–71; snipers and, 187–89; telephone cables used in, 119–20. *See also* battlefield reports; front lines
Turkey, 99, 102

United Press (UP), x, 16n9, 39n3, 41–42, 170, 193n1
United States: arms sales to Allied Powers, 32–34, 48; army in World War I (*see* American Expeditionary Force [AEF]); declaration of war against Germany, 83, 129, 140; domestic propaganda, xiv, 3, 7, 46, 83, 129, 194–95 (*see also* censorship; Committee on Public Information); military mission in

United States (*continued*)
  Germany, 33–34, 36, 141, 207–8; military secrets, 130; military spending, 122, 140–41, 143–46; neutrality, 3n6, 8, 11, 17, 23, 29, 50–51, 68–69, 90, 115, 127; pacifism, 48–49, 115, 124, 149; pro-German sentiment, x, 18n11, 36–42, 39n3, 47–50, 68–74, 121; support for Allied Powers, 61–62, 68–69, 83–88, 122–28, 129, 140, 194–95 (*see also* Allied propaganda)
U.S. Department of Justice, 32
U.S. Navy, 16n9, 34, 44–45, 47, 130, 142
U.S. State Department, 125, 128
U.S. War Department, 55n2

Van Dyke, Henry Jackson, 11, 50
van Loon, Henrik Willem, 23
Venice, Italy, 89
Verdun, France, 82, 97
Versailles Treaty, xixn30, 41, 211
Victory Loans, 16
Viereck, George Sylvester, 18
von der Marwitz, Georg, 36
Vosges, 187–89

Washburn, Stanley, 82
Waterloo (battlefield), 49
weapons, 169; advances in, 123; American arms sales to Allies, 32–34, 48; gas, 63, 83, 114, 190–92; "light heavies" (guns), 178–80. *See also* bayonets; bombings; shell fire
Western Front, 38. *See also* front lines
Wiegand, Karl von, 39, 41–42
Wile, Frederic William, xviiin1, 42–43
Wilhelm I, Kaiser, 18n10
Wilhelm II, Kaiser, 33, 39, 44, 62–63, 207, 209
Williams, Jay, 124
Williams, Wythe, ix, xii, 139, 210

Wilson, Harry Leon, 147–48
Wilson, Woodrow, xiv, 3n4, 11n3, 204; Armistice and, 210–11; decision to enter World War I, 122, 125–27; France and, 144–45; propaganda and, 129n1 (*see also* Committee on Public Information); re-election of, 125; "too proud to fight" speech, 115; war information and, 87–89
wire services, viii, x, 37, 158
Wise, Frederick, 149
women: American, xvi, 19–20, 147–49; American "old ladies," pro-war attitudes of, 3, 7–8, 46, 83, 129, 140, 183; British, 20–21, 98–99, 190; French, 156–157, 178–80; heroism of, 190–92
Women's Army Auxiliary Corps (WAAC), 20
Wood, Junius, xvii, xixn33, 55n2
World War I: beginning of, 96n1; Corey's opinions on, xv, 1–9, 10–18, 19, 40, 44–47, 123–28; effects on humanity, 56–57; end of, xixn30, 41, 204–8, 211; news coverage of (*see* correspondents; newspapers); potential victor, 24, 38, 84, 86, 88, 125–26; public opinion on, 61–62; rules of war and, 63; science of, 123 (*see also* weapons). *See also* Allied Powers; American Expeditionary Force (AEF); Germany
World War II, xii, xv, 77n2, 211
wounded soldiers. *See* casualties
Wright, Henry J., 37–38, 84

YMCA, 2
Youell, Rice H., 176–77
Young, Owen, 31–32
Young Turks, 100
Yugoslavia (Jugo-Slavia), 97, 100, 140

Zimmerman, Arthur, 127–28

CPSIA information can be obtained
at www.ICGtesting.com
Printed in the USA
LVHW111738130522
718731LV00002B/68